The Future
of Nuclear Deterrence

The Future
of Nuclear Deterrence.

George H. Quester
University of Maryland

Lexington Books
D.C. Heath and Company/Lexington, Massachusetts/Toronto

Library of Congress Cataloging-in-Publication Data

Quester, George H.
  The future of nuclear deterrence.

  Includes index.
  1. Deterrence (Strategy)   2.   Nuclear warfare.
3. Warfare, Conventional.   I. Title.
U162.6.Q44   1986   355.4'3   85–45343
ISBN 0–669–11565–7 (alk. paper)
ISBN 0–699–12321–8 (pbk. : alk. paper)

Published simultaneously in Canada
Printed in the United States of America
Casebound International Standard Book Number: 0–669–11565–7
Paperbound International Standard Book Number: 0–669–12321–8
Library of Congress Catalog Card Number: 85–45343

The paper used in this publication meets the minimum requirements of
American National Standard for Information Sciences—Permanence of
Paper for Printed Library Materials, ANSI Z39.48–1984.

The last numbers on the right below indicate the number and date of printing.

10 9 8 7 6 5 4 3 2 1

95 94 93 92 91 90 89 88 87 86

for Aline

Contents

Figures and Table

Figures

Table

Preface

As they commemorated the fortieth anniversaries of the end of World War II in Europe and in the Pacific, and the corresponding anniversary of the nuclear age's beginning at Hiroshima and Nagasaki, Americans and others expressed great concerns about the nature of the international system we have been living with these four decades. Doubts about the morality of having ended World War II by the use of atomic weapons are connected to doubts about the morality of relying since then on threats of nuclear attacks as the basis of deterrence.

People naturally celebrate a fortieth anniversary more than a thirty-ninth or a forty-first. It is interesting to speculate what the tone of such commemorations will be in 1995, for the fiftieth. Will Germany by then be as much forgiven as Japan was in 1985? Will there still be as much Japanese bitterness about Hiroshima and Nagasaki? Will there indeed still be a world left to take part in such commemorations—that is, will we have avoided nuclear war for another decade, so that we do not see any duplicates of Hiroshima or Nagasaki around the world?

Yet there is a different reason why 1985, the fortieth year after Hiroshima, was the right time to put together a book like this one. We are now just about twice as far into the nuclear age as when the first "golden age," between 1956 and 1965, of thinking on the problems of nuclear war and limited war was completed. In those years a great number of very basic analyses were done on deterrence, escalation, tacit bargaining, and limited war, analyses now under extensive attack from the right and from the left, but analyses this author believes still make a great deal of sense.

There are thus a great number of Americans in 1985 who are discovering the problems of nuclear deterrence and are not yet so convinced or so aware of the "best of a bad bargain" solutions that were converged upon twenty years ago. Many or most of the Americans who have become excited by the idea of "nuclear winter" or by President Reagan's "Strategic Defense Initiative" do not themselves remember Hiroshima and Nagasaki. Many of them do not remember the "missile gap" that was allegedly about to close in on the United States after 1957, or the Cuban missile crisis of 1962.

It is possible, therefore, that we should measure the nuclear era not in decades, but in pairs of decades; that is, in generations. It took about two decades for the majority of Americans, and perhaps the majority of the world, to understand the changes that had been imposed on international relations by nuclear weapons; and in a similar length of time another generation has emerged, in the United States, in West Germany, perhaps in every country in which we can measure public opinion, a generation that is reluctant to accept the answers that had been written down, however cogently, by 1965.

This book, it will be obvious to the reader, concludes that nuclear deterrence does indeed have "a future." Yet this future is under attack on various counts, each of which requires at least a chapter of response. The technical underpinnings of nuclear deterrence are in question, amid visions of "windows of vulnerability" which pale in comparison with the earlier spectres of a "missile gap." The moral future of nuclear deterrence is similarly questioned, driving some of the questioners to seek nuclear freezes or substantial nuclear disarmament, and others to seek after elegant new counterforce capabilities and/or an ABM system such as has been proposed by President Reagan. Fred Iklé published an article in 1973 entitled "Can Nuclear Deterrence Last Out the Century?"[1] At the time, the moral arguments offered by Iklé attracted the attention mostly of specialists. Deterrence rence indeed may well last out the century, and decades more, but by 1985 the criticisms offered in 1973 have attracted a much larger following.

Perhaps most important of all, the future of deterrence comes under periodic and repetitive challenge with regard to its extendability to Western Europe. If the threat of nuclear war is usable to keep Soviet paratroops from landing in Colorado (the plot line of the movie *Red Dawn*), is it usable to keep Soviet tank forces from rolling into West Germany? This last question, like the others about the future of nuclear deterrence, is hardly new. One can yank out of the literature of the 1950s and 1960s exactly the same worries and exactly the same answers. But what are we to make of the fact that the worried questions are being posed all over again and that the same answers may not be so quickly accepted as satisfying?

Aside from the simple turnover of the generations, there is one other explanation for today's noticeable uneasiness about the future of nuclear deterrence. The morality of mutual assured destruction is questionable, and the concept of mutual deterrence is in so many ways something new. A defense policy that has been in place for the past four decades is morally out of step with the Western moral tradition that has existed for at least the past four centuries, and perhaps the past twenty. As will be discussed in this book, it is also out of step with centuries of military professional practice.

It may thus take six, or eight, or ten decades for the average person to come to terms with the logic by which the antiballistic missile system is bad if it protects people, and good if it protects weapons. And in the meantime, our concerns about the future of such a new and different deterrence system will periodically boil over.

While they can agree on little else, hawkish and dovish critics of mutual assured destruction (MAD) and nuclear deterrence both tell us that we are somehow escaping the problems of nuclear deterrence, that we are living on borrowed time, with a moment of truth ahead. At the least, such challenges deserve a response, when attentions around the globe are so focused on the nuclear deterrence issue. Yet it may still be that a closer study of the problems will in the end produce a return to the solutions we have lived with, however imperfect they may be.

The overall point of this book is that the problems of the future of nuclear deterrence are indeed manageable, that we can survive to do another taking of stock in 2005, and another in 2025, and that the concepts and mechanisms of nuclear deterrence as we have known them will indeed play a major role in carrying us forward.

There are admittedly many things wrong with the U.S. situation in analyzing the problems of nuclear deterrence. Yet one of the good things about the U.S. situation is the development of patterns of intellectual interaction in the handling of such problems, drawing together faculty, graduate students, and undergraduates, and midcareer professionals as at the National War College, drawing together civilians and military officers, decisionmakers and detached analysts, advocates of one approach and advocates of another.

As authors get older, they thus owe debts to increasingly long lists of people for stimulating exchanges, for good questions, and for ideas that have been deliberately or inadvertently stolen. Rather than trying to construct a list of all of such individuals, I will thus simply express my especial thanks to my faculty colleagues at the University of Maryland, at the National War College, and at Cornell University, and to a still larger number of students at the same institutions.

Substantial portions of this book have appeared as journal articles and as chapters in books. A fair amount of editing has been done to bring issues to date, to eliminate duplication, and also to present the themes of the book in a more orderly manner. I am indebted to the journals and publishers in question for providing the necessary permissions so that these materials could be used here.

As in other writing ventures, my most direct and immediate thanks have to go to my wife, Aline, and my children, Ted and Amy, who bore up with my distractedness as various logical gaps got closed. Whether these gaps are as closed as this author believes must be left for the reader to decide.

Note

1. Fred C. Iklé, "Can Nuclear Deterrence Last Out the Century?", *Foreign Affairs* 51, no. 2 (January 1973):267–85.

Abbreviations

ABM	antiballistic missile
ALCM	air-launched cruise missile
ASW	antisubmarine warfare
ATGM	antitank guided missile
C³	command, control, and communication
C³I	command, control, communication, and intelligence
CEP	Circular Error Probable
CIA	Central Intelligence Agency
GCD	General and Complete Disarmament
GLCM	ground-launched cruise missile
IAEA	International Atomic Energy Agency
ICBM	intercontinental ballistic missile
INF	intermediate-range nuclear forces
MAD	mutual assured destruction
MBFR	mutual and balanced force reduction
MIRV	multiple independently targeted reentry vehicle
MRBM	medium-range ballistic missile
NATO	North Atlantic Treaty Organization
NEACP	National Emergency Airborne Command Post
NPT	Nonproliferation Treaty
OPEC	Organization of Petroleum Exporting Countries
PAL	permissive action links
PD	Presidential Directive
PGM	precision-guided munitions
PRC	People's Republic of China
SAC	Strategic Air Command
SALT	Strategic Arms Limitation Talks
SEATO	South East Asia Treaty Organization
SLBM	submarine-launched ballistic missile
SLCM	sea-launched cruise missile

1
Security and Arms Control

Any average American, when asked to balance considerations of controlling arms against considerations of military security, feels himself in something of a dilemma. Just as in ordinary life, in which we do not wish to be abusive, but also do not wish to be abused, we do not want the United States to be bellicose, but we also do not want it to be submissive to others who may be bellicose. What do we then conclude when advocates of greater armaments portray the Soviet Union as relentlessly out to conquer more and more of the world and then accuse those who favor disarmament (and those who talk of arms control) of being naively submissive or worse? And what do we do when the advocates of disarmament instead blame the bulk of international difficulties on the United States' own provocative acquisitions of arms (voicing a suspicion that even the term *arms control* amounts to a euphemism for further acquisitions of weaponry)?

The Difficult Choices of International Security

We live in a world of suspicions and of dangers. Even if some were to conclude that the suspicions about Soviet aggressiveness were groundless or exaggerated, others would be difficult to convince of this. And the mere fact that one side can thus not free itself totally of such suspicions then provides plausible grounds for the other side's suspicions: "They may attack us, only because they groundlessly fear that we are about to attack them."

This essay was prepared for the Global Understanding Project of National Public Radio, with support from the Annenberg/Corporation for Public Broadcasting Project. The essay is published and distributed for classroom use by the American Political Science Association.

The Soviet Union can devastate the United States through nuclear attack, and the United States can do the same to the Soviet Union, and either of these nuclear powers can devastate any other corner of the earth. The Soviet Union could also very possibly use its conventional forces to occupy Western Europe, a most valuable peninsula sticking out from the Eurasian land mass. One does not have to read Mackinder[1] or attach much significance to the concept of geopolitics to conclude that this possibility may constitute a permanent source of suspicion and tension between the two superpowers, since American ground forces slated to defend the European members of the North Atlantic Treaty Organization (NATO) will always have to cross an ocean by sea or air transport while Soviet reserves could arrive in Germany by railroad or highway.

There is no reason to suppose that leaders in Washington or Moscow ever look forward to inflicting nuclear destruction on each other's homelands or that they would ever want a nuclear war (the kind of strategic nuclear war the United States fears and has to take steps to make less likely, would occur instead because either side feared that the other was about to strike). But might the leadership in Moscow not like to impose a Marxist system of government on places like West Germany and Belgium and France by the power of Soviet tank forces, much as they have done in Poland and East Germany and Czechoslovakia? Here the answer must always be less sure. We may never know whether Stalin or his successors would have seized Paris, for they were not offered the opportunity, as the West began putting up its guard soon after the German defeat and the end of World War II. Having lost Western trust and confidence by the violation of their Yalta pledges about places like Poland, the Soviets have never been given a chance to prove a lack of interest in places like France.[2]

The United States may be concerned for many corners of the globe, but it feels especially close ties with the economically advanced industrial democracies of Western Europe. And it has similar ties now with the advanced industrial society in Japan. Yet the differences between the geopolitical situation of NATO and Japan goes to the heart of many U.S. problems with international security and arms control. The Soviets could not easily invade and conquer Japan, but they could conceivably invade Western Europe. If only the Elbe River were as wide as the Japan Sea; then there would have been no need for the United States to threaten escalation in order to reinforce the deterrent to Soviet aggressions in Western Europe.

To complicate the situation a little more, both Western Europe and Japan are very much dependent on the Persian Gulf region for their energy needs, a region also conceivably open to land invasion from the center of Eurasia, a region beset as well by a great many local conflicts and instabilities. Can the United States, to protect the energy supplies of its friends in Western Europe and Japan, somehow deploy forces into the Persian Gulf region to impose a deterrent barrier, posing threats of nuclear escalation comparable to those that have been in place for NATO? Or are the local instabilities in the region too much greater than anything comparable in Western Europe, so that this would be far too hazardous an exercise?[3]

Similar problems apply to one other appendage to Eurasia, the Republic of Korea, sitting south of the 1953 truce line, also burdened with the possibility of larger forces being brought down upon it from the interior of the continent. South Korea has grown very much in industrial value because of its internal energies and substantial economic growth since the Korean War, but its value to the United States is still very different in nature from that of Western Europe. In Korea, American lives were lost in resisting Communist aggression in 1950, so that the precedent of tolerating any repetition of this aggression would seem unbearable. By contrast, Americans' attachment to Europe derives not only from the vast economic power of Western Europe, but also from centuries of cultural, political, and philosophical tradition, and from a blood kinship affecting most American citizens.

The threats posed by nuclear weapons can thus almost never be forgotten, because they are so awesome. But they can never be forgotten by either side, which allows each side to continue the contest of imposing the larger portion of the burdens of restraint on the other. These can be dangerous contests, but they are central parts today of what could be called strategy, or arms control.

As one moves farther away from the most central territorial concerns of the United States and the Soviet Union (perhaps to Thailand, Grenada, or Chad), one encounters a diminishing role for nuclear weapons. They are less of the problem, and they are less of the solution, as the countries threatened by invasions are not valuable enough for either side to make credible threats of nuclear escalation. Here the arms control agenda turns more to possible restraints or qualitative sortings of conventional armaments, and the applications of military strategy look more like the strategy of World War II battle planning. Yet the need for restraint is unforgettable in every one of these situations too, as strategy and arms control still cannot be allowed to diverge. The strategic goals, above all, will always have to include keeping a conventional war from escalating into something much worse.

Any nuclear retaliation that would punish Communist aggressions in Europe, Japan, the Persian Gulf, or Korea would automatically entail the nuclear devastation of the United States itself, so plans for such retaliation must at the very least be carefully tuned to avoid false alarms, in order to avoid punishing Moscow for actions of which Moscow is not yet guilty. Ideally, punishment should be inflicted on any foreign power that aggresses militarily against the United States or its allies (thus, one hopes, deterring such aggressions in the first place), but these punishments should be inflicted *only* if such aggression occurs (that is, the United States wants its adversaries to know that they are safe from punishment as long as they themselves do not initiate warfare). This sounds a little like wanting a burglar alarm that goes off whenever a burglary occurs, but never gives off a false alarm; or wanting a judicial system that always apprehends and punishes criminals, but never punishes any innocent parties, never drives anyone into criminality by the injustice and hopelessness of false accusations.

Just as such perfect burglar alarms and perfect judicial systems are impossible to attain in domestic life, such a balancing between vigilance and provocation will be difficult to achieve in the anarchic world of international politics. The task in arms control is thus to understand the difficulties of choice involved and to seek national security for the U.S. side without menacing the security of the other side.

Arms Control

Arms control is a term often used and often misused. It has hardly yet become a household expression, for a great number of Americans might still wonder if it did not mean "gun control." Among those familiar with its international context, it continually draws criticism from both the Right and the Left. Advocates of greater American defense preparation and of lesser trust of the Soviets tend to equate arms control with disarmament or with formal negotiations about disarmament, treating the whole matter as an exercise in naiveté and Soviet deception. Advocates of greater disarmament and of accommodation between the superpowers tend to view the concept of arms control as a deception, as an excuse for maintaining more armaments than the United States needs, and at times as just a euphemism for ordinary foreign policy and self-interested strategy.

Not everything that draws criticism from both the Right and Left merits endorsement thereby as some kind of middle ground. Yet there is instead a great deal to be said in favor of the logic of arms control, for it is something different from a simple endorsement of disarmament or of trust of the Russians, and it is also something more than a simple euphemism for whatever the United States was planning anyway as foreign policy. At its core, arms control is a more rational and more goal-oriented way of looking at weapons procurements and weapons use in light of the tremendous increase in the destructive power of such weapons ushered in by the discoveries of nuclear physics and in light of continuing national interests. As articulated at the end of the 1950s, especially by analysts like Thomas Schelling and Morton Halperin,[4] it resulted in some lessons of great value to the United States *and* to its Soviet adversaries. The heated criticisms that arms control draws from its right and left flanks may show how far the policy's advocates still have to go in selling these lessons to all of the public, but the issues that are involved are important.

Arms control is basically different from disarmament in that it focuses on the outputs we desire from all of policy, rather than assuming that disarmament (which, after all, is only an input) automatically takes care of such outputs. What are the outputs that policymakers would care about so much in considering whether to procure any particular weapons system, or where to deploy it, or even whether to use it—in some limited war?

First and foremost, policymakers probably will always care about reducing the likelihood of war. Many factors play a role in predicting the likelihood of war, including the political natures of societies and men, the values of pieces of land that are in dispute, and so forth. Yet the nature of weapons also plays an important role, because some weapons systems and arrangements seem to reward whoever takes the initiative, while others tend to punish the side taking the initiative, rewarding instead the side that sat still and took the chance of letting itself be attacked. This elementary distinction may coincide with what intuition or tradition would have sorted into the categories of "offense" or "defense"; for the moment, let the argument simply be that weapons make a difference, in some cases making wars less likely even when men hate each other, in others making wars more probable, sometimes generating (as perhaps in the outbreak of World War I, or in a standard apprehension about the possibility of a World War III) "a war nobody wanted." Americans do not want their own country to be attacked or those of their friends. And they probably do not wish their adversaries to be in constant fear of attack, lest this fear breed an inclination toward preemptive attacks.

Second, policymakers care—if fighting were nonetheless to break out—about reducing the destructiveness of war when it occurs. All war is bad; but some wars kill millions, while others kill thousands. Some destroy all the civilian targets within the proximity of military targets, while others spare such civilians. No one can be morally indifferent to such distinctions, anymore than one can be indifferent to the *likelihood* of war in the first place. As long as doing so does not increase the likelihood of war, policymakers will generally want to reduce the destruction in any war that happens.

As a third important consideration, policymakers will wish to cut the costs in peacetime of such preparations for war. If arrangements have been made to make wars less likely and to make them less destructive when they occur, Americans will at the same time not wish to see huge fractions of each state's gross national product wasted on military weaponry or to see many months of young men's lives tied up in military service. The nation also generally opposes the kinds of militarism, dictatorships, and repressions that can result from peacetime military preparedness.

Arms Control and Disarmament

But are not all three of these categories of desirable human gains already automatically covered by any possibilities of disarmament? An advocate of such disarmament might complain that talk of arms control is a distraction, since common sense suggests that beating swords into plowshares will address all of these moral concerns.

To begin with, it is indeed the most plausible that disarmament will cut the peacetime burden of military preparedness. Weapons cost money, and long periods of military service for a nation's young men are also a major economic and social burden. Spokesmen for the military-industrial complex sometimes tend to play down these costs by suggesting that spin-offs of military research and development can be found in the civilian world; yet one should be skeptical about these claims, for most of these spin-offs cost much more than if they had been produced in a purely civilian research and development program. (In noting that this matter of spin-offs is not an easy one for the advocate of straightforward disarmament, we will have to consider the nuclear proliferation question, which suggests the nasty possibility that weapons are a free by-product of purely civilian electric-power projects; this situation implies that a nation might only keep itself reliably free of such arms by foregoing some benefits for its civilian economy.)[5]

Weapons can also increase in destructive power while actually decreasing in economic cost. The nuclear weapons that have helped guard Western Europe against attack for all the years since 1949 are surely more destructive than the conventional weapons they replace, threatening to devastate the very territory on which they are deployed. Yet, by sparing West Europeans the burdens of maintaining numerous tank battalions, they may have made possible the dramatic economic growth of the NATO countries over subsequent decades, a growth that otherwise could have been stunted by the burdens of military spending.

The argument for simple disarmament becomes more difficult when one approaches the other two categories of human concerns upon which arms control focuses. On the second category, some weapons definitely increase the destructiveness of wars, but others may decrease it. One should always be skeptical about the advertising claims made for very accurate new weapons, because (like the Norden bombsight of World War II) they do not always deliver as much capability for discriminating among targets as they promise. Yet some accretions of accuracy do emerge, whereby one can direct more fire at enemy soldiers and weapons systems and less at the adversary's civilians. And some kinds of military spending on command, control, and communications systems might be very helpful for moderating any wars that break out.

There is another link between retaining arms and moderating war. For example, states lacking smaller options may—if attacked—feel driven to use the only weapons they have, that is, relatively larger weapons. If the United States has nuclear weapons *and* large conventional forces with which to try to defend NATO, then it does not have to escalate as quickly to the use of the nuclears. If the nation somehow disarms, leaving itself with only nuclear weapons, then its choices in the event of a Soviet attack would be narrowed to surrendering or escalating—and the choice might not be to surrender.

Furthermore, the argument for a simple endorsement of all forms of disarmament is even more troubled. There are certainly weapons that make wars more likely, in such a way that disarming ourselves and our adversaries of them would be beneficial for humanity. But there are other weapons that tend to make war less likely, in that they make aggressions less profitable and attractive, and disarmament in their category could have a real price.

Even if two out of five conceivable weapons systems were in the war-inducing category, one might still have to conclude that as many as one out of five was in the war-preventing category (given the suspicions and hostilities of the world), with the other two in five perhaps making no difference in either direction (being simply a waste of taxpayers' money, thus to be objected to on the basis of cost-cutting considerations).

Would it be good for the chances of peace to reduce the current Soviet and U.S. missile inventories by perhaps 40 percent? Very possibly it would (and it might certainly be a contribution to reducing the damage if a war were to break out). Would it be good for the chances of peace to remove the remaining 60 percent? Almost certainly not, for the temptation to cheat in the last rounds of such disarmament, and the temptation to strike at the other side (reinforced by natural rumors and fears that the other side might be cheating, or might be about to strike) would be overwhelming, making war much more likely.

Straightforward advocates of disarmament often declare that they wish as much disarmament as possible, converting swords into plowshares until there are no more swords, with zero armaments as the final goal. This policy, often called General and Complete Disarmament (GCD), is officially endorsed by both the United States and the USSR at the United Nations General Assembly. Yet the prospect of total disarmament, or even of total disarmament only in the category of nuclear weapons, is fraught with enormous problems of verification and reliability, so much that the chances of war might rise spectacularly as the powers approached the zero-arms goal. Each side might try to hide away a few nuclear weapons somewhere, just in case the other side had done the same, or (if the other side had foolishly not done the same) to leap into a position of nuclear monopoly and world dominance.

Anyone looking at the safeguard and verification problems connected with halting only the further horizontal spread of nuclear weapons to additional countries (normally spoken of as "nuclear proliferation") will encounter major problems of the technical and political reliability of such International Atomic Energy Agency (IAEA) inspections, even where the gain in trying to beat the system, by cheating and fooling the IAEA inspectors, would merely be to become the "nth" country possessing rudimentary nuclear weapons, far outclassed by the arsenals commanded by Washington and Moscow.[6] How much greater would be the temptation, and the worries, when a nation cheating might become the "only" one again to have nuclear weapons.

With regard to general and complete disarmament in all the rest of the conventional weapons categories, endless and basically unsolvable problems of definition and verification would also apply. What about police forces on each side, some of which have considerable latent military capability (especially when ordinary military forces have been disbanded)? What about "workers' militias," like those that played such a role in the Communist 1948 coup in Czechoslovakia? What about gymnastics societies, which in some cultures practice a very military drill? What about hunting rifles? What about ordinary kitchen knives? What about groups of muscular bullies?

Most of the objections that can be raised against GCD can be raised with equal justification against attempts to eliminate the nuclear menace by a perfect defense against missiles, as was proposed earlier in various ABM (antiballistic missile) projects, and more recently in President Reagan's SDI (Strategic Defense Initiative) program, so often labelled as "Star Wars" by its critics.

In each case, "being there" might be fine (a world disarmed by negotiation, or by the erection of unilateral defensive barriers eliminating the power of arms); but in each case "getting there" would be fraught with perils and tensions, because one side might be cheating, or one side might attain antimissile coverage for itself before the other side obtained it. The temptations when one nation alone had the ability to devastate someone else's cities and the tensions caused by a fear that the other side might strike when it alone had such an ability would raise the risks of World War III far above what they are today.

The easiest criticism of Reagan's SDI proposal is that it probably cannot work physically. Billions of dollars will be spent to blunt Soviet missile capabilities, and these billions will then be cancelled out by hundreds of millions of Soviet rubles restoring the grip of such missiles on U.S. cities.[7] But the more important criticism of SDI, just as with GCD, is that it would be very dangerous even *if* it could work, because of the tensions that would be produced while the process of eliminating the nuclear menace was underway and was not reliably completed for all concerned. Perhaps we just "cannot get there from here."

Arms control's claim to legitimacy would thus be the focus it directs to the ultimate outputs about which the United States cares. Disarmament is not desirable per se, but is desirable only if it contributes to the outputs listed. And we have noted some situations when it would not contribute to such outputs. Formal negotiations on arms reductions similarly cannot be desirable per se, but are desirable only if they contribute to the outputs human beings must care about.

Arms control compares with disarmament, therefore, just as program-budgeting compares with line-item budgeting. Any student of operations research could explain the advantages of the former over the latter, because it focuses the decisionmaker's attention on the guidelines that really matter, and because it eliminates the disappointments that occur when intermediary goals are pursued mindlessly as if they were final goals.

Arms Control versus Formal Negotiations

If arms control is not synonymous with disarmament, it is also not synonymous with formal negotiations about armaments, even though many press commentators and political figures still misleadingly use the term in this sense.

Let us say a few words here about the role of such negotiations, since a great many Americans welcome negotiations just as automatically as they welcome any and all forms of disarmament. To repeat a point that should be painfully obvious by now, such formal and explicit negotiations are often desirable, but *only* when they indeed contribute to the goals we stipulated as the essence of arms control, that is, reducing the likelihood of war, or the costs of war, or the peacetime burden of preparations for war. It would be pleasantly simple if the process of negotiations always worked in these desirable directions, but does it?

Formal negotiations are hardly indispensable. Anyone familiar with the logic of limited war, whereby two adversaries use some weapons against each other, but withhold others from use in a mutual bargain of restraint, would recognize that agreements do not always have to be openly and explicitly negotiated to be effective. "Watch what I do, rather than what I say" is the implicit principal message on each side, in a process of tacit bargaining whereby each country calibrates its own restraints on the basis of restraints noticeable on the other side.[8] Why should not the same methods of tacit bargaining apply to restraints in the *procurement* of arms, as effectively as restraints on the *use?* The same basic logic applies, that each side holds itself back somewhat, in exchange for the other side holding itself back somewhat, for a limited arms race is only an ultimate form of limited war.

The intuition of the public, however, is that something is added by open negotiations, with diplomats talking to each other across a table, culminating in a formal document decorated with signatures and seals and ratifications. This intuition may not be altogether wrong here, but we must now ask ourselves a little more precisely what such formality really adds.

Formality of negotiations may make each side's intentions clearer, of course. The tacit bargaining process in limited war depends heavily on clarity of distinctions ("south of the Yalu, but not north"; "conventional weapons, but not nuclear"); such bargaining restraints and limits are always in danger when the distinctions get blurry, for then each side has difficulty knowing what it is supposed to expect from the other side, and what the other side is expecting in return. It is possible that two powers could restrain their arms procurements by simply watching each other's practice, but some verbal (that is, formal and nontacit) communication might ease possible confusions and reduce the risk of mutually unwanted rounds of increased arms competition.

Formal public declarations also introduce the mechanism of the "promise." A promise is a statement of future intentions that would not have been true until it was made. It is more than an outline of what the country would have done in any event. Rather, it is a public assurance before witnesses (with the country's future honor and credibility at stake) that we will restrain ourselves in the future, if our adversary has restrained himself in some parallel way. The promise mechanism, needing formal negotiation and declaration, gets around problems of timing, for someone usually has to commit himself first, wondering whether the other side will not pull a double cross once the initial concession of restraint has been delivered. When we keep a promise, we pass up the temptations and opportunities of such a double cross. We give up what would have been an advantage in terms of our national interest, because we have already mortgaged our national honor in such a way that a double cross would damage our national interest. The on-going exchange of promises and compliance with promises in the longer run serves the national interests of both sides; formal contracts, publicized to the world amid rounds of champagne toasts, guide the two adversaries into a less expensive version of arms competition, perhaps making wars less likely, certainly making military preparedness in peacetime less costly.

A third kind of advantage for the more formal version of arms reduction negotiations stems from the political signals and side effects of any reduction in adversarial competition between two military powers. One of the "peacetime costs" lamentable in any arms race is the political poisoning by which two publics nurture a dislike for each other, and whereby their mutual propaganda assaults make both sides look less attractive to the rest of the world. If the formal negotiation of an arms agreement, even an agreement relatively trivial in substance like the denuclearization of outer space, can be publicized widely enough, it might have a political multiplier effect whereby Russians and Americans come to think better of each other and whereby Swedes, Indians, Japanese, and Kenyans come to think better of both Russians and Americans.

Yet for each of these possible advantages of formal negotiations, there are corresponding possibilities of problems. To begin with the last item on the list, the political multiplier can work in either direction. When Moscow and Washington are in the mood to compliment each other (when, say, the objective political or military situation is brewing less deep conflict between the two), then negotiations at the United Nations, or on the Strategic Arms Limitations Talks (SALT), or the mutual and balanced force reduction (MBFR), can work to amplify this mood. When they are instead in a mood to challenge each other (perhaps because the objective situation is more suggestive of conflict), the same formal negotiations amplify such conflict, as each side can use negotiations to try to embarrass the other.

Almost everything that gets put forward in any formal discussion of armaments thus has to be assayed for its propaganda content, as well as for its substantive value. The U.S.–Soviet agreements on Antarctica and Outer Space and the Seabed were probably low in substantive value, but at least had a very positive propaganda value. The hotline agreement, and especially the nuclear Nonproliferation Treaty

(NPT), were much higher in substantive value (in terms of real impact on the future likelihoods or nature of war), and were also quite positive in their propaganda value. Yet one should also remember the long period from 1945 to the 1960s when the great majority of Soviet or American formal proposals on arms reductions were functionally very negative as propaganda, inadvertently or deliberately shaped to make the opposing side look bad. One fear for the 1980s is that the two superpowers may be returning to this style in using formal negotiations, with each side putting forward proposals designed to look reasonable to the neutral gallery, even if it knows in advance that its adversary will have to reject such proposals.

The 1946 United States Baruch Plan for the elimination of nuclear weapons might be criticized on these grounds, for it looked like a very generous renunciation by the United States of its "trump suit" in such weapons, but it ignored the fact that American nuclear scientists would retain knowledge of how such bombs are made, which would have been a major source of power leverage in any future crisis. Soviet proposals in the early 1950s for "one-third" slashes in conventional forces were similarly suspect; ostensibly, it was the Soviets' trump suit, but would a one-third reduction on each side not have given each even more of an overall advantage, an even easier trip for the Red Army down the road to Paris? The Soviets also typically proposed disarmament without inspection or verification, a proposal that looked very disingenuous, coming from a society as closed as that of the USSR. If the United States had accepted such unverified disarmament schemes, the result might well have been a unilateral Western disarmament, as Moscow merrily failed to comply with its share of the disarmament obligation, hiding behind the secrecy of the Iron Curtain. But if the United States had rejected the proposal, it could then have been pilloried for "opposing disarmament," as Moscow scored points with the neutral gallery.[9]

It would be wrong to contend that the dialogue at the beginning of the 1980s has descended to the level of the early 1950s. Yet the exchanges are more propaganda-oriented again (to be precise, more oriented toward negative propaganda) than they were at the beginning of the 1970s. Under such circumstances, the goals the United States wishes to advance might be served better by an absence of formal negotiations, rather than by a diplomatic game of beggar thy neighbor.

In addition to the possibility of negative propaganda, another undesirable aspect of formal negotiations can appear, namely, the litigiousness that follows in the wake of negotiations. As noted earlier, negotiations can help to clarify relationships, but they also typically lead negotiators to call in lawyers to assist in the clarification process; such lawyers often then encourage their clients to demand more and to concede less. Concessions are held back as bargaining chips, to be delivered only if the opposing side delivers something. When a bargaining chip is a weapons system that otherwise looked wasteful and unpromising, something one side would not have wished to procure per se, the bizarre result can be that an ongoing process of formal negotiations causes higher defense spending on each side.

The argument can be illustrated with a homely analogy. Suppose that we wish to clarify our relationship with a next-door neighbor, with regard to one man's apples falling into another's yard, or one man's amateur radio generating interference with another's television set, for example. Such relationships are typically sorted out in a relatively light, informal, and "neighborly" atmosphere, rarely put down in the form of a contract on paper. If each property owner were to decide to enhance the clarity of the relationship, however, by hiring a lawyer to draft a contract, many more issues might suddenly be introduced as part of the general quid pro quo, or as what we have come to refer to as bargaining chips in the negotiations about strategic or theater missile forces.

There are thus pessimistic analysts who, after looking at the domestic political processes of the two superpowers and at the general process of formal arms negotiations, have concluded that fewer weapons would have been purchased or retained on each side if there had never been a SALT negotiation. They point to the enormous number (some fourteen hundred) of B-47 jet bombers built by the United States at the beginning of the 1950s and then scrapped as wastefully obsolete in the mid-1960s. If formal disarmament negotiations with Moscow had already been under way in the years these bombers were slated for the scrap heap, might not someone have counselled that they should be retained as a bargaining chip until the Soviets offered to scrap something in exchange? Might they not then still be in our force inventory today?

Military Strategy

If the logic of arms control thus meshes, but only somewhat imperfectly, with the more traditional advocacy of disarmament or of formal negotiations, how does it compare with more traditional notions of military strategy? As hawkish supporters of Ronald Reagan helped him win the 1980 election by denouncing arms control, how much conflict (or confusion) is there in this area?

The traditional notion of military strategy was indeed often simply to defeat one's enemy, to disarm enemy military forces so as to protect one's own civilians and to achieve the political goals of the war. When war was declared, considerations of bargaining or reasoning with the enemy tended to be suspended, as the military operation became a straightforward counterforce exercise in striking the weapons from the enemy's hands.

The introduction of nuclear weapons in 1945 made a tremendous difference, however. For the first time, any nation that had been defeated on the oceans and on the battlefields might still be able to inflict horrendous destruction on its enemy's civilian population, perhaps doing so in a last-gasp burst of spiteful retaliation. Barring some kind of splendid first strike, which would cripple all the nuclear forces on the other side before it could inflict any retaliation in a second strike, the United States now would always have to keep the adversary's motives in mind, even after war had been declared.

Military strategy today still includes moves to weaken the enemy in military strength, but it also must include substantial bargaining with the same enemy, to dissuade him from doing the very worst he can do. For the purpose of dissuasion or deterrence, it helps to be able to inflict horrible punishments on the enemy's cities and population, *and* not to have inflicted such punishment as yet, holding this power in reserve and holding his people as intact hostages for the welfare of Americans.

The entire meaning of *strategy* has thus changed from simply how to disable the enemy, to how to disable and at the same time dissuade him, by a bargaining combination of threats and promises, facilitated by restraints in U.S. behavior, from inflicting the greatest possible damage. Each side has an enormous interest in keeping a lid on the volume of warfare, in keeping the worst round of nuclear exchanges from occurring. Each side will also be playing the game of trying to get the other side to carry more of the burden in moderation, of holding down such escalation.

The choices here are hardly easy. What follows is offered as a modest proposal for the goals of U.S. military strategy in today's nuclear environment, a list that could easily belong to the Soviet Union as well.

A Plausible List of the
Categories of Gains to be Sought in Strategy

A. 1. deter attacks on the United States itself

    2. but—in event they happen, reduce physical damage

    3. but—in event they happen, prevail politically

B. 1. deter attacks on our closest allies abroad (Western Europe, Japan—and the Middle East?)

    2. but—in event they happen, reduce physical damage

    3. but—in event they happen, prevail politically

C. 1. deter attacks also on our less valued allies

    2. but—in event they happen, reduce physical damage

    3. but—in event they happen, prevail politically

D. 2. reduce the physical (economic and otherwise) costs in peacetime

    3. prevail politically in peacetime

A first crucial point about this list is that every item on it may conflict with every other item. For a problem-set examination in a course on defense policy and arms control, one could list each of the pairs of considerations here and ask students to cite one policy choice or weapons-procurement choice to illustrate each of these tensions. What makes an attack on North America less likely may sadly and bizarrely make an attack on Western Europe more likely. What makes a war in Western Europe more destructive may make such a war less likely.

The current debate about deployments of intermediate-range nuclear missiles to Western Europe illustrates these dilemmas and needs for choice all too well. Such weapons almost certainly (despite some reassuring statements from the U.S. administration) will be difficult to control once they come into use in any war, thus causing very substantial damage to both Western and Eastern Europe and perhaps to the Soviet Union, and then perhaps to the entire world in a final escalation to World War III. Hence the arguments of former Defense Secretary McNamara and others that all such nuclear weapons ought to be withdrawn from the NATO theater, as the United States would adopt a "no first use" policy on such weapons, not employing them unless the Soviet Union did so first.

Yet such escalation and destruction also make it less likely that the Soviets will invade Western Europe in the first place, as Moscow will have to be appalled and deterred by the prospect. Choosing between making wars less horrible or less likely is surely an unwelcome task, but it is a task we can not escape.

The decisions on the MX as a replacement for Minuteman intercontinental ballistic missiles (ICBMs) illustrates some of the same worrisome needs for choice. The MX will be less vulnerable to an attack by Soviet ICBMs, which might seem like a general gain, discouraging Soviet attacks and enhancing some American positions if an attack should nonetheless come. The MX will also be considerably more accurate than Minuteman, a much more mixed blessing.[10]

Accuracy allows one to hit Soviet military targets without inflicting as much destruction on Soviet civilians, a clear gain from a humane point of view (reducing the destructiveness of war); such accuracy might also reduce the damage suffered by U.S. civilians, since the United States might destroy some Soviet ICBMs poised to strike once again at its cities. Yet this very threat to Soviet missile silos might panic the Soviet leadership, as they felt themselves pushed into a "use them or lose them" situation, driven to fire off their missiles in a crisis for fear of what the United States might be about to do, with the result of raising the likelihood of nuclear war, a most undesirable result indeed.

All military capabilities thus have to be reexamined by the logic of arms control in light of the awesomeness of the destructive power of nuclear weapons. The moral intuitions of the disarmer are a very imperfect guide here. Equally imperfect are the moral intuitions of the traditional professional soldier, taught to seek to disarm an enemy and to protect his own civilians. Much as such behavior might seem appropriate in a war occurring if deterrence fails, it might make war much more likely; that is, it might cause deterrence to fail where it otherwise would have succeeded.

The choices are even more spread out than was initially described. Beyond choosing between making war less horrible and less likely (with the two seldom going together), the United States must choose between making war in Europe or the Far East less likely, and making war in North America less likely. Increasing the chances that North America would be exempted from any future war in these regions might sadly increase their probability of war. The need for choice here is at the center of all discussions of national security and arms control. It is unhelpful for critics from either the Left or the Right to brush aside such needs for choice, for our analysis would only suffer in the disappointments that ensued.

When discussing deterrence of enemy aggression, we must now continually distinguish between two very different approaches. The first, that of conventional warfare preparations, is what was the United States' only military option prior to Hiroshima and Nagasaki: strengthening U.S. infantry and tank forces so that they can repulse any Soviet attack on Western Europe, on the Persian Gulf, on South Korea, or on whatever other piece of territory is that important. This approach might be viewed as stressing defense rather than deterrence, or, in Glenn Snyder's phrase, it might lead to a "deterrence by denial," as Soviet attacks might never actually have to be repulsed, since Moscow would realize in advance that its troops could not capture any of these territories and that such troops would only undergo needless suffering and humiliation in the attempt.[11] The pains that deterred would be pains typical of warfare, the dead and wounded of the battlefield, the lost tanks and aircraft, all with no redeeming prospect of victory.

A very different approach to deterrence comes with the introduction of nuclear weapons. In this situation "denial" may not occur, as Soviet tanks reach Frankfurt and Paris soon enough, but as cities like Leningrad, Kiev, and Moscow are destroyed in the meantime, perhaps for military reasons, perhaps merely as spiteful retaliation. Deterrence rather than defense is being stressed here. In Snyder's typology, we have "deterrence by punishment" rather than "deterrence by denial," a much more costly and brutal form of war, but perhaps a more reliable and effective deterrent.

However more brutally destructive nuclear war would be, if war were to come, the probability of war may be reduced. Even more assuredly, the peacetime costs and economic burden of nuclear weaponry has been far less than the costs and burden of mounting a conventional defense would have been. It is difficult to believe that the Western European recovery after 1948 could have moved as it did, with economic miracles and unprecedented economic growth, if nuclear weapons had not existed and if the NATO countries had been forced to maintain large standing armies to ensure against Soviet attack.

To repeat a point made earlier, very few observers believe that the Soviets would ever want to destroy Western Europe in a nuclear attack; the worry is rather that Moscow might like to seize and incorporate this area by conventional military aggression, with its industrial potential and population largely intact.

To make a crude analogy, Western Europe does not have to worry about murder as much as about rape, for it is very attractive to the East. In Gothic novels, one classic defense against rape was for the heroine to plunge over a cliff, preserving her honor, killing herself and her assailant; if the potential assailant had read such a novel in advance, however, he might not have attempted the attack. This prospect of deterrence by the prospect of suicidal nuclear retaliatory punishment has thus played an important, if often not fully admitted, role in U.S. and Western European strategic planning for all the years since World War II.

How do we decide whether to stress decreasing the costs of wars (which might well entail pulling nuclear forces, and perhaps all U.S. forces, out of possible theaters of conflict), or decreasing the likelihood of wars (which might mean leaving such forces in the path of possible invasions—making wars much more destructive if they break out—but perhaps deterring invaders from launching such wars in the first place)? Balancing all these considerations is difficult, but it is not yet impossible. Happily enough, when the United States is known to care very much about an area (the closest allies on its list), the likelihood of deterrence increases; that is, the likelihood of war decreases, because the adversary is all the more convinced that an aggression would bring unacceptable levels of retaliation.

One could thus propose the following as a rule of thumb: Where the likelihood of war is high (as in Lebanon or Thailand, for example), the United States should devote most of its efforts to keeping the costs down (as by keeping nuclear weapons away from the scene). Where the likelihood of war is already low, however, the United States might instead tailor its efforts to keeping it low, as with the continued deployment of U.S. forces and nuclear weapons to Western Europe.

Arms Control and Military Strategy

The first major point about the list of goals for strategy was that choices are inevitable, the kind of choices that may lead to relatively satisfactory solutions, but hardly to perfect ones. A second crucial point about this list is that it is remarkably similar, simply being a longer and more disaggregated version, to the list of arms control outputs cited earlier. The lists are indeed so parallel that the more diligent and perceptive student would suspect that he is being cheated of value for his tuition money, since he is in effect getting the same lecture twice.

But the congruence here is no coincidence, for the logic and the goals of strategy should now indeed be the same as the logic and the goals of arms control. Arms control is either the opposite side of the same coin of strategy, or it may even be functionally identical to it.

The difference then is not in where we must land conceptually and intellectually, but in where we will have been coming from. The former believer in disarmament, reluctantly accepting instead the more realistic and somewhat more pessimistic calculations of arms control, enters the stage through a very different door from that of the admirals or generals, who now must demonstrate an awareness of the need for continual restraint and continual bargaining (even in wartime) with the "enemy," for "fighting with one arm tied in back."

It should be welcome news that such an awareness of arms control considerations has permeated the thinking of U.S. military officers, so that they would no longer automatically applaud General MacArthur's comments on the Korean War, that "in war there is no substitute for victory." In war and in peace, there is simply no substitute for concentrating on what the nation really cares about, which includes some (but not all) kinds of "victory," but also includes the avoidance of most rungs of escalation. Air force or army colonels and navy captains must now demonstrate a familiarity with this logic if they are to have any prospect of reaching the ranks of general or admiral. They are exposed to this logic at the war colleges, at the civilian universities to which they are sent, and on a host of other occasions.

The arms control approach will often enough favor reductions in armaments, thus matching the intuitive feelings of disarmament advocates and of a great many ordinary citizens. Some weapons are destabilizing in that they reward whoever strikes first in a crisis, at either the nuclear or the conventional level, and thus make war more likely. Other weapons do not change the likelihood of war in one direction or other, but waste the resources of the nations investing in them.

Yet at times the arms control analysis will have to depart from such intuitive feelings by endorsing some weapons, even arguing that more would be better than fewer. We could begin with some fairly obvious examples of "good" military hardware, for example, the permissive action links (PAL) that make it impossible to fire nuclear weapons without the approval of higher command authority, or the enhanced command and control links that also ensure that the president and high-ranking officers can communicate with each other during a crisis or during a war and that they can reach all their military subordinates. Reconnaissance satellites (often still labelled "spy satellites" in the popular press) are also desirable, in that they allow each side to be surer of how many missiles the other side has, thus somewhat dampening an arms race that otherwise would have expanded in the wake of uncertainties.[12] The first two military systems here are desirable because they can reduce the damage if a war comes, and the third because it may help to reduce the volume and costs of a peacetime armed confrontation.

Also highly desirable are secure second-strike retaliatory forces, such as the submarine-based missiles of the Polaris, Poseidon, and Trident varieties, based so that an adversary has almost no opportunity or temptation to find and attack them.[13] Rather than being condemned for military research, the engineers who speeded the development and deployment of the original Polaris submarine-launched ballistic missile (SLBM) systems might better have been nominated for the Nobel Peace Prize; the existence of such secure systems, really usable only for retaliation and not for trying to prevent someone else's retaliation by a sneak attack, greatly contributed to the peace and stability of the 1960s and 1970s. Rather than smaller numbers, the production of larger numbers of these missiles can thus be endorsed in some of these categories (although today's numbers certainly seem large enough), because they make war less likely.

To endorse such weapons goes against the grain of most of what many peace-minded Americans have believed all their lives. Going against the attitudes of some other Americans, the arms control analyst might further endorse the possession of such weapons by U.S. adversaries as well. The United States is better off if the Soviets also have "spy satellites," the capability for verification by national technical means, because this allows them to relax somewhat more, having reliable information on the totals of U.S. missile forces. The United States is better off if the Soviets have submarine-based missile forces of their own, because having them will allow the Soviets to feel more secure in a crisis, less worried that the United States might try to launch some kind of "splendid first strike." The Soviet SLBM forces might increase the destruction in the United States if war comes, but (more important) they might make such a war less likely.

This last category best illustrates the disturbing novelty of arms control analysis, stemming from the disturbing novelty of the magnitude of the threat of nuclear war. One can find some examples in earlier history when Americans may have wanted to deny their own country some kind of military capability. But one can not find instances of Americans' wishing the nation's principal adversary to have a military capability, actually hoping that it would move a little faster to develop and reensure such capability.

Even harder for the typical American to accept would be the next logical step in policymakers' worries about the likelihood of war. If an adversary does not himself follow good advice by purchasing the more stabilizing weapons and instead buys the destabilizing, should the United States then feel free to follow suit? It is destabilizing for a power to acquire multiple warhead missiles and to enhance their accuracy, because this tends to make a first strike advantageous in a missile exchange, rather than sitting still and letting the other side fire first. If Moscow invests in MIRVs (multiple independently targeted reentry vehicles) or in very accurate guidance systems for intercontinental missiles, does it not naturally follow that the United States is somehow redressing the balance by matching such procurements?

At the conventional level, too much reliance on rapid deployment forces, carried to future crisis situations by new troop-carrier aircraft or landing ships, could similarly set up a situation in which whoever moved first had the best prospects of victory, an unstable and undesirable situation. But what if the Soviets acquire such greater troop-carrier capability? Does the United States not have to follow suit?

Rather than redressing the balance, such a matching procurement on the U.S. side could work to compound and intensify the imbalance, in the sense of making a first strike all the more attractive, in making crisis situations all the more unstable. A situation is referred to here as unstable whenever rumors of war tend to be self-confirming, when they tend to drive political and military leaders to precautionary actions that push everyone into war. Conversely a weapons system is regarded as stabilizing when it causes leaders to respond to any rumors by moves that do not amount to war, by moves that instead amount to reinforcements for peace as well as reinforcements for their national interest.

If the Soviets acquire MIRVs or troop-carrier capabilities, it may thus be a far from appropriate response for the United States to acquire the same systems. Yet one can hardly convince patriotic Americans that the U.S. response should be to do nothing. The appropriate response, by the logic of arms control, by the logic of responsible military strategy, would instead be to find new weapons that would undo the impact of the Soviet procurements, rather than duplicating and mirroring that impact. In the end, this approach almost becomes another plea for defensive weapons, despite all the abuse and criticism that the offense-defense distinction has suffered over the past four decades.

Some weapons reward, in terms of the counterforce exchange, the side that is moving forward, the side that takes the initiative to strike first. These weapons should be labelled offensive. Other weapons have the opposite impact, imposing higher disablement and casualties on the side that takes the initiative, rewarding instead the side that elected to wait and let the attack come. These weapons we would define here as defensive.

All these considerations are also sometimes discussed in terms of different notions of stability. We speak of crisis stability in the sense of keeping nations from panicking out of fear of being attacked in a crisis, to prevent rumors of war from becoming self-confirming. With the application of sound arms control analysis to the design of weapons, however, we might thus hope to have systems in place that allow each side to wait and see, systems that strengthen the defense and weaken the offense in each direction.

We speak then of deterrence stability in terms of discouraging aggressions, the kinds of attacks based on simple greed and power-lust rather than preemptive anticipations of U.S. attacks. It is crucial to discourage the first without encouraging the second, and vice versa. As in the domestic arena, policymakers want everyone to know that criminal behavior will be punished and that noncriminal behavior will not be punished. The United States wants neither to tempt the Soviets into attacking, nor to stampede them out of fears that the United States is so tempted.

Finally, we speak of arms race stability. The first two categories of stability pertained to the impact of the production of any new weapons system on the likelihood of war. This third category pertains to the impact on the likelihood of further arms procurements by the Soviets, and then again in another round by the United States. When weapons lead to the use of weapons, policymakers worry a great deal. When weapons lead instead merely to the procurement of more weapons, policymakers may worry a little less, but there is still damage to be considered.

Making wars unlikely and reducing the costs of military preparations in peacetime (along with moderating wars if they occur) continue to be very appealing goals for U.S. policy. If Americans were perplexed by the challenge of balancing considerations of security against considerations of arms control, they do not need to feel hopelessly perplexed. Americans can serve the nation's foreign policy goals, and wider goals as compassionate human beings, always having to make tough choices, but at the least making such choices clearheadedly and wisely.

Notes

1. Halford J. Mackinder, *The Scope and Methods of Geography and the Geographical Pivot of History* (London: Murray, 1951).

2. On the evolution of U.S. concerns about Soviet intentions in Europe after World War II, see Adam Ulam, *The Rivals* (New York: Viking, 1971).

3. The special problems of the Persian Gulf are discussed in Anthony Cordesman (ed.), *The Gulf and the Search for Strategic Stability* (Boulder, Colo.: Westview, 1984).

4. Thomas C. Schelling and Morton H. Halperin, *Strategy and Arms Control* (New York: Twentieth Century Fund, 1961), 2.

5. See William C. Potter, *Nuclear Power and Nonproliferation* (Cambridge, Mass.: Oelgeschlager, Gunn, and Hain, 1982).

6. For a careful evaluation of the difficulties of the IAEA's task inspecting peaceful nuclear facilities, see Lawrence Scheinman, *The Nonproliferation Role of the International Atomic Energy Agency* (Washington, D.C.: Resources for the Future, 1985).

7. Some well-stated criticisms of the SDI proposal are to be found in Sidney D. Drell, Philip J. Farley, and David Holloway, "Preserving the ABM Treaty: A Critique of the Reagan Strategic Defense Initiative," and in Charles L. Glaser, "Why Even Good Defenses May Be Bad," *International Security* 9, no. 2 (Fall 1984):51–122.

8. The dynamics of tacit bargaining are outlined in Thomas C. Schelling, *The Strategy of Conflict* (Cambridge: Harvard University Press, 1960), chapter 3.

9. On the earlier tone of disarmament negotiations, see John W. Spanier and Joseph Nogee, *The Politics of Disarmament: A Study in Soviet–American Gamesmanship* (New York: Praeger, 1962).

10. For a criticism of the MX missile, see Herbert Scoville, *MX: Prescription for Disaster* (Cambridge, Mass.: MIT Press, 1981).

11. Glenn Snyder, *Deterrence and Defense* (Princeton: Princeton University Press, 1961), 14–16.

12. A good survey of the early role of reconnaissance satellites can be found in Philip Klass, *Secret Sentries in Space* (New York: Random House, 1971).

13. On the contributions of submarine-based missile systems to the reensurance of peace, see Oskar Morgenstern, *The Question of National Defense* (New York: Random House, 1959).

2
Six Causes of War

T
he reader of this chapter will be asked to use a very simple game-theoretical matrix in order to distinguish among some very different causes of war. When the blurring tendencies of the language make such causes seem the same, we are less able to understand what is happening. We are probably also less able to keep the peace.

Can wars come about because states trust each other too little? The answer is yes. Wars can come about also because states trust each other too much, as will be shown as the matrices are developed. Indeed, are we sure of what we mean by such words as *trust, defense, deterrence, pacifism,* and *surrender?* It is to be hoped that the numerical relationships here will clarify such concepts.

The intention of this chapter is hardly to be rigorous in working within the canons of mathematical game theory. It is rather to apply game theory so as to be more rigorous in discerning and separating differing kinds of causes of war. The game-theoretical notation will at times thus be adapted and amended from normal usage, with the hope of contributing to the political analysis.

It is hoped that the reader will find it easy to relate such elementary concepts of game theory as "prisoners' dilemma" and "zero sum" to the shape of the international system. Similarly, he should be able to apply game-theoretical matrices in the future to trace out the complicated interactions that follow the introduction of yet another new weapons system. And he should be able to sort out and avoid the semantic confusions of ordinary-language analyses of international conflict.

Reprinted from the *Jerusalem Journal of International Relations* 6, no. 2 (Summer 1982):1–23.

Above all, the stress will be on demonstrating how different wars in history were produced by differing causes, such that supposed antidotes to conflict have to be administered with great caution, lest the administration of the wrong antidote worsen the situation.

Causes of War

Operations Research Error

Many of us might be quick to conclude that war is always caused by some sort of foolishness, that only stupidity could lead two nations into the mutually disadvantageous payoffs of war when they could both have peace. The most important function of this entire exercise may be to sort out the occasions on which such foolishness or stupidity is in fact to blame and when it is not.

Some wars are indeed directly caused by a straightforward mistake, by the simple misanalysis of battlefield outcomes, of "who will win." Greek generals in 1940 told their prime minister that they could hold back Italian armies; Italian generals at the same time were telling Mussolini that their armies could easily plunge from Albania into Greece. The Italian staff officers were wrong, and the war (as shown in matrix 1A) simply reflected the folly in two sides expecting to win, when by definition only one could.

Matrix 1A

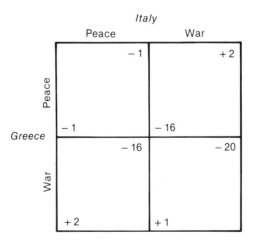

Matrix 1B

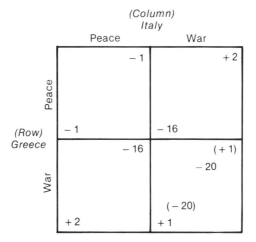

An adapted notation will now be used here whereby a payoff within parentheses depicts an illusory payoff as seen by one of the parties. When the parenthesized payoff is to the lower left of the unparenthesized one, it indicates that "Column" sees the return correctly, while "Row" is misreading it, incorrectly expecting the payoff indicated within parentheses; the reverse is indicated, of course, when the parentheses are to the upper right of the real payoff (as in matrix 1B).

Perhaps there is a tendency everywhere for foolish mortals to overrate their own military prowess. Perhaps all losing generals should be fired, or even shot. However, the scientific accuracy of attempts to predict war outcomes has not yet become so great that neutral bystanders can always know for certain who has and who has not correctly judged the battlefield possibilities. It would be a more peaceful world if one could trust outside experts to settle the outcomes of wars in advance, much as good lawyers can settle legal cases out of court, sparing both sides the costs of litigation, by their expert predictions of how a court trial would go. One could thus imagine teams of experts from the Rand Corporation being flown into every crisis to make the predictions that would spare all sides the grief and expense of a war. Yet neither Rand nor the accumulated military professional research agencies of the world seem as yet to have this sort of prescient competence.

Matrix 2A

Lloyd George

	Peace	War
Peace	− 1 − 1	+ 2 − 16
Kaiser War	− 16 + 2	− 20 − 20

"Tug-of-War"

If it is difficult to predict war outcomes for the case just sketched, predictions may be even more difficult, though just as important, in the
war situation outlined in matrix 2A. Each side here is overrating not
necessarily its own military capability, but rather its own resolve. Each
is wagering that its opponent will soon surrender, if only the war can
be prolonged a few more months; each is thus also overrating and
misreading the opposite side's aversion to war.

In a sense, therefore, this also is a situation in which error produces
or prolongs war. Which side would surrender first in World War I?
Lloyd George and the kaiser were each betting that the other would
have to give in first.[1] Similarly, mutually contradicting bets were made
by Lyndon Johnson and Ho Chi Minh.

The war of attrition here, or "tug-of-war," closely resembles the
game of "chicken," wherein young men drive automobiles directly at
each other to see who will be the first to veer off the collision course.
The major difference in "chicken" is that the material costs of the
"war" are not borne minute by minute, but are to be found in the
continually increasing risk of disaster, which, of course, generates a
psychological cost on the two drivers minute by minute. The persistence of each side in such a costly and dangerous exercise nonetheless
is to be traced to the same calculation as was noted earlier, each side's
assumption that the other will be the first to buckle under the strain.[2]

This endurance contest pattern indeed shows up in much of politics apart from war. From any situation that is less than ideal, a spectrum of moves is possible that should result in an improvement for both sides. Since each side knows this, each may be tempted to hold out at the position least favorable to both, in an attempt to win the bulk of the improvement for itself. The failure to reach the optimality frontier thus becomes an endurance contest in which each side is betting that the other will give up first. One side, of course, is wrong in its bet, but it is hardly pathologically stupid in making this error. The matrix as it stands does not determine any behavior; it dictates peace when the other side chooses war, and war when the other side chooses peace.

Seeking clues to predict the ultimate outcome, each side may watch for supposed asymmetries in the value patterns, whereby one side hates war more than the other. While this involves an interpersonal comparison of utility that is of questionable logical validity, it will nonetheless be the factor that drives the sides on. One form of error prolonging war would thus be that shown in matrix 2B, whereby each side exaggerates the other's disutility in war (the two misperceptions again being shown in parentheses).[3]

Matrix 2B

Ho Chi Minh

	Peace	War
Peace	− 1 / − 1	+ 2 / − 16
War	− 16 / + 2	− 20 (− 30) / (− 30) − 20

Lyndon Johnson

"Prisoners' Dilemma"

A third kind of war situation may not depend at all on any mispredictions or mistakes of the kinds cited above, but may be simply a function of a strategic situation that very much allows either side to gain by double-crossing the other and gives neither side any warning of a double cross by the other.[4]

Prisoners' dilemma, shown in matrix 3, may thus explain a great deal of war. What if the geographic and strategic situation between two nations is such that whoever strikes first comes out ahead for having done so? And what if there is no way for either side to know in advance whether or not the other is striking out on a path of violent hostility, until the blow is felt? The gains of a double cross in this case always turn out to be greater than those for cooperation (and the costs of a mutual double cross are severe, but less than the costs of foolish unilateral cooperation when the other side has decided on a double cross). In effect, each side knows that the other must betray the peace by shooting. Because we know that they will shoot, we also are better off shooting. Indeed, we would be better off shooting even if they were to stop.

Each side prefers peace to the wasteful war that results, a war in which both armies are actively defending themselves and attacking the other. Yet each side prefers still more a war in which it alone has attacked, as the other has laid down its arms. When peace is preferred to bilateral war, but unilateral war is preferred to peace, the result, almost inevitably, is bilateral war.

Matrix 3

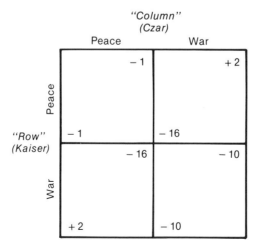

The original prisoners' dilemma scenario depicts two vagrants—"Column" and "Row"—taken into custody by an unscrupulous sheriff on false charges of burglary and held in adjoining separate prison cells as the sheriff attempts to extract confessions from them. Each prisoner is informed that he will get two years' employment as a deputy if he turns state's evidence against the other, if the other has still not confessed, and that the other will then get sixteen years in prison. If both plead innocent, both will receive shorter sentences (one year); but, if both confess in order to turn state's evidence, both will get ten years in prison.

Since the wall between the two prison cells is soundproof and the prisoners are not able to communicate, neither can be sure that the other is not betraying him to the sheriff, or that his own betrayal would be detected by the other in time for counteraction. Each prisoner is thus better off confessing no matter what the other does and each therefore "confesses" to receive ten years in prison, although honest cooperation would have gotten both men off with a one-year sentence.

The "error" or "misinformation" here lies wholly in the absence of a reliable communications and monitoring system, one that would let each player know if he were about to be double-crossed, in time to allow retaliation. The outcome of the prisoners' dilemma situation thus is directly related not to the wisdom or stupidity of the "prisoners," but to the presence or absence of devices that assure each side that it will know in time if the other is about to cheat, devices whose presence generally would make cooperation safe and advisable. Achieving this kind of warning device, however, is often very difficult.

The real-life international relations equivalent of the prisoners' dilemma was exemplified by the outbreak of World War I and the decisions of the kaiser and the czar to mobilize their armies. Each side was better off mobilizing, no matter what the other side did. If the other failed to follow suit, one could win a decisive victory; if the other side also had a mobilization underway, one could at least stave off a decisive defeat. The result, of course, was a war that neither side may have wanted. If Swedish or other observers could have been previously posted to the barracks and railway terminals of the major European powers, they might have served as the equivalent of a warning device "window" between prisoners' cells, and the war of 1914 might have been avoided.[5]

Mirror-Image Misunderstanding

A fourth case of war is not quite a prisoners' dilemma but has much of the same instability. In this case, shown in matrix 4A, each side would actually prefer peace to double-crossing the other side, but each is deeply afraid of the consequences should the other side want to commit a double cross.

Matrix 4A

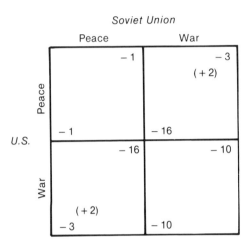

We again use the special notation of parentheses to show where each side may be misperceiving the preferences of the other. Each nation cannot be sure that the other side prefers peace to attacking. Moreover, it cannot be sure that the other side knows it prefers peace to unilaterally attacking it. For either reason, each must prefer to defend itself, which will appear as preparations for attacking the other. Furthermore, when the other similarly seems to be preparing to attack, one's own preparations must be accelerated. Hence any slight increase in the perceived probability of war becomes self-confirming.

Unlike the previous case, peace here does not fully require that both sides know that they could not get away with a sneak attack. In truth, neither side would *want* to get away with it even if it could; rather, peace depends on each convincing the other of that. This may seem easier in some ways than installing the monitoring system noted above, but it may be harder, too. Technology gave us reconnaissance satellites that can warn us of Soviet missile procurements. Could

Kremlinologists and their opposite numbers in the Soviet Union ever really convince each side that the other had never been tempted by war and aggression?

This model has often been put forward as the explanation of the Cold War between the United States and the Soviet Union after 1945, and as the likely cause of World War III, should it happen, perhaps because bombers or accurate missiles heavily favored whoever attacked first in nuclear war.[6] Supporters of the model of course presume no real hostility between the powers, no real intent to achieve world conquest for Communism or capitalist pluralism by surprise attack; in this model, it is only the false assumption of aggressive intentions on the other side that threatens war.

To demonstrate the basic instability of all such cases, we now introduce an asymmetrical confrontation (matrix 4B) imputing an aversion to aggression to only one of the adversaries, that is, blending Column's payoffs from matrix 3 with Row's payoffs from matrix 4A. The result produces war just as surely as if both sides preferred aggression, since both powers must race to start the war. It is, of course, precisely the fear of matrix 4B that causes the wars of matrix 4A.

Matrix 4B

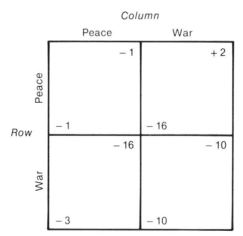

It should be noted that such matrices can describe hostile confrontations short of war, for example, arms races, as was illustrated by Soviet and U.S. arms procurements during most of the Cold War.

Perhaps the United States would have preferred not to run the arms race, but felt it had to match any further Soviet procurements; the Soviet leadership, in contrast, may indeed have preferred to try to buy arms whenever it could hope that the United States would not follow suit. We can depict this simply by replacing the Peace and War labels in matrix 4B with DA (for "disarm") and A (for "arm"), respectively, as in matrix 4C.

Matrix 4 C

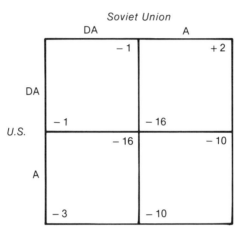

As with the pure prisoners' dilemma and the mirror-image mis-understanding, this mixed case would benefit from reliable surveil-lance and monitoring systems, systems giving each side fair warning of the other side's moves before those moves can be finalized.

The reader should note that this cause of war is precisely the oppo-site of the "tug-of-war" model presented above. War happens here because each side underrates the other's attachment to peace; in the tug-of-war model, each side overrates the other's attachment to peace, betting that the other will want to surrender first in order to end the war. As the causes are opposite, the antidotes also would seem oppo-site. Here we serve peace by teaching each side that the other really is peaceful; in the earlier war situation, we serve peace by teaching each side that the other is determined and bellicose and is unlikely to give in so easily.

"Zero-Sum" Total Hostility

The kinds of war situations discussed so far are based on mistakes in predicting the outcome of war (the first two cases) or on the inability to establish sufficient mutual trust between potential adversaries (the next two). Yet not every war results from these kinds of causes. To turn to perhaps the most depressing social relationship imaginable, one side might actually prefer war, in a sort of symbiotic conflict, rather than offering the minimum required for the other to surrender. Such a case is depicted in matrix 5A.

Matrix 5A

Carthage

	Peace	War
Peace (Rome)	−7 / −7	+2 / −16
War (Rome)	−16 / +2	−15 / +1

A game-theory-oriented reader will quickly note that this matrix describes a zero-sum game, that is, a set of outcomes such that neither side can gain in any shift without the other losing an equal amount. It is often noted that international politics is never a zero-sum game— indeed, that the concept may be meaningless since one cannot devise a meaningful interpersonal comparison of utility. This leads to the possibly joyous discovery that further possibilities for cooperation may exist. Yet the strict notion of zero sum is not as necessary for war here as we might have hoped. As shown in matrix 5B, which produces a result identical to that of matrix 5A, all that is required is that the two nations disagree on every possible choice between two outcomes. Since either side can start a war, war instead of peace is guaranteed,

Matrix 5B

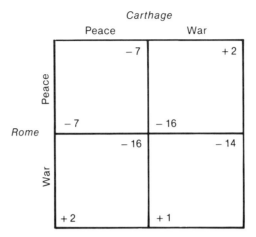

because one side at least prefers the outcome in mutual war to the outcome in mutual peace.[7]

If the numbers are allowed to have interpersonal significance here, moreover, it would be impossible for the loser to offer sufficient side-payment to the winner to make him peace-minded (impossible, that is, without first making the loser war-minded). The weaker side thus can never sue for peace, can never deliver enough ransom to make surrender an alternative. Each side would most prefer to fight and have the other not resist. Yet can it really be that the net utility for the two sides is greater if they both fight than if they both consent to "peaceful coexistence"? Unfortunately, it can be.

Perhaps the two populations would severely cramp each other's life-style by mere existence in the same region, so that one cannot easily offer the other life and peace, even in exchange for its surrender. For illustrative cases, one might consider the treatment of American Indians by white pioneers, or even the attitudes toward each other of some Israelis and some Arab Palestinians. People usually have an option for surrendering and agreeing to submit to the governance of new rulers in the territory they have populated. As POWs or as a captive nation, they could earn their keep, perhaps hoping for rebellion and political victory far into the future.[8] If the conquerer has absolutely no desire or need for their labor, however, he may not even feel able to offer them the option of staying. The extent to which the two groups would irritate and bother each other in any state of coexistence is thus shown by the worsened negative payoffs in the Peace–Peace box, where the net disutility is higher than in the War–War box. In such horrible instances, both sides will prefer war to peace even if they are fully aware of all the consequences. For at least one side, the war has become one of extermination or eviction of the other; for the resisting side, armed struggle is no more horrible than peace, for the latter entails being murdered or driven from their homes.

If zero sum were more often the case, war would more often be "totally rational"; war would be less tragic and far more common, and life might be grim indeed. Happily, such an array of payoffs and preferences is rare. Peoples do not normally dislike each other so much that they find the costs of war straightforwardly lower than the costs of coexistence.

Love of War

In a final discrete form of war situation it is, of course, possible that one side or both will actually prefer war to peace, as shown in matrix 6.

Matrix 6

	Peace	War
Peace	-1 -1	$+2$ -16
War	-16 $+2$	$+1$ $+1$

Such a positive desire for war could emerge because of some special interests that stood to gain from war and that were capable of ignoring the contrary preferences of the masses who must suffer. Or it could emerge because of deep economic, social, or psychological problems in the general society of the country choosing war, problems that could be eased only by the diversion of battles abroad. One can also, of course, imagine a society so "naturally" warlike that most of its citizens genuinely prefer combat to peace, for example, the Huns or the Mongols, to omit more recent examples of this extreme militarism.

It is difficult to determine how much, or how little, of war is explainable by such a direct preference for it. All of our other models of war are different in assuming that people generally prefer some form of peace to war, other things being equal. Here we would see war being found preferable to peace, other things being equal. Many of us like some violence, otherwise no one would play football. Yet how many of us like the violence of a modern battle? Statistics on suicide show that such self-directed violence usually declines at the outbreak of war, suggesting that some disturbed individuals can find value for their lives only when their country has committed itself to an armed struggle. In a well-functioning society, however, we would arrange for such persons to receive therapy and thus lead happy lives without battlefield carnage.

Marxist and radical economists sometimes argue that the needs of modern capitalism similarly cannot be satisfied without substantial expenditures on weapons and, therefore, without a positive liking for war, or at least for preparations for it. In the Marxist view, a well-functioning society would find other ways to keep aggregate demand properly in balance and to provide full employment; without a fundamental rearrangement of domestic society, however, the lust for war will persist.

There is a different version of the Marxist argument that is much more like the zero-sum war situation outlined above, that is, that advanced capitalist societies are so desperate for overseas markets that they are driven into war, not because they have come to like war itself, but because none of them can stand a peace in which they do not have control over these markets. Such an analysis sees World War I or the Spanish–American War or even the Japanese–American portion of World War II as a simple life-and-death struggle among capitalist economies. Such capitalist economies may have no particular desire for war, but they are in the grip of an unbridgeable incompatibility, in that what one needs for its own economic health stands in the way of what the other needs.

It should be noted that both such radical claims of a link between capitalism and war are not easy to prove. While we have some evidence that defense industries like war preparations, other forms of industry typically do not, and even the defense industry has shown no particular lust for actual fighting, as opposed to mere preparations. With regard to competition for markets, the radical analysis must show more than that markets are attractive, for everyone surely welcomes a regular customer; it must, rather, show that the overseas markets involved in political conflict loomed so large in the economies of the advanced capitalist states that war became the necessary and thinkable way to get them. The data for World War I, the Spanish–American War and World War II in the Far East do not suggest any such dominant role, any such zero-sum game.

Summary of Section One

What kind of typology of causes of war have we constructed here? A reader might conclude that, by setting up six kinds of situations that can explain a war, we have generated six yes-no questions about the world, which would thus give us $(2)^6 = 64$ possible complicated combinations of causes of war. In truth, this is not the case.

The cause of war that was discussed first, simple stupidity, can, of course, coexist with all the others. Foolishness can increase the chances of war in any of the situations presented. The intent in outlining the next five cases was to examine whether ignorance is *required* in order for a war to break out; in a way, each of these cases produces a war that does not need to be accounted for by simple foolishness and error. If there is an "error" in the "tug-of-war," for example, it is an "error" that each side is making, where the "right answer" does not exist until the two adversaries settle the matter by their very behavior.

As a study of the matrices shows, moreover, all of the causes of war but the first are discrete from and incompatible with each other. To change the numbers in the boxes, to reverse one or both players' preferences for a certain alternative, is to convert one model into another.

Steps toward Peace

If these cases represent six discrete turning points in the international system that can cause war, what can one propose or hope to achieve in the way of eliminating such causes? What changes in the nature of the situations can one seek in order to increase the chances of peace?

Eliminate Love of War

A first kind of change would have the highest priority almost by definition: the elimination of most situations in which states actually prefer war to peace, actually "enjoy war." If one accepts theories that blame war on psychological, sociological, economic, or political pathologies of societies at their domestic level, or that blame individual human beings themselves, one must work for peace mainly "at home." Changing our domestic arrangements would strike some readers as a desirable goal in its own right, as reforms are needed for altogether domestic reasons. Achieving such domestic reforms is not always easy, however.

Fortunately or otherwise, such domestic social and economic ailments may not so typically be the international problem with respect to the causation of war. People rarely look forward to war in today's world. The solution to the war problem often will let us move on to other steps.

Eliminate Disagreement

A second comparably basic approach to peace would be to eliminate the total (zero-sum) hatred that constitutes the fifth kind of cause of war, a situation in which each side finds unacceptable what the other finds acceptable. Here neither side prefers war to peace, but both prefer war to a peace that would let the other side remain to live in peace.

Again one must begin by stipulating how little leverage can be applied against the preferences of societies and individuals. If people hate each other and are uncomfortable in each other's presence, what can we do to change that?

Again, however, we can reassure ourselves by the fact that at least such zero-sum hatred is rare as a cause of war, for it is very unusual now for people to disagree so totally about their goals in life. The Arab–Israeli conflict is perhaps the closest approximation we have to this kind of conflict today. But other examples are hard to find, and the ideological conflict between capitalism and Communism is clearly of a different sort.

Continuing with our effort to eliminate causes of war, we might note the advisability of stressing cooperation and agreement in general, thereby not just eliminating zero-sum conflicts but perhaps eliminating conflict altogether. Would not peace become very likely if nations were to come to agree on their first choices about life, such that whatever one saw as optimal the other saw as optimal too?

At an extreme, this might be a world in which the two sides agree totally on their ranking of preferences all through the list, as shown in matrix 7A. As a perhaps less demanding alternative, but one offering the same benefit of reducing the likelihood of war, the two sides could at least agree on their first choices, even if they differed in evaluating their second, third, fourth, and so on (matrix 7B). (One must note, however, that in both of these cases, even in the totally cooperative

Matrix 7A

Matrix 7B

matrix 7A, peaceful behavior by Column would depend on its trusting the intentions and *competence* of Row. If Row were foolishly to opt for war, Column would be wise to do so as well.)

Eliminating disagreements about first choices would do far more than by definition eliminate the possibility of zero-sum conflict. It also would eliminate three of the other causes of war, the prisoners' dilemma situation, the tug-of-war, and the simple operations research error. (Curiously, it might not rule out "love of war" if both sides agreed in enjoying war for its own sake, just as two gangs of boys may enjoy playing football—an unlikely situation, but not an unimaginable one.)

Would it not be a fine world if no one could improve his own lot without improving that of fellow members of the community, and if no one could worsen anyone else's lot without in the same move worsening his own? This, presumably, is what the theology and philosophy of love and compassion have tried to inculcate in man over the centuries, with some, but not total success. How much war would be possible if this final elimination of substantive disagreement among countries could be accomplished?

Eliminate Counterforce Potential

Unfortunately, there is at least some risk of conflict and counterproductive behavior, and of war, even where the two sides agree on their first choices; and this is where we would have to return to the model of mirror-image misunderstanding presented as the fourth cause of war. If there is imperfect mutual communication and understanding between the two sides, so that they do not really comprehend each other's preferences, so that they mistakenly assume disagreement about first choices and mutual hostility, then a stampede into mutual checking and war may still set in.

This is in effect to argue that even where hostility towards goals has been largely eliminated, another important step in reducing the likelihood of war is to eliminate preemptive counterforce capability, what is sometimes called the offensive in warfare. We are now addressing military *capabilities* rather than intentions, the kind of capabilities that give each side the means for taking the initiative into its own hands to inflict damage on the other side and/or to ward off damage to itself. The misunderstanding of the other side that produces precautionary preparations for possible war, and in turn then cycles into matching preparations, and so forth, would not occur if neither side could find anything to do in the way of such preparations, if neither side seemed capable of achieving anything by taking the military initiative. Reducing the capability for taking the counterforce military offensive is thus a valuable contribution to peace, because it lowers the risk of a mirror-image misunderstanding causing war; but its contribution goes considerably beyond this.

We cannot normally hope to be very effective in getting all the powers to come to share first choices about the political nature of the world. An identity of interests would rule out prisoners' dilemma and operations research error as causes of war; but what if an identity of interests cannot be achieved?

Where it cannot be achieved, the reduction of offensive weapons potential again becomes an excellent substitute, making prisoners' dilemma much less likely and making operations research error less likely as well. A world in which military technology severely penalizes whoever sends his troops, ships, or airplanes charging forward is a world where the stampede psychology of prisoners' dilemma or mirror-image misunderstanding is very unlikely, and where far fewer generals would ignorantly and foolishly leap to the conclusion that they are sure to win.

Can one thus come up with matrices that would be more conducive to peace? For a number of the cases described above, peace becomes more likely, and even certain, if one simply restructures force exchange rates and battlefield outcomes to favor the side on the defensive, the side sitting still, over the side taking the offense initiative, moving in for the attack. This might involve replacing multiple-warhead missiles with single-warhead missiles again, or tanks with pillboxes, minefields, and precision-guided antitank weapons, or torpedo boats with dreadnoughts. In matrix terms, it converts the prisoners' dilemma, matrix 3, into matrix 8, in which each side welcomes an attack by the other but would never be so foolish as to lunge out to attack. The payoffs within each of the two War–Peace boxes simply have been reversed.

In such cases, political crises or even declarations of war might be followed by "phoney wars," as with troops in the Siegfried and Maginot Lines in 1939 sitting and waiting for the opposition to attack, or the two major fleets waiting on opposite sides of the North Sea in 1914. Military systems that punish the initiative rather than rewarding it are by and large good for peace.

Matrix 8

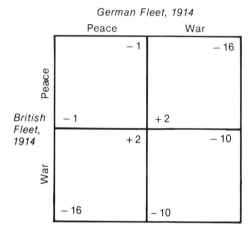

German Fleet, 1914

	Peace	War
Peace	− 1	− 16
British Fleet, 1914	− 1	+ 2
	+ 2	− 10
War	− 16	− 10

Add Mutual Verification Capabilities

Where the capabilities for taking military initiatives cannot be eliminated, an important contribution to peace can still be made if one
develops and institutes mutual means of monitoring and surveillance,
whereby each side will have advance warning if the other is about to
attack, or is about to purchase new weapons. Prisoners' dilemma situations tend to cease to be binding in their horrible effects when the wall
between the cells is broken down, when the two sides can watch each
other. Mirror-image misunderstanding situations similarly become
easier to defuse, as each side has a reassurance that the other indeed
does not want to launch an attack. Wars and arms races that otherwise
would have been stampeded into existence can thus be avoided.

Some verification capability can be achieved by technology, as
with reconnaissance satellites that let each superpower know how
many missile silos the other has built. Some can be achieved by human
means, as a positive result of what otherwise is seen as espionage. At
other times, of course, such mutual surveillance becomes impossible,
as each side develops or stumbles into ways of concealing its activities.
The result then is a resumption of prisoners' dilemma or mirror-image
misunderstanding in all its glory, a resumption of arms races and of
wars.

Reduce Countervalue Capabilities

If there were an agreement among the powers about first choices, there would not be any tug-of-war situations either. Neither side could improve its own position by imposing penalties on the other. Where such an agreement on goals has not been achieved, however, the risk of this cause of war again comes to life, and we must then seek yet another change in the environment as a step toward peace.

The references above to preemptive offensive advantages amounted largely to a discussion of what can be called the "counterforce" aspect of war; that is, how one can cripple an enemy's forces by preemptive moves and/or head off the crippling of one's own forces. The tug-of-war situation relies not on the incapacitation of forces but on the mutual imposition of pain, on what could be called the "countervalue" aspect of war. Destroying an enemy's landing fields by an air raid is counterforce; destroying its cherished cathedrals and cultural monuments is countervalue. Blockading and destroying its commerce also is largely countervalue.

What if this countervalue capability were to be reduced? At certain stages of history the defenses against air raids or coastal raiders became so effective that no damage to cities or cathedrals was likely. At certain stages the trade and economic well-being of nations became so autarchic and independent that warfare could not impose much pain. When the two sides cannot inflict much pain on each other, wars of endurance are not so likely to be pursued (matrix 9A).

Matrix 9A

	Peace	War
Peace	− 1 − 1	− 16 + 2
War	+ 2 − 16	− 20 − 20

A very important qualification must be attached, however, to this endorsement of the shielding of countries against each other's countervalue efforts. The contribution to peace of such a change will depend very much on whether the offensive military capabilities on the counterforce side have been trimmed back first. Where they have not been trimmed back, where one or both sides might see chances for grand victory in moving on to the offensive, the presence of probable countervalue costs of war may well serve to reensure peace more than to damage it.

Here we come at last to the subject of deterrence. The discoveries of nuclear physics will add a great deal of damage to any future war, a kind of countervalue damage that can eliminate all the attractiveness of fighting out a counterforce war. Without the retaliatory damage threat posed by nuclear weapons, we might at various stages be faced by a clear prisoners' dilemma in the confrontations of intercontinental missiles, or by a very precarious mirror-image misunderstanding situation. With the addition of some extensive war costs to all the appropriate boxes in matrices 3 and 4A, however, we arrive at matrices 9B and 9C, which promise to be considerably more conducive to peace. Each of these is still a mirror-image situation comparable in form to matrix 4A; yet the awesomeness of the damage a side would suffer now if it chose to attack would greatly reduce the risk that the other side might misread its intentions.

A certain kind of countervalue pain is thus now very necessary for peace, as long as missiles and jet bombers are with us. This under-

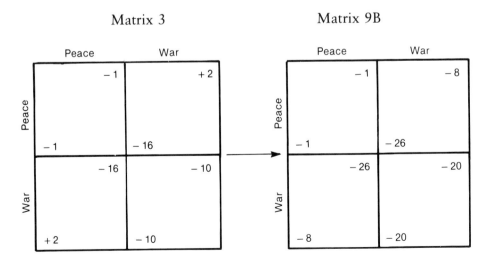

Matrix 3   Matrix 9B

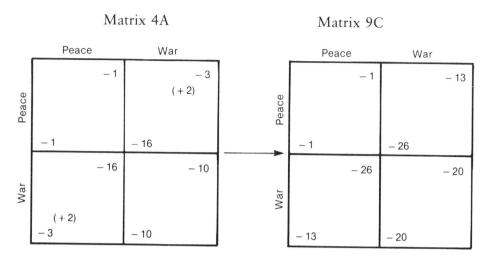

Matrix 4A   Matrix 9C

scores the importance of noting the differences between defense against counterforce attack and against countervalue. The defenses that protect missile silos against missiles, or bomber bases against bombers, or infantry against tanks, or ships against ships are normally very conducive to peace, for the reasons just cited. But a very different meaning of defense arises when we think of something like antiballistic missile (ABM) protection of cities against nuclear missiles, an ABM protection that might reduce the costs of war by shielding people.

The latter kind of defense, of people rather than of weapons or soldiers, can now be introduced only in moderation and at specified portions of the scale. As noted, where the other incentives to war have been stabilized away, the elimination of countervalue capabilities can take the sting out of, and thus remove the incentive for, contests of mutual resolve and tug-of-war. If we went so far as to remove the ultimate fallback of massive retaliation, however, by which the sides have deterred and prevented World War III, the result would simply be to replace a more manageable mirror-image situation with a more precarious one or with a war-causing prisoners' dilemma.

We might thus propose the following as a way out of this choice. As long as the modern weapons of missile warfare remain in place, one serves peace best by leaving intact and reensuring the ultimate fallback of the *nuclear* second-strike countervalue retaliatory threat, while, where possible, working at the same time to reduce the *conventional* capabilities for inflicting countervalue pain.

Eliminate Planning Error

Last, but not least, is the possibility of reducing the incidence of planning errors, to avoid bad predictions about who will win any future war or who will give up first. As noted, this kind of error would not matter, would not cause wars, if the two sides could be brought to agree fully about the ideal arrangements of a peaceful world. When the two sides do not agree, however, the significance of such errors returns.

As also noted, the risks of a war being caused by an error about who will win decrease as counterforce capabilities recede and increase as they reappear. Errors about who will give up first similarly are less likely to cause a war when conventional countervalue capabilities recede and are more likely to do so when they reappear.

What was said at the outset must be repeated, however. We may do what we can to avoid miscalculations regarding the outcomes of future battles, but the skill of predicting is not likely to become nearly as good here as in the legal profession (and even legal matters are often taken to court because the two lawyers cannot be sure who will win). Moreover, if predicting the outcome of battle is difficult, it is even harder to make accurate predictions, and to condemn "foolishness," on the question of who will give up first. In many ways, this last question is self-confirming, as we are continually tempted to put in a little more effort, to endure war a little while longer, in the hope that this will convince the other side that we will not give up first.

Foolishness can cause wars, just as love of fighting or hatred for one's fellow men can cause them. We should do what we can to change people so that they will not be foolish or warlike or full of hate. Yet this may be difficult to achieve, and often we may be able to make a quicker contribution to peace by changing capabilities.

Recapitulation

Figure 2–1 recapitulates the six kinds of causes of war we have outlined, setting them opposite the six kinds of ameliorative turning points in progress toward peace that we have described. The arrows running from right to left are meant to suggest how the improvements in environment would be tied to the kinds of war problems.

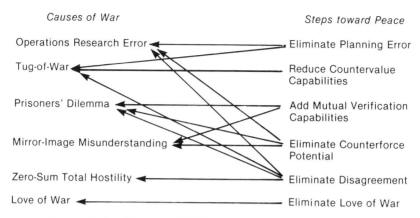

Figure 2–1. Causes of War and Steps toward Peace

Wars versus Arms Races

One should note that we might find each of these modes of conflict plausible explanations for arms races just as for wars, but a few significant differences of emphasis then emerge.

Simple error could explain an arms race just as much as war. Each side might have been told to expect that it would attain the best weapons, even when only one was correct in such a technological forecast.

The tug-of-war model might also explain either. Just as each side persists in some wars simply in hopes that the other will quit first, so each side might persist in building missiles or dreadnoughts, expecting the other to throw in the towel.

Situations resembling prisoners' dilemma and mirror-image misunderstanding similarly can explain arms procurements as well as wars. Sometimes each side dares not hold back its attack, for fear that the other will attack, and a war results. At other times, each side might not dare hold back on its weapons procurements for fear that the other side was procuring new weapons, and another new round of the arms race results.

Although the U.S. government is often assailed for overstressing the need for verification in the limitation of arms, such verification can certainly defuse prisoners' dilemma situations. Foreign observers in the Sinai Desert can make it less tempting or less urgent for either the Egyptians or Israelis to use their weapons. And outside inspection and verification can assure each side that the other is not procuring weapons, not diverting resources from civilian purposes to the accumulation of greater military strength.

When talking about kinds of stability in arms control analysis, we often, as noted, draw distinctions between a weapon's impact on crisis stability and its impact on arms race stability. The former situation involves the question of whether some kinds of weapons will bait, tempt, and worry the sides possessing them into attacking, into *using* weapons. The latter situation involves the question of whether such kinds of weapons will bait, tempt, and worry the sides into *obtaining* more weapons.

We will repeat later how much of arms control logic is addressed to the particular problems and risks of situations looking like the prisoners' dilemma with a view to enhancing the stability of the system and thus making less likely a "war nobody wanted." By a roundabout analogy to physics, a weapon produces instability when it tends to make thought-of-use lead to use, or when, by its very existence, it tends to bring additional weapons into existence. Conversely, it is more stable as it lacks these characteristics.

The fifth model of conflict outlined here, zero-sum hostility, may apply only to wars and not to arms races by its very logic. If two sides cannot agree on anything, cannot agree on any form of coexistence, they can hardly be counted upon to agree on having only an arms race and not a war.

By comparison, the sixth model (love of war) may be a much better description of arms races than of wars. Generals do not typically look forward to wars, but they often may welcome preparations for wars, since promotions and appropriations are made easier and as the social status of being a professional soldier goes up. Military-industrial complexes, in every corner of the world, might fairly be suspected of having a vested interest in a continuation of international anarchy and military confrontations, even if none of them is so insane as to look forward to the thermonuclear World War III, or even to conventional wars.

Solutions and Academic Disciplines

The approach of academic analysts to issues of war and peace in North America or elsewhere has not been a single, integrated multidisciplinary and interdisciplinary effort; this may only very partially be caused by the legendary aloofness of the academic departments of a typical university and may be caused on a much more profound level by the separateness of the components of the peace problem, a separateness that will irritate and baffle that observer who wishes a simple and once-and-for-all solution.

We of course would wish to stamp out any national inclinations toward liking war for its own sake. Reasonable men might agree that the Vikings were such a people, but the thoroughly civilized outlook of today's Swedes, Danes, and Norwegians suggests that a people can indeed reform.[9] We remember the earlier "Huns" and also how this appellation was then applied to twentieth-century Germans. Indeed, one premise of the Allied effort in World War II was that the Germans and Japanese might be societies liking war for its own sake and that they might inherently pose threats to peace.

As noted, however, reasonable people will differ in judging most of the more recent cases. Marxists may claim that capitalist societies are inherently warlike and that socialist regimes are inherently peaceful (and they thus have to swallow hard when China, Vietnam, and Cambodia fight wars after their "liberation"). Liberals suspect Marxist regimes of being warlike, and see liberal regimes as being inherently peaceful (have two political democracies ever fought a war against each other?).

Centuries of history changed the descendents of the Vikings into peaceful people, but another difficulty with this approach in any event is that such basic reforms of human nature are not easily engineered, or even explained. If the Germans were reformed after 1948, perhaps it was only because they were first conquered militarily and thus neutralized as a power.

We would also like to stamp out that kind of selfishness or hate that creates zero-sum situations. Indeed, if we could substantially eliminate disagreement around the world, we would take the steam out of many of our models of war. Mistaken analyses by generals would be less likely to produce conflicts, endurance contests would be less probable, and prisoners' dilemma situations would also be less nerve-wracking (although in the prisoners' dilemma case, however, the risk remains that two sides that did not disagree might still very much suspect each other falsely of hostile intentions and then act upon such suspicions in ways that worked to confirm them). It is thus just as desirable to operate education programs generating mutual human compassion as it is to educate people to stop enjoying the prospect of war; yet doubts must also be entertained about the feasibility of such educational programs.

The avenues of improvement discussed so far are those that might appeal more to sociologists or psychologists. They address the "indifference curves" of people and regimes (in the terminology of the economist) rather than the "opportunity curve." Sociology and psychology are disciplines whose practitioners, in any discussion of international relations, will tend to talk about the "root causes" of conflict and war. Such a focus on root causes, often becoming a discussion of poverty and injustice, perhaps reflects a greater bias among sociologists and psychologists toward the political left, for the professionals in these disciplines are indeed typically somewhat to the left of their colleagues in political science or economics (with all of such academics, of course, probably being somewhat to the left of many of their countrymen). More probably, the focus comes rather from the normal level of analysis of the disciplines, amid inherent differences of focus on "what part of the problem can I do any good trying to treat?"

By comparison, political scientists, economists, and peace-minded people from the physical sciences are more inclined to focus on the next several steps, steps that are probably more at the heart of arms control. These are steps intended less to change the basic attitudes, preferences, and indifference curves of people, and more to steer them away from the physical fears and opportunities that pull them into war.

We thus have more than one problem in avoiding war since the sources of war come from different levels of analysis, responding to different specialties in the social sciences. It is hardly proof of folly or of academic intransigence that the social science disciplines have not concentrated on a single effort for reducing the likelihood of war (or for reducing its destructiveness when it happens, or reducing the likelihood and magnitude of the arms race); special aspects of the overall risk have required specialization in responding to it.

The fractionation and complexity this approach requires have inspired pessimism, as too many people in North America and elsewhere come to the issue seeking a quick and simple solution and then walk away lamenting that arms control cannot be achieved this way. The fractionation also produces some internal arguments between disciplines, as analysts stressing human motivation as the root cause of war begin to argue with and distrust those stressing the problems caused by situations and opportunities, and vice versa. Each side begins to accuse the other of having "hidden agendas" and of pursuing an ideological bias. Each defends its own priorities of approach by claiming that it has focused on the part of the problem that is easiest to treat and then accusing the other of not wanting to treat the whole problem.

This author is most committed to a notion of arms control that focuses on the opportunities nature offers, opportunities that sometimes relax all sides by reinforcing the defense and at other times unfortunately plunge parties into war because everyone has to anticipate a preemptive strike from everyone else. Societies that show very little liking for war or very little animosity toward each other might then nonetheless wind up fighting each other. If we can simply monitor and alter the future shape of weapons systems to reduce the number of these instances, we will have accomplished a great deal. This author is convinced that we have already accomplished a great deal, even if more is to be done.

How then does all this information reach the public? Much of the current North American dissatisfaction about arms control may simply reflect the gaps in public understanding of the concepts outlined here rather than any manifest failings in the concepts. Given the newness of nuclear weapons, of mutual deterrence, and of the logic of the quest for mutual stability as a means to international security, the existence of this gap should hardly be surprising, for old traditions die hard. The intuitively familiar idea that military forces should be aimed at opposing military forces and not at innocent civilians continues to draw lip service from Soviet spokesmen (who probably know better) and from churchmen who probably do not know better. Yet such a classical approach to strategy is terribly destabilizing and is to be avoided as much as possible.

The simple words we use in discourse can get us into trouble or out of it. As a particular example, we might consider the terminology that has been used and proposed at various times for the appropriate goal of U.S. strategic weapons programs. In an earlier day, this goal was labelled "superiority," but the obvious logical problem with such a term is that only one side can be "superior" at a time, so that this goal would always be politically and strategically unacceptable to the Soviet Union. U.S. government pronouncements have referred more recently to "parity" or "essential equivalence," more reasonable-sounding terms. The difficulty with these expressions is that they connote a great urgency of measurement, whereby any slight increase of an adversary's military arsenal would have to be matched, lest the crucial equality be upset.

Far better as a phrase was that used for a short time by President Nixon and his adviser Henry Kissinger: *sufficiency,*[10] a word suggesting much more elbow room, a tolerance whereby a 10 percent variance or uncertainty in the Soviet stockpiles of armaments would make little difference. The notion of sufficiency is then logically linked to the idea of avoiding weapons systems that reward preemption and the first strike; it is linked similarly to strategies of aiming at cities in countervalue retaliation, rather than of aiming counterforce attacks at opposing missile forces. The "assured" in mutual assured destruction (MAD) conveys the same tone as "sufficiency."[11]

In addressing the public mood on arms control, policymakers thus have a twofold task. As much as possible, policymakers must direct defense spending toward defusing prisoners' dilemma situations. And they must direct the debate so that the public can see prisoners' dilemma as central to the general problem. No single factor covers all of the peace problem. Yet the mutual fears and mutual temptations of the prisoners' dilemma situation are certainly an unignorable part of the problem, a part to which arms controllers have devoted a considerable portion of their energies.

We may have to wait decades for the key lessons to settle in, that it is better for civilians on both sides to be vulnerable, unprotected by ABM or by their own missile forces' counterforce options, and that it is better for each side to have means of espionage or "verification by national technical means." But the logic of this argument is sound and applicable to the situation and the hope of winning public acceptance is still there.

Arms controllers may have little new to say on this subject, having laid out all the basic points in the literature at the end of the 1950s. Yet they will continue to render an important service if they simply continue to make these points, otherwise the alternative propositions will still be intuited and made too often. One can illustrate with a story told by the late Adrian Fisher about waiting to address a Fourth of July audience and having to listen to a terrible-sounding high school band. Leaning over to one bandsman banging away on the bass drum with more gusto than skill, he said, "You know, son, you don't play much good music." The drummer responded, "Yeah, but I drown out a lot of bad."

Notes

1. For a valuable discussion of the motivations prolonging World War I, see Fred Charles Iklé, *Every War Must End* (New York: Columbia University Press, 1971).

2. The relationship of "chicken" to prisoners' dilemma is spelled out in Glenn Snyder, "'Prisoners' Dilemma' and 'Chicken' Models in International Politics," *International Studies Quarterly* 15 (March 1971):66–103.

3. An analysis of the motivations at the heart of the endurance contest is presented in Robert Jervis, "Bargaining and Bargaining Tactics," in *Coercion* (Nomos XIV), ed. J. Roland Pennock and John Chapman (New York: Aldine, 1972), 272–88.

4. Extended discussions of the workings and implications of prisoners' dilemma can be found in Anatol Rapoport and A.M. Chammah, *Prisoners' Dilemma: A Study in Conflict and Cooperation* (Ann Arbor: University of Michigan Press, 1965), and in Anatol Rapoport, *Fights, Games and Debates* (Ann Arbor: University of Michigan Press, 1960).

5. For a most detailed account of the real-life playing out of the mutually preemptive beginnings of World War I, see Luigi Albertini, *The Origins of the War of 1914* (New York: Oxford University Press, 1957), vol. 3.

6. For examples, Charles E. Osgood, *An Alternative to War or Surrender* (Urbana: University of Illinois, 1962), on the origins of the Cold War, and Thomas C. Schelling, *The Strategy of Conflict* (Cambridge: Harvard University Press, 1960), 207–9, on a World War III wanted by neither side.

7. A comprehensive and formal analysis of zero-sum games can be found in Anatol Rapoport, *Two-Person Game Theory: The Essential Ideas* (Ann Arbor: University of Michigan Press, 1966).

8. See Paul Kecskemeti, *Strategic Surrender* (Stanford, Calif.: Stanford University Press, 1958), for a fascinating discussion of the underlying rational basis of surrender.

9. On the life-style of the Vikings, see David Howarth, *1066: The Year of the Conquest* (New York: Viking Press, 1977), 106–11.

10. The short period in which Kissinger and Nixon were using the "sufficiency" term is discussed in John G. Stoessinger, *Henry Kissinger: The Anguish of Power* (New York: Norton, 1976), 86.

11. For arguments analogous to those presented here on the need to avoid anxiety-producing comparisons of numbers, see Gen. Maxwell D. Taylor, "START: Let's End the Numbers Game," *Washington Post,* 25 April 1983, p. 11.

3

The Newness of Deterrence

I s deterrence credible as a concept? Can deterrence survive into the future, or has it outlived its moral, psychological, and political acceptability? These are ways of phrasing a question that seems to be bothering people around the world in the 1980s. Since the competition in nuclear arms procurement does not show signs of abating, people who might have been relatively content with mutual deterrence, though not wanting to dwell upon its mechanisms, are now forced to think about it and are often upset by what they see.

Can we even conclude that deterrence has worked? How can one ever prove that the threat of nuclear destruction prevented any enemy attack, when the prospective enemy (the USSR) is so secretive about all of its decision processes, making it impossible for Americans to read any meaningful Soviet documents or diaries, or logs of Politburo meetings? Some alarmed skeptics would lead us into a discussion of psychological constructs, citing theories or definitions of "rationality"; but if deterrence presupposes rationality, how do we deal with most studies of individual or mass psychology, which suggest that we are all rather lacking in this category?

Yet another, very different reaction to "deterrence" has all along been one of "ho hum" and "much ado about nothing." Is deterrence something so very new, a different approach to international security since 1945; or is it merely old stuff, something that we have used much longer, with anyone touting its alleged novelty merely displaying an ignorance of history? Some of those who see nothing new are trying to ease our concerns, of course, but others would use this argument to amplify our concerns, noting how arms races often became wars in

---

This chapter was delivered as a paper at a conference on "Deterrence in the 1980s," in April 1984 at York University, Toronto, Canada.

earlier decades and noting some striking similarities between the outbreaks of a World War I and a World War III.

Yet, as Glenn Snyder pointed out very clearly some two decades
ago, there is indeed a major difference between what might have
amounted to deterrence in an earlier age and what it became after
World War II. The difference is illustrated, in his terms, in the distinction between "deterrence by denial" and "deterrence by punishment."[1]
In the past, peace has, of course, often enough been maintained because potential aggressors were dissuaded (deterred) from engaging in
war by a reckoning of the likely consequences if they attacked, and
(with only a modicum of "rationality" being presupposed) they responded to this reckoning by holding their forces back. The reckoning
in earlier times was, however, normally that of "who would win" if
someone launched a war. If one simply loses soldiers and equipment
by attack, failing to gain any territory thereby, and perhaps even losing
some territory, one sees no point in launching the attack. Perhaps the
other side is too strong (should the other side therefore launch the
attack?). Perhaps there is an advantage for the defense (the side which
does not move forward to attack), so that either side would lose soldiers and tanks (and prestige) by attacking.

Fear of the destruction of one's own cities thus did not play much
of a role in deterring military adventures in earlier centuries. To be
sure, cities were sometimes devastated, as by the Huns or the Mongols, but such was only the fate of the losers in battle, and not a dis-
suading factor for those who could win. The winner on the battlefield
ipso facto maintained safety for his women and children; all that one
had to fear, all that normally could work as a deterrent, was the prospect of defeat on the battlefield and of being denied the gains one was
seeking (and perhaps, in a badly executed military adventure, even of
losing some of what one had begun with).

Contemporary deterrence is based much more on the suffering
that can at the very end be imposed on the winner, for a victory on
the battlefield no longer ensures a victor against the punishment and
destruction of his cities. The punishments thus inflicted would not be
simply the normal wear and tear of combat. Rather, these punishments violate the normal ethics and laws of combat by making civilians
into targets along with the men in uniform. The deterring retaliation is
very much a move of spite and revenge, intended to be painful and
mean, and is thus intended by its very prospect to preclude aggressions,
even where victory on the battlefield would have gone to the aggressor.

This is a new approach to warfare, new enough to seem untested, jarring to our traditions and moral sensibilities, and perhaps therefore it does not seem fully "credible."

It is easy enough to sketch out some of the changes that made such deterrence by punishment possible. First, there had to be a third-dimensional means of delivery, so that the stout, forward-moving line of a victorious infantry or fleet could no longer shield the home front. The airplane and the missile offered this option; so do the submarine and the submarine combined with the missile. Looking for earlier examples of deterrence by punishment, we occasionally find them in the fogginess and the porousness of battle lines at sea, as punitive raiders might slip by a preponderant navy in order to harass the home front of those who had counted on victory.

The second prerequisite for deterrence by punishment was a form of destructive power so compact that this third-dimensional delivery approach would become unignorable, even for a power that would otherwise have gone to the limit in pursuing total victory. The atomic bomb definitely offered what was necessary; and if the A-bomb was not quite awesome enough, the thermonuclear hydrogen bomb surely is.

Forerunners in Air Warfare

A list of early analogs to contemporary deterrence by punishment will thus not be very long. Indeed, many readers may have assumed that deterrence reasoning could only date from the introduction of nuclear weapons in 1945, or even later, from the introduction of thermonuclear weapons after 1952. Yet the discussions after World War I about the strategic possibilities of air warfare are a little richer in this regard than we might normally realize.[2]

In the years between World War I and World War II, it was typically projected that an ordinary explosive or poison-gas attack delivered by airplane or submarine might suffice for this ultimately painful deterrent role. Such projections were clearly premature, but they nonetheless amounted to premises for what could be considered forerunners of contemporary theories about mutual assured destruction. For example, note the expectations of Giulio Douhet:

> In general, aerial offensives will be directed against such targets as peacetime industrial and commercial establishments; important

buildings, private and public; transportation arteries and centers; and certain designated areas of civilian population as well. To destroy these targets three kinds of bombs are needed—explosive, incendiary, and poison gas—apportioned as the situation may require. The explosives will demolish the target, the incendiaries set fire to it, and the poison-gas bombs prevent fire fighters from extinguishing the fires.[3]

It is remarkable how most such analysts who won a public reputation for their early discussions of air power came very close to outlining the modern concept of deterrence, but did not quite make the connection. Writers like Giulio Douhet and J.F.C. Fuller presented versions of future air attacks on cities that certainly read very much like the actual firebombings of Hamburg, Dresden, or Tokyo in World War II, or even the atomic bombings of Hiroshima and Nagasaki. But their descriptions of "knockout blows" ordinarily place such air attacks in the category of a counterforce or countercapability strike, designed to win the war, to eliminate the enemy's ability to fight, rather than to eliminate his will to fight by the mere prospect of airborne retaliation.

Stressing the penetration capability of the aerial bomber, such theorists again and again concluded that the bomber would always get through. They treated this confrontation, however, as a simple race of who would get his bombers through first. Following out this logical trail leads to the conclusion that the losing side would still be able to get its bombers through as well, to wreak retaliatory havoc on the winner's cities, and thus perhaps to deter anyone from despatching his bombers in the first place.

Douhet sketched out all the premises, but did not push through to the conclusions of contemporary deterrence theory. Perhaps he was held back, as many military professionals have been over the decades, by a need to pretend some compliance with the traditional canons of proper targeting philosophy, by which civilians are never aimed at as a countervalue spite target, but are struck only accidentally when they are close to some legitimate military target. Douhet puts it this way:

> To simplify the situation, then, let us admit that both independent Air Forces could begin operations simultaneously. We have already seen that the fundamental concept governing aerial warfare is *to be resigned to the damage the enemy may inflict upon us, while utilizing every means at our disposal to inflict even heavier damage upon him.* An Independent Air Force must therefore be completely free of any

preoccupation with the actions of the enemy force. Its sole concern should be to do the enemy the greatest possible amount of surface damage in the shortest possible time, which depends upon the available air forces and the choice of enemy targets.[4]

J.F.C. Fuller similarly imputed horrendous capabilities to aircraft using poison gas and to submarines landing tanks at some remote coast, where they would quickly make their way inland, again using poison gas (the functional equivalent of today's SLBM—submarine-launched ballistic missile—submarines firing missiles at our land base, after having escaped all detection at sea).

> I believe that, in future warfare, great cities, such as London, will be attacked from the air, and that a fleet of 500 aeroplanes each carrying 500 ten-pound bombs of, let us suppose, mustard gas, might cause 200,000 minor casualties and throw the whole city into panic within half an hour of their arrival. Picture, if you can, what the result will be: London for several days will be one vast raving Bedlam, the hospitals will be stormed, traffic will cease, the homeless will shriek for help, the city will be in pandemonium. . . .
>
> If we meditate for a moment on the above possibilities, rendered practical by wedding tank to submarine, two facts will strike us forcibly; these are:
>
> (i) The secrecy and celebrity of the operation.
> (ii) The vulnerability of the civil target.
>
> If to these two weapons we add the aeroplane, this secrecy and this vulnerability becomes enormously enhanced. Consequently, we may well ask ourselves, as Fontenoy courtesies have become completely out of date, will not formal declarations of war follow suit. Bearing in mind that the main tactical problem in war is to hit without being hit, is it common-sense to expect a nation, reduced to fight for its life, a nation which possibly possesses scientific weapons of tremendous power, and the development of the power of which demands surprise in its positive form—an unexpected and terrific blow, moral or physical, according to the theory of warfare held—to place its adversary on guard by saying: "On August 4 I am going to hit you." What is far more probable is that the enemy will say nothing at all, or: "On August 4 I will agree to your terms," and then launch a surprise attack on the 3rd.[5]

The destruction such forces could inflict on London would be quite horrible, but Fuller never considered the possibility that the British military might have its own submarines at sea, carrying tanks equipped with poison gas, and its own aircraft, similarly capable of striking back to inflict the same horrible destruction on the enemy's cities. What Fuller feared was that the enemy attack could stun and incapacitate the British government and military command, as well as impose terrible suffering on the British people. Yet what good would it do a French or German government to stun the British command, if the existing aerial and submarine units could impose a comparable suffering on Paris or Berlin?

The connection between aerial bombardment vehicles and mutual deterrence (deterrence by punishment) was made by J.M. Spaight, a British strategic writer of the interwar years who never commanded an audience as large as those of Douhet, Fuller, or Liddell Hart, but who indeed in 1938 predicted that aerial bombardment might be held back on each side in future wars as a deterrent to the other side's launching of such bombardment:

> The very magnitude of the disaster that is possible may prove to be a restraining influence. Because the *riposte* is certain, because it cannot be parried, a belligerent will think twice and again before he initiates a mode of warfare the final outcome of which is incalculable. The deterrent influence may, indeed, be greater than that. It may tend to prevent not only raids on cities but resort to war in any shape or form. No one can tell what will happen if war does come. Its momentum may carry it to lengths not intended before it began to gather speed. Wars have a way of deteriorating in their course.
>
> *Omne ignotum pro magnifico.* At present air attack is regarded as a menace, a withheld thunderbolt, an impending calamity. All nations fear it. For that very reason it should be a deterrent influence against war.[6]

Having thus actually opened the "deterrent" vocabulary in his argument, Spaight foresaw a pattern of restraints very like what we have experienced since World War II, whereby the worst bombing capability of each side deters the other side from using its worst bombing capability, and also deters it from a great deal more.

Since the deterrence will usually not be totally effective on each side, however, something like contemporary "limited war" emerges, a limited war that is indeed the conceptual twin of deterrence, since limits on what weapons get used are now accepted for fear of what the other side could do—and is not yet doing—rather than for any of the other traditional reasons for limits. For a nice interwar illustration of this kind of argument, we can turn to a piece published pseudonymously under the name of "Ajax" that offered a prediction of limited wars in the future, a prediction that held for less than a year of World War II, but that certainly has been confirmed in practice many times since, with the current adversary being Soviet rather than German or Italian:

> It is more than probable that if either Germany or Italy were ready for a colony-snatching adventure, or a trade war supported by arms, they would carry on with the enterprise using only such military means as conform to established civilized warlike custom and tacitly defy us to bomb them at home. If this happened the author feels very sure that Britain would have to keep her "strategic bombers" at home and the people who would decide this would not be the British War Cabinet but the British people.[7]

The decisions made by the British Royal Air Force and its civilian superiors at the onset of World War II in 1939 stand as examples of actual implementation of such deterrence and limited war theory. Convinced (somewhat prematurely and erroneously) that the Luftwaffe would be able to inflict horrendous damage on London and Paris, the British and French governments held back their own air forces as war was declared, striking at only the most explicitly military targets. While the Luftwaffe was imposing substantial devastation on targets in Poland during the German invasion of that country, Hitler claimed that the bombing was directed only at "tactical" targets, close to advancing German ground forces. Hitler also restrained the Luftwaffe with regard to any attacks on British and French cities, for the German dictator feared his people's reaction to being bombed. Had this pattern persisted (based, as it was, on the exaggerated premises developed between the wars on how much damage could be inflicted in an aerial attack with ordinary high-explosive bombs), we would now be dating our discussion of deterrence theory back to 1939, rather than to 1945 or later. In a process of escalation after the fall of France in 1940, however, the two sides began a maximum effort to cripple or intimidate each other by air attack, efforts that (at least until the introduction of nuclear weapons at Hiroshima and Nagasaki) are typically considered as a failure by most strategic analysts.

Forerunners in Naval Warfare

As was discussed earlier, one reason why the credibility of deterrence is questioned is because it is new, something lacking much historical testing. And another reason is that it is of such dubious morality, intended somehow to prevent wars by threatening those on the other side who would have been relatively innocent in any decision to launch a war. Yet before we draw any final conclusions, we should examine all possible evidence with bearing on these issues. In addition to warfare in the air, the sea offers ways of retaliating against the enemy's civilian sector, for the ability of navies to harass commerce and bombard coasts generates some nontrivial countervalue options. A very nice theoretical opening of the issues in this area can be found in the arguments of the British historian Sir Julian Corbett, who wrote at the beginning of the twentieth century after the first works of Mahan had appeared but before the outbreak of World War I. Corbett contended that Mahan's emphasis on counterforce uses of a fleet was overdrawn and that the countervalue punishment role of naval power might ultimately be as or more important than driving the enemy fleet from the seas.

> It ignores the fundamental fact that battles are only the means of enabling you to do that which really brings wars to an end—that is, to exert pressure on the citizens and their collective life. "After shattering the hostile main army," says Von der Goltz, "we still have the forcing of a peace as a separate and, in certain circumstances, a more difficult task . . . to make the enemy's country feel the burdens of war with such weight that the desire for peace will prevail. This is the point in which Napoleon failed. . . . It may be necessary to seize the harbours, commercial centres, important lines of traffic, fortifications and arsenals, in other words, all important property necessary to the existence of the people and army."
>
> If, then, we are deprived of the right to use analogous means at sea, the object for which we fight battles almost ceases to exist. Defeat the enemy's fleets as we may, he will be but little the worse. We shall have opened the way for invasion, but any of the great continental Powers can laugh at our attempts to invade single-handed. If we cannot reap the harvest of our success by deadening his national activities at sea, the only legitimate means of pressure within our strength will be denied us.[8]

Corbett's argument, that Britain should retain freedom of action for its fleet to cripple the commerce of an adversary, in effect set the stage for British policy during World War I and interestingly opened up much of the moral debate about air attacks as well. In World War I, the British stopped all ships going to Germany, not just those carrying explicitly military goods, but also those carrying food or anything else. To satisfy the moral demands of neutrals, or of British fighting men, this action was always officially labelled a counterforce operation rather than countervalue, intended (even in the case of food) to reduce Germany's *ability* to fight, rather than specifically to punish the Germans by imposing on them malnutrition and diminished resistance to disease. The official rationale was much the same for the U.S. submarine attacks during World War II, which obstructed the travel of *all* ships going to Japan, not just those carrying soldiers or weapons; the argument was that cutting off food would reduce Japanese military *capabilities* and only incidentally make life miserable for Japanese civilians.

This same kind of doublethink was, of course, applied to the aerial bombardments carried through in World War II. Critics of the final use of atomic weapons against Japan (Hiroshima was officially a "military target") or of the massive conventional firebombings of Tokyo have suggested that Japan was about to surrender in any event, so that such destructive aerial assaults were unnecessary brutality.[9] But when asked to explain how they conclude that the Japanese government would have surrendered anyway, such critics typically cite "the naval blockade." Since the blockade was of this same dual nature, officially intended to weaken Japan militarily and only unofficially torturing the civilian population in order to reduce the government's willingness to continue the war, it seems that we are hypocritically comparing the moralities of two kinds of countervalue torture. If Japanese civilians had not been suffering, if civilian homes had not been bombed, and if civilian cargo ships had been allowed to enter under neutral flag, it is questionable whether Tokyo would ever have surrendered. If the war had thus been fought honorably and cleanly, the Japanese would not have surrendered until beaten on the battlefields of their own islands, a terribly costly process for the Allies.

As an illustration of an earlier version of such naval deterrence by punishment, we might look at the way in which Canada was secured against U.S. invasion during the years between the War of 1812 and the beginning of the twentieth century. The favorite British plan (analogous to the favorite plan of many Americans today for defending NATO against Soviet attack) was that the Canadians should generate a larger militia capability and otherwise prepare to defend themselves effectively against any U.S. invasion (that is, the policy was one of deterrence by denial).[10] Since the Canadians (like the NATO countries) did not generate the forces required for this plan, the ultimate assurance against a U.S. invasion was the ability of the British fleet to retaliate by destroying U.S. cities along the Atlantic seaboard. Burning out Boston, New York, Washington, or Baltimore would not have prevented an advance of the Union Army intent on "liberating Canada," but it would have imposed enough pain and destruction to make the military adventure a bad bargain from the perspective of Washington, and the Fourth of July speeches calling for the absorption of Canada thus never led to any military move north.

Such an ability to burn out the Atlantic coastal cities of the United States was qualitatively different from approaches that prevailed in the days of the Mongols. It is not so different in the level of destructiveness, because the depredations of Mongol or Viking armies (or the armies of the Thirty Years War) may have been comparable to what a nation losing in war would suffer today. But it is qualitatively different because today the military victor is also exposed to this kind of attack and suffering in the form of revenge taken by the side whose troops or fleets lost the battles. "Don't you dare beat me on the battlefield, because I will get even in a way that makes you sorry you won" is the modern message, and it is part of what we call "deterrence"; this approach does not have much historical precedent.

The Slow Development of
Nuclear Deterrence Reasoning

In the immediate aftermath of the atomic bombing of Hiroshima and Nagasaki, followed by the surprisingly sudden Japanese surrender, it took some time for serious analysts to establish a consensus interpretation on the impact of such weapons on the international system. Indeed, no such consensus may exist even now, some four decades later.

As in the earlier, more general analysis of air power by Douhet and others, one could choose to stress the *counterforce* impact of such weapons, or their countervalue impact. In their ability to cripple an enemy's military cabability, thus settling quickly who the "winner" of any war was to be, nuclear weapons delivered by aircraft work far more rapidly and decisively than any of the weapons or plans of the past, surpassing even the most smoothly functioning Schlieffen Plan, indeed taking the point out of any industrial and troop mobilizations after war was declared. This possible use of nuclear weapons was consistent with traditional thinking about the purpose of weapons and about what a professional and moral approach to thinking about the use of weapons was. It was the emphasis presented in a book by William L. Borden published in 1946, *There Will Be No Time*.[11]

A somewhat different conclusion would be reached by stressing the countervalue damage that could be inflicted by nuclear weapons, the damage they would inflict on cities and on all of civilization, regardless of who "won," since the victor would probably be unable to keep the losers from imposing such damage on his cities. This interpretation, premised on what we now would call assured second-strike retaliation, or mutual assured destruction, has had great influence on contemporary notions of deterrence. It was outlined by Bernard Brodie in his chapters of his 1946 book, *The Absolute Weapon*.[12]

As long as only the United States possessed nuclear weapons, of course, such issues of second-strike retaliation could not play any role. The Japanese had no way of retaliating for Hiroshima and Nagasaki, and the United States used its atomic weapons, officially claiming that these nuclear attacks were intended to cripple the Japanese *ability* to continue fighting the war, in actuality also hoping (probably correctly) that these new bombs would eliminate the Japanese *willingness* to fight.

Any hopes that this monopoly would persist, that it would take the Soviet Union many years to produce nuclear weapons of its own, were dashed, however, when the first Soviet nuclear detonation was detected in 1949. A National Security Council study (NSC-68) was commissioned by President Harry S. Truman to consider the implications of the Soviet detonation. The study was itself not to be declassified for public perusal until 1975, but various accounts of its analysis and conclusions leaked to the public earlier; at the end of the 1950s, accounts emerged along with a flood of academic analysis on arms control and deterrence.[13] The NSC-68 study addressed, though only in an imprecise way, the possibility that the two nuclear forces might now deter each other, with neither side using its nuclear weapons until the other did, but with the Soviets then being free to pursue nickle-and-dime aggressions using purely conventional forces.[14] But the study also devoted a fair amount of attention to the counterforce possibility that nuclear weapons might be used by either side to try to win a victory by crippling the other side militarily.

This NSC-68 study was not as crisp in its analysis as it was credited with being. Many of the academic authors dissecting the issues of limited war and mutal deterrence by the beginning of the 1960s assumed that NSC-68 had already preceded them on the same analytical path within the government, but this was true in only very general terms.

What should one make, then, of this slowness of the strategic analytical community to assign priority to the deterring significance of the countervalue retaliation that a nuclear force could inflict? One explanation is simple wishful thinking on the part of the analysts, who had trouble facing the horrors of war in a nuclear age. Sheer momentum from the past is another explanation. Furthermore, similar countervalue predictions had been made in the 1920s and 1930s, only to be disproven, as bombing during World War II did not force either Britain or Germany to surrender. Another explanation of this delay in regarding the atomic bomb as "the absolute weapon" stemmed from the traditional professional outlooks of the military men, who are still not conditioned to thinking of their weapons as destroying civilian homes, except when this happens incidentally to attacks on military targets.[15] Preparing for spiteful retaliation resembled the felonies indicted at war crimes trials.

In addition to this resistance by Western strategists to accepting any revolutionary implications of mutual deterrence, Soviet spokesmen generally persisted in claiming that nuclear weapons were not important (at least for as long as the USSR had none of its own, and even for a while longer) and that aerial bombardment in general was pointless; they portrayed the World War II destruction of Hiroshima and Dresden as purposeless brutality by American leaders, with such destruction of population centers presumably being unlikely to change anyone's feelings about persisting in a war or about beginning a war.

Continuing Problems

Deterrence works, but will it always work? And is it not beset with some terrible logical and psychological tensions? It will be argued here that there are at least four major unresolved problems or tensions with nuclear deterrence, problems that can never be solved once and for all, but that must be confronted in explaining some U.S. military and political difficulties of the moment. The four kinds of tension are:

1. The assurance of second-strike survivability of the strategic nuclear systems—whether both sides can be certain of the ability to retaliate if the other has struck first;

2. The assurance of responsibility in this system of all the nuclear powers—whether the United States can be sure that no one will retaliate prematurely and without cause, that no one will first use his nuclear force because of a false alarm, or because of another less rational stimulus;

3. The extendability of nuclear deterrence protection—whether allies of the nuclear powers can be covered by the same dissuasive threats that cover the nuclear powers themselves, without thereby greatly increasing the risks of a nuclear war nobody wanted;

4. The basic immorality of the deterrence approach—whether the threatening of the innocent, as a way of controlling the guilty, can continue to be an acceptable mode of preserving peace, in a philosophical and cultural environment that would ordinarily not tolerate such a mechanism.

These four kinds of tension will be discussed further in chapters 4 through 6.

Notes

1. Glenn Snyder, *Deterrence and Defense* (Princeton: Princeton University Press, 1961), 14–16.

2. For a longer discussion by this author of earlier examples, see George H. Quester, *Deterrence before Hiroshima* (New York: John Wiley, 1966).

3. Giulio Douhet, *The Command of the Air* (New York: Coward-McCann, 1941), 20.

4. Ibid., 59.

5. J.F.C. Fuller, *The Reformation of War* (New York: E.P. Dutton, 1923), 150, 184.

6. J.M. Spaight, *Air Power in the Next War* (London: Geoffrey Bles, 1938), 126.

7. "Ajax," *Air Strategy for Britons* (London: George Allen and Unwin, 1939), 61–62.

8. Sir Julian Corbett, *Some Principles of Maritime Strategy* (London: Conway Maritime Press, 1911), 90–91.

9. For an example, see Gar Alperovitz, *Atomic Diplomacy* (New York: Simon and Schuster, 1965), 94–95.

10. An extended discussion of British strategic thinking on the protection of Canada can be found in Kenneth Bourne, *Britain and the Balance of Power in North America* (Berkeley: University of California Press, 1967).

11. William L. Borden, *There Will Be No Time* (New York: Macmillan, 1946).

12. Bernard Brodie, ed., *The Absolute Weapon* (New York: Harcourt Brace, 1946).

13. For a valuable extrapolation on the strategic logic of NSC-68, before the document was published, see Warner R. Schilling, Paul Y. Hammond, and Glenn H. Snyder, *Strategy, Politics and Defense Budgets* (New York: Columbia University Press, 1962), 267–378.

14. The declassified text of NSC-68 was published in *Naval War College Review* 27, no. 6 (May–June, 1975):51–158.

15. For a very thoughtful articulation of the arguments against treating nuclear weapons as we would have treated weapons in the past, see Robert Jervis, *The Illogic of American Nuclear Strategy* (Ithaca, N.Y.: Cornell University Press, 1984).

4

Assured and Responsible Retaliation

Second-strike survivability could easily be viewed as the most central of the four kinds of tension listed in chapter 3, for the very definition of deterrence presupposes that it *must* be solved. Deterrence would be upset, indeed, would cease to exist, if either side could use its military forces so effectively as to preclude second-strike retaliation by the enemy's nuclear forces. What many or most military officers are taught to think of as their true mission as members of the profession, shielding their own civilian population against enemy attack by attacking the enemy forces that would threaten such civilian populations, would become practicable again. (Part of the problem, to be discussed more later, is that such a "counterforce" approach continues to have a morally positive ring for the layman as well as for the military professional; yet this counterforce threat to the adversary's countervalue retaliatory capabilities is basically inimical to deterrence and to the international peace that is based on such deterrence.) If such a "splendid first strike" were possible, we would be back to the days when Genghis Khan's armies could be assured that no retaliation would be visited on their homes back in Mongolia while they were devastating towns in Europe.

Threats to Strategic Stability

We tend to take for granted the survivable existence of second-strike countervalue retaliatory capabilities. Missiles buried in concrete silos

This chapter appeared as part of a chapter in a book edited by George Thibault, *The Art and Practice of Military Strategy* (Washington, D.C.: National Defense University Press, 1984).

promise that a number of enemy missiles will have to be expended in the attempt to dig them out, thus (in a situation involving roughly equal forces) discouraging either side from trying to wipe out the opposing force. Other missiles deployed on-board submarines promise to be still more secure against an enemy attack, thus even more sure of an ability to inflict retaliatory damage if such an enemy attack comes.

Yet this relative security of strategic forces facing each other has not always been taken for granted. In retrospect, some of the arrangements developed during the years of U.S. nuclear monopoly look extraordinarily relaxed and complacent, with all the U.S. nuclear warheads being stored (disassembled and apparently in a state of decay) at a single location in New Mexico and with all the B-29 aircraft capable of carrying them based at a single airfield nearby. What a wonderful target for a Soviet leader inclined to gamble on a splendid first strike with his own first nuclear weapons!

While this situation did not last long, a feeling of confrontation caused continual anxiety all through the 1950s. A Rand Corporation study of basing alternatives for the Strategic Air Command (SAC) suggested that the aircraft might be quite vulnerable to a Soviet preemptive attack.[1] A sense of the inherent insecurity that would be caused by such a confrontation, whereby a single bomber of one side might destroy a great number of the other side's grouped on a single airstrip, penetrated to the general public as well. A Sunday afternoon television documentary on Strategic Air Command would have focused in those years mainly on bomber crews racing to man their aircraft, hurrying for fear that their takeoff would be prevented by an incoming Soviet bomber attack; such an image would transmit a subliminal signal of anxiety, of a "delicate" balance of terror. These were the years of "bomber gap" reports, when the Soviets were even (mistakenly) for a time suspected of having surpassed the United States in the total number of jet bombers capable of carrying nuclear weapons.

Causing even more anxiety was the "missile gap" that was discussed after 1957. By being the first to orbit a satellite around the earth (Sputnik), the Soviets suggested that they would surge ahead of the United States with a clearly superior mode of strategic weapon. Amid all the discussion of a possible "window of vulnerability" in the 1980s, none of the scenarios advanced has been as fearsome as what such authors as John Medaris, Maxwell D. Taylor, or James Gavin were projecting for the early 1960s.[2] Their nightmare was of a truly splendid Soviet splendid first strike, in which the USSR could strip the United States of virtually all its nuclear forces while escaping almost all damage to its own territory, being free then to dictate peace terms and the future of the world. (Those contemporary scenarios in which the USSR is somehow tempted to attack all U.S. Minuteman missile silos, while the U.S. submarine-based strategic forces would remain in being as a threat to Moscow and other Soviet cities, pale in comparison to this original version of a missile gap.)

Soviet intercontinental ballistic missiles for a time did pose two threats to strategic stability. First, until the United States had some of its own, these ICBMs might be capable of targeting all the U.S. bomber bases, hitting such bases so quickly and effectively that only a weak retaliatory strike against the USSR could get through.

Second, even after the United States obtained its first ICBMs, the fear was that such liquid-fueled systems would (on both sides) be too vulnerable to an enemy attack, in some cases standing out in the open without any concrete silos for protection, which would suggest that a preemptive counterforce first strike might preclude a countervalue second strike.

All of this anxiety about the basic strategic stability of mutual deterrence then abated somewhat by the mid-1960s, as the United States and the Soviet Union procured the next generation of more easily secured missiles, deployed underground in hardened silos or on-board the submarines whose location would be difficult for an adversary to detect. Television documentaries on strategic forces were focused more on bored-looking missile silo crews rather than on frantic bomber crews, and the subliminal message to the American public reinforced the idea that strategic deterrence was reasonably secure.

Threats to strategic stability can never be finally dismissed, of course. Such threats, for two important reasons, have seemingly become more real again for the 1980s, at least in a diminished version of the nightmares of the 1950s. First, ICBM accuracies have been dramatically improved on both sides, greatly increasing the likelihood that a warhead aimed at any particular silo will destroy the missile inside it. Second, the introduction of multiple warheads for such ICBMs, when combined with the enhancement of accuracy, makes it possible once again that the force initiating a war will use up fewer of its own missiles than it destroys in the forces of the other side; this would leave the initiator a robust and meaningful countervalue capability, while the side suffering such a first-strike attack might thereafter lack such a capability.

What possible threats does this situation pose to the United States? The first worry, as always, must be an actual Soviet capacity for a splendid first strike. If the accuracies of Soviet multiple-warhead missiles allow for a very good kill-ratio against U.S. land-based missile silos, they could then be combined with new breakthroughs in Soviet antisubmarine warfare (ASW) capability to leave all of the U.S. strategic force too vulnerable. Adding antimissile defenses to stop whatever bombers escaped the Soviet first strike would then work to reduce the Soviet suffering in American retaliation, with Soviet protection then being augmented by the Soviet civil-defense system. If the Politburo were perhaps ready to accept the same twenty-five million casualties suffered by the USSR in World War II, deterrence would be in a great deal of trouble.[3]

Needless to say, many flaws exist in this scenario for Soviet world conquest. The Soviets have a long way to go (farther than the United States) before they develop the necessary effectiveness in ASW. The effectiveness of Soviet ABM defenses, civil defense, and air-defense systems is at least open to question. Soviet civil-defense manuals are required reading for every Russian high-school student, but the United States has detected no real drills of the evacuation and sheltering plans, and some skepticism is in order about whether anything this big ever goes according to plan in the USSR. Soviet moves toward an ABM system can be criticized (just as can U.S. moves toward such a system, as proposed in President Reagan's Strategic Defense Initiative) for being destabilizing in the doubts they would raise for the survivability of the mutual deterrence system. Yet such Soviet moves, just like the U.S. moves, can also be criticized as a waste of effort and money, very unlikely to make Moscow and other Soviet cities safe against a thermonuclear attack.

Finally, we must question any inference from World War II that a Soviet leadership would be willing to accept twenty-five million casualties as retaliation in a World War III. The current Soviet leadership is, first of all, probably less callous than was Stalin, with a greater vested interest in the Soviet population and the cities in which it resides. Even Stalin did not willingly agree to such losses, moreover, having done everything he could to appease Hitler and head off the German invasion.

To return to the question of destabilization, the erosion of strategic stability by the introduction of MIRVs (multiple independently targeted reentry vehicles) and the enhancement of missile accuracies is real;[4] most of the rest of the suggested threats to such stability remain more hypothetical, however. If the MIRVing of land-based missiles set up tempting targets, the MIRVing of submarine-based missiles vastly reinforced the amount of destruction that could be inflicted on second strike. To repeat, Soviet capabilities for the location of such submarines are not "just around the corner."

But the lowered stability in the confrontation of strategic nuclear forces has also generated worries about other possible applications of Soviet nuclear capability, applications far less ambitious than the splendid first strike, but that would nonetheless amount to a substantial failure of mutual nuclear deterrence. One such scenario calls for the Soviets to attack only U.S. land-based bombers and missile forces, for the moment leaving alone the submarine-based forces whose location they can not detect, in strikes carefully orchestrated to hold down the number of American civilians killed (thus to impress on the U.S. president a powerful continuing disincentive to retaliate against the Russian people). This approach allegedly would demonstrate Soviet resolve and the superiority of the Soviet overall military and political situation, a demonstration perhaps crucial for the settling of some crisis in Europe or in the Middle East.

Among the many flaws in this scenario, one of the greatest would paradoxically be the Soviet task in holding down the number of Americans killed, killed as "collateral damage," when the Minuteman missile silos were being destroyed. For, if the effectiveness of Soviet missile aiming and the effectiveness of U.S. civil defense could not be allied to keep U.S. casualties from creeping up into the tens of millions, it is still altogether likely that any U.S. president would order a full retaliatory strike at the Soviet Union. It is thus hard to believe that the Soviets would willingly and cheerfully launch such a "limited strategic nuclear war," especially since Soviet strategic literature has never openly speculated about any such applications of Soviet missile capabilities (virtually all of such speculation originates in the United States). Yet the mere fact that either side could feel "better off" by attacking the other side's missile silos, rather than waiting to have its own missile silos attacked, is worrisome, because it runs counter to what stabilizes the main elements of mutual nuclear deterrence.

The next round of fears about Soviet missile capability translates a "window of vulnerability" into a "window of coercion"; the worry here is not that the USSR would begin either a full or partial version of a thermonuclear World War III, but rather that the United States might be intimidated by the fear of such a Soviet attack, or that the West Europeans and the Japanese would be intimidated by such a fear, or that the West Europeans and the Japanese would be intimidated by the fear that the United States would be intimidated, and so forth. This is an example of what is sometimes labelled "Finlandization": likening the impact of Soviet nuclear threats to the impact of post-1945 Soviet conventional threats directed at the government in Helsinki. The result of such actions might be a severe setback politically for much of what Americans care about.

Perhaps this last kind of concern is the most real of all the threats considered here for the 1980s. It basically relates also to the idea of extendability of deterrence, a subject to which we shall return later.

We should not leave this discussion of the basic need for assured second-strike forces on each side without asking about the nature and significance of the period when only the United States had such weapons. What should we make of these years of U.S. monopoly? Wasn't the unique U.S. nuclear force, faced by no counterdeterrent, free to be used, just as it had been used against Japan at Hiroshima and Nagasaki?

Perhaps the biggest question of all is whether this nuclear monopoly could not have been applied in such a way that it would perpetuate itself, as the Baruch Plan would not only have been proposed to the Soviets, but imposed on them.[5] The United States was hardly happy with Soviet policies in the years between 1945 and 1949, as Stalin reneged on his promises regarding the future of Eastern Europe and showed in many other ways that the USSR would cause problems for the United States. Is it not totally consistent with the logic of nuclear deterrence, as outlined here, that the Soviets must have lacked the necessary deterrent at that time to keep the United States from attacking? Would it not have made sense for the United States to have taken the offensive, to force conventional disarmament on the Soviets, along with a submission of their nuclear laboratories to international controls, to force an acceptance of self-government in Eastern Europe, and ultimately to force a democratization of the government of the Soviet Union itself? In terms of making the world secure against conventional and nuclear war in the future, would not such a U.S. offensive have indeed been a contribution to world peace?

Various interpretations of this period are possible, as we try to relate it to our understanding of nuclear deterrence today. Many of us might conclude that this period simply demonstrates that the United

States is the most moral of countries, incapable of beginning a war, capable only of responding when someone else has attacked it. Perhaps this means that the United States is naive, incapable of seeing the fundamental realities of international politics. Stalin would not have allowed a nuclear monopoly to slip out of his hands, but would have launched a war to perpetuate it, making the world over in the Soviet image, and ensuring the world against even the slightest amount of nuclear proliferation and against the concomitant possibility of nuclear war; but the United States could never be as realistic or as Machiavellian as Stalin.

A very different kind of explanation would make the United States look less unrealistic. This explanation cites the quite limited number of nuclear warheads the United States had on hand in the years after 1945 and a widespread skepticism about strategic bombing, including atomic bombing, that had emerged in the aftermath of World War II. When nuclear weapons were test-detonated at Bikini in 1946, most Americans indicated that they were surprised by how *small* the explosive impact had been, with the test being most memorable thereafter for naming a bathing suit. Hitler had not surrendered, even when some German cities suffered more casualties in a single night as a result of nonnuclear bombing than had been imposed on Hiroshima or Nagasaki. If the Japanese had surrendered because of these atomic bombings, other analysts could claim that they were about to surrender anyway, having been beaten on the battlefields and starved by the U.S. naval blockade. The atomic bomb might thus still have been a powerful instrument, in this view, but only comparable in power to the inherent threat of the Red Army to Europe. Nuclear threats might deter a Soviet advance on Paris. But the threat of a Soviet advance on Paris might conversely deter any exercise of nuclear threats, with no guarantee that Stalin would surrender as his cities were being hit with A-bombs.

It was much harder to shrug off the thermonuclear hydrogen-bomb, of course. Yet the race to acquire H-bombs may have been close to a dead heat, close enough to keep the possibility of thermonuclear monopoly from being so real. The United States detonated the first such device in 1952, but hardly in a form deliverable as a bomb. The Soviets were perhaps the first to test such a bomb delivered by air.

The tensions resulting from the uncertainty as to which side would be the first to develop H-bomb warheads were then combined with the tension, already discussed, regarding the development of jet bombers.

A "balance of terror" was brought about that remained "delicate" for a decade or more, producing continuous fears and possibilities of a splendid first strike; it was finally made less delicate with the deployment of a thousand Minuteman missiles in the 1960s.

Responsibility and Rationality

We now turn to the second major problem with deterrence: the fear of an irresponsible launching of a nuclear attack. Deterrence, as has been noted, would fail if either side could not launch nuclear weapons in retaliation. It would also fail if either side launched such weapons when there was as yet nothing to retaliate for. If Moscow is destroyed for no good reason by a U.S. (or other) nuclear attack, New York and Washington will be destroyed, if only because the hostage ensuring the safety of U.S. cities has been lost.

Various possible causes of such an irresponsible initiation of nuclear war have burdened our imaginations over the years.[6] One kind of worry pertains simply to the physical reliability of nuclear weapons systems. With thousands of nuclear warheads in the arsenals of both sides, may not one of them go off by accident sooner or later, either destroying its home base and the city nearby, or going off as a missile, perhaps fired by a computer malfunction, destroying a city of the adversary? The intuition of the man on the street is that anything mechanically complicated has to malfunction sooner or later. An ordinary dynamite bomb may go off if caught in a fire. Don't the same problems exist with A-bombs and H-bombs?

The truth, of course, is that the nuclear weapons are complicated in ways that make them relatively easy to make safe. They will not explode if caught in a fire or if they are on-board a plane that crashes. All kinds of safety features can and have been added to ensure that such weapons will explode in a fission or fusion chain reaction only when this result is desirable. Missiles can be wired in a similar manner to prevent their firing by physical malfunction. Given the large numbers of nuclear weapons that have been deployed in the military forces of the United States and the Soviet Union, and by Britain, France, and China, among others, it is remarkable that no accidental explosions or accidental firings of such weapons have taken place (that we know of).

More serious concern relates to the possibility that human beings such as insubordinate junior officers or "irrational" heads of state might launch these nuclear weapons. Nuclear deterrence obviously fails if any of the people with control over such weapons become indifferent to the consequences of nuclear war. If someone with access to these weapons were actually neurotic or unusual enough to welcome nuclear war, convinced that the cities of the world had become places of evil, peace would be in great jeopardy.

At lower levels, a great deal of attention has been paid to the psychological screening of Strategic Air Command crews and the officers in missile silos or on-board missile-carrying submarines. Complicated systems of checks and balances have been devised, so that no single officer can fire off such weapons. One would like to know more details about the parallel arrangements on the Soviet side, but there is evidence that the same concern has prompted matching systems of double checks and controls. For nuclear weapons deployed close to the battlefield, the United States has devised systems of permissive action links (PAL) combination locks, precluding the activation and firing of such warheads without the prior transmission of an enabling code released from higher authority.

Some inherent risks remain, such as that nuclear weapons might yet one day be fired because an individual or several individuals together had gone berserk, but the thought and arrangements that have gone into guarding against this possibility are reasonably reassuring.

Perhaps less well thought through but equally worrisome is safeguarding against such an "irrational" initiation of nuclear war by a national leader, whether he be the president of the United States, the prime minister of India, or the head of the Communist Party of China or the Soviet Union. Americans cherish the idea of military subordination to the duly elected civilian leadership, and thus have focused much of their nuclear concern on ensuring that military officers cannot begin a nuclear war unless authorized by the president. As was illustrated, however, by the nervousness in Washington during the days just before Richard Nixon resigned his office in 1974, insufficient attention may have been given to what checks there might be or need to be on the head of state.

It is important to address the question here of how rationality relates to deterrence. It is common for critics of current defense arrangements to voice the sentiment that "deterrence depends on rationality; since most people are somewhat neurotic, and very few are rational, deterrence is thus sure to fail."

As yet another version of a general intuition by which things are bound to go wrong, this kind of expression is often more persuasive than it deserves to be. A certain kind of rationality is indeed required, but it is considerably less than total rationality or total freedom from neurosis or psychological ailment; there is simply a requirement that crucial decisionmakers must be averse to nuclear war. Most people would consider it irrational for someone to prefer nuclear war to peace or to be indifferent to the choice; this definition seems commonsensical, although it could draw some objections from a serious social scientist. But we would fool ourselves if we then concluded that nuclear deterrence was in serious trouble because of lack of either side's "rationality" in some more demanding sense.

Just as the tension about the Soviet first-strike capacity will persist, so will the problems of a possible irresponsible nuclear launching, problems incapable of a perfect solution.[7] As more countries obtain nuclear weapons, in an ongoing process of nuclear proliferation, this strain on the responsibility of the system will indeed grow. Yet these problems are certainly not beyond management.

Notes

1. On the precariousness of the survivability of bomber forces, see Albert Wohlstetter, "The Delicate Balance of Terror," *Foreign Affairs* 37, no. 2 (January 1959):211–34.

2. On the magnitude of the fears of the "missile gap" anticipated for the early 1960s, see Maxwell D. Taylor, *The Uncertain Trumpet* (New York: Harper and Row, 1960), James E. Gavin, *War and Peace in the Space Age* (New York: Harper, 1958), and John G. Medaris, *Countdown for Decision* (New York: Putnam, 1960).

3. An example of this kind of view of Soviet intentions and capabilities can be found in Richard Pipes, "Why the Soviet Union Thinks It Could Fight and Win a Nuclear War," *Commentary* 64, no. 7 (July 1977):21–34.

4. For a carefully researched view of some threats to U.S. nuclear retaliatory capability in the 1980s, see John Steinbrunner, "Nuclear Decapitation," *Foreign Policy* 45 (Winter 1981–82):16–28.

5. A good discussion of the Baruch Plan and of the atmosphere of the time in which it was offered can be found in Michael Mandelbaum, *The Nuclear Question* (Cambridge: Cambridge University Press, 1979), 23–35.

6. See Joel Larus, *Nuclear Weapons Safety and the Common Defense* (Columbus: Ohio State University Press, 1967).

7. See Philip Green, *Deadly Logic* (Columbus: Ohio State University Press, 1968), for an extended and critical discussion of the problems of rationality as they affect nuclear deterrence.

5

The Extendability of Deterrence

We turn now to a third tension associated with nuclear deterrence, perhaps the most critical tension through the years since 1949: whether such deterrence can be extended to shield not only the territory of the nation possessing such weapons, but also the territory of its allies, allies as important as the Western European members of NATO, South Korea, or other states.

Would the United States destroy Soviet cities because U.S. cities had been hit by Soviet nuclear warheads or because the continental United States had been invaded by Soviet troops? Very probably yes, even if the exact "rationality" of this kind of revenge requires some further discussion and scrutiny. Would the United States inflict massive nuclear retaliation if a city like Saigon were invaded by Communist forces? We know that the answer is negative. Would the United States retaliate if Paris or London were attacked by Soviet rocket forces, or if Frankfurt or Paris were occupied by Soviet tank forces? Here the question is much more debatable, with the answers affecting many of the political and security decisions of the entire NATO alliance.

It should be stressed that the dilemmas of extended deterrence here, of "nuclear umbrellas," are not confined to the western side of the line. Would the Soviet Union destroy the United States if Soviet cities had been destroyed, or if the homeland of the USSR were invaded by the United States? Almost surely it would. Would the same Soviet retaliation come if a Marxist regime in Guatemala or Chile were deposed? We know the answer to be negative. And what of Soviet retaliation if the West embarked on a military liberation of Hungary or

This chapter appeared as part of a chapter in George Thibault, ed., *The Art and Practice of Military Strategy* (Washington, D.C.: National Defense University Press, 1984).

Czechoslovakia? We do not know what the Soviet response would be; this ignorance works to deter any Western plans for such an operation.

The most abstract logic on either side would question all such extensions of deterrence beyond the nuclear power's own homeland. The United States must keep the Soviet cities intact as hostages for the safety of its own cities, so the logic runs; thus the United States could not destroy such Soviet hostage cities merely because French cities had been devastated or German cities occupied. The ultimate deterrent cannot be used twice. The ultimate threat cannot be executed in response to one contingency and at the same time reserved to deter yet another one.

French strategic writers, most prominently Pierre Gallois,[1] used such abstractly logical arguments to justify a separate French acquisition of nuclear weapons on the basis that no United States president would risk the safety of U.S. cities for the protection of European cities. In 1957 Henry Kissinger published a best-selling book, *Nuclear Weapons and Foreign Policy*, in which he argued basically the same thing, that the threat of U.S retaliation against the Soviet homeland would have to be held back, reserved only for the deterrence of Soviet attacks on the U.S. homeland.[2]

Kissinger could thus be praised for having predicted today's problems twenty-five years in advance, thus beginning a career of insightful analysis that ultimately made him secretary of state. But, the tone of his book implies that Western Europe would surely have been invaded by now, since no defenses or deterrence by denial were put into place. So, what should we make of the fact that this geopolitically vulnerable peninsula has not been invaded for these twenty-five years, even in the absence of any significant defenses? The truth is that various ways have been found of making the links of nuclear deterrence more credible again,[3] despite the abstract logic of the strategic writers. A discussion of some of these links will help to make the point clearer.

Mechanisms of Extension

First of all, as was demonstrated all too well by the press conferences and other public statements of President Eisenhower, it is possible for the president to be a good actor in feigning a lack of awareness of any "rational" reasons for being reluctant to punish the Soviets for aggression, and in pretending to be fully intent on such retaliatory punishment, just as he would retaliate for any attack on the United States itself. Whenever the arguments of an analyst like Henry Kissinger were presented at a press conference, Eisenhower would always give a confusing response, so that no one could be sure that he had understood the reasoning. Critics passed this off as demonstrating Eisenhower's intellectual limitations. An astute strategic analyst, however, would see this way of responding as evidence (inherently imperfect evidence, of course) of what a clever old fox the Republican president may have been, for any Soviet observer at the press conference would have had to report back to Moscow that the Soviet free ride into Frankfurt was by no means yet assured. The American president was either too foolish or too uncomprehending to realize that he would have to hold back the nuclear weapons of the Strategic Air Command during the Soviet armored advance into West Germany.

The Democrats under President Kennedy and Secretary McNamara began their time in office by trying to be more clear and rational, aiming for a conventional defense of Western Europe such that the United States would not have to use bluffs so patently irrational. Faced with European resistance, however, to the increases in economic expenditure and to the compulsory military service that conventional defense would entail, they soon enough came back to playing the extended deterrence game, not playing it as well as Eisenhower because they were too intent on looking intelligent rather than stupid, but still playing it well enough.

President John Kennedy visited West Berlin in 1962 and proclaimed "Ich bin ein Berliner." Kennedy's identifying himself as a "Berliner" illustrates another way in which nuclear deterrence continues to be credibly and plausibly extended, as the United States identifies various countries as the "fifty-first state." Nuclear deterrence works credibly enough, it is widely held, for the fifty United States, but not for anything else (perhaps it only works for the continental United States plus Hawaii, and skipping over Alaska, since Secretary of Defense Schlesinger proposed to augment the conventional forces of the U.S. Army in order to shield the Alaska pipeline against hostile attack).

If deterrence can work for the fifty, cannot deterrence include Canada, Britain, Australia, Japan, or West Germany? When citizens of any of these countries ask us, after a few drinks, whether the United States would be willing to defend them, be willing to risk nuclear war in their defense, our response is typically that "we think of you Australians (or whoever) as the fifty-first state."

All of such extensions of deterrence thus amount to "jawboning," maintaining pretenses on political attitudes, and it all can work; in fact, it has worked now for a quarter century or more. Reinforcing the jawboning are the formal alliances, like NATO and the mutual defense treaties the United States has signed with Japan, Australia, New Zealand, and South Korea. Such alliance documents have now come to have a role and function very different from those that similar legal documents would have at an earlier time, in the days before nuclear weapons arrived upon the scene.

The alliances of an earlier time, for example between Japan and Britain in 1902, amounted to mutual insurance treaties, as each side wanted to be assured of military and political help in the future contingency of a war, and so each reluctantly agreed to bind itself to give such help to the other for the other's worrisome contingency. Like all normal insurance policies, neither party very much liked having to pay in, while each partner wished to be assured of getting help paid out if the dire need arose.

The alliances that the United States has negotiated since 1949, by contrast, are much more one-sided, with the United States contributing continually to the defense of countries like Belgium and Luxembourg, but with Belgium and Luxembourg not really being expected to make a contribution to the defense of the United States. Rather than amounting to a mutual insurance policy, which is what treaty arrangements like NATO still pretend to be, such agreements have the more real function of tying the hands of the United States in advance, so as to make its commitment to the defense of Western Europe more credible. U.S. policymakers could not have announced in advance that this was what the real function of a NATO agreement had become, for such candor would have undercut the new function of treaty agreements; rather the United States must pretend that these agreements are simply the legal, mutual assistance contracts of old. Since Americans are law-abiding people who fulfill contract obligations, the message to potential aggressors is that the United States has one more reason, irrationally or otherwise, to plunge into nuclear war in defense of these threatened territories.

Unlike the British 1902 alliance with Japan, by which Britain wanted to be sure of Japanese aid but did not particularly want to be committed to give aid to Japan (agreeing to do so only because Britain came out ahead in the swap), the United States in its current alliance with Japan *wants* to be committed to assisting Japan and to assisting

South Korea and all the countries of NATO, because such tied hands help deter Communist attack. The United States does not just accept the commitments of alliances, but rather seeks commitments.

The ludicrousness of the defense agreement that is ostensibly mutual between the United States and Luxembourg is illustrated by the discussion at a NATO Council meeting in a year in which the Soviets used the propaganda ploy of suggesting that NATO and the Warsaw Pact guarantee each other's security, a ploy to which the West at least had to respond. After most of the other NATO foreign ministers had gone through the drill of explaining why the Soviets' plan was unworkable, the Luxembourg foreign minister took the floor to explain his own nation's response: "If the Soviet Union wishes to guarantee the safety of Luxembourg, we do not object. But if the Soviet Union expects Luxembourg to guarantee the safety of the Soviet Union, well, gentlemen, I submit that this would be a bit too ambitious."

Yet another approach to ensuring the credibility of nuclear escalation might seem a bit bizarre, although it may have been part and parcel of the success of this approach ever since 1957; that is, to *fail* to prepare conventional defenses, thus showing the Soviet Union that the United States has no choice but to respond at the nuclear level, or at least to hold back any evidence that the United States is entertaining serious doubts about nuclear war and its consequences.

All contests about the comparative resolve of the two sides in a crisis will resemble a game of "chicken." In this game, each side tries to show a maximum of determination and a minimum of concern for ways of avoiding a crash. Too much discussion of the alternative of a conventional defense, especially if such discussion only leads to half-hearted efforts without meaningful results, would in this game be worse than doing nothing, for the Soviets would simply gain the information that the United States was beset by deep doubts about the wisdom of a nuclear response.

A different part of the escalation-plausibility strategy might at first seem contradictory to the strategy just described, but actually it is not. This strategy would involve deploying some U.S. troops near the front lines of a future conflict as a tripwire moral commitment. When U.S. soldiers are overrun by an aggressor's advance, their parents and the rest of the American public can be counted upon to become angry enough to wish to respond, and perhaps to respond by an escalation to the use of all the other weapons in the U.S. arsenal.

The U.S. troops deployed forward can never be allowed to admit that their role is merely to get in the way, merely to mobilize American outrage, for doing so would once again cast American resolve into doubt. Rather, they would have to go through all the motions of seeming to prepare for combat, with the message to the Soviets being that the rest of the United States would be sucked into the melee merely as part of the normal course of events, just as was the case in some wars of the past when the United States redeemed the honor of the *Maine,* of Pearl Harbor, and Bataan.

A perfect miniature illustration of this entire phenomenon can be seen in the stationing of the U.S. Army garrison in West Berlin. The garrison is small enough that it could probably be overwhelmed and disarmed by the East German police force, to say nothing of the East German and Soviet armed forces surrounding the enclave. The role of the force is clearly to commit American honor to the city and to force any hostile force to rise above a certain threshold of violence in seizing the city. Yet the commander and troops of the West Berlin garrison will never admit to this simple trip-wire role, always training for and asserting a role involving the defense of the city, a "deterrence by denial." The "denial" on which the U.S. military forces are so intent would, of course, involve some significant additions of force if it proved necessary, in the end perhaps bringing all the U.S. forces into play, and greatly adding to the costs for all concerned, possibly amounting even to a World War III (that is, "deterrence by punishment").

We will thus never see Army shoulder patches with the Latin for "trip-wire" as the unit motto. The units engaged in this role must pretend to be doing something else in order to be effective as trip-wires. Just as an actor must always pretend to be the character he is playing (and never admit to being an actor if he is to be a good one), so it is with the garrisons and forces deployed to Western Europe.

Suppose, however, that such forces were defensively proficient enough to throw back any Soviet onslaught without escalation, imposing enough simple battlefield costs on the advancing Soviet tank columns that the Soviets learned a nasty lesson, but so that neither side had to escalate to all-out war. Such a capability might by its prospect deter any aggressions in advance. But while it might be desirable to attain this level of conventional warfare proficiency, it would be highly undesirable to stress any reliance on such a capability and then fall short of it. The proper quantity of forces to be maintained is thus either enough to defend Europe without any escalation to nuclear war

("defense by denial"), or is instead a considerably smaller force sufficient to ensure U.S. involvement in any hostilities, but only pretending
to be ready to hold the line conventionally, in a manner calculated to
convince the Soviets that the United States would have to escalate to
nuclear warfare in the end.

Another move to reinforce the nuclear escalation commitment is
straightforward enough; that is, to deploy some tactical nuclear weapons in the path of possible aggressors, weapons that are ostensibly
intended to repulse a Soviet advance, but which by their presence
make it all the more likely that any war in Europe (or in South Korea)
will go nuclear, if only because a weapon in place is a weapon likely to
be used. The role of such tactical nuclear weapons has always thus
been a double one, either (as officially described) to make escalation to
all-out war unnecessary or (as perhaps more realistically interpreted)
to make such escalation very likely and thus deter invasions in the first
place.

Henry Kissinger underwent an interesting evolution of thinking on
tactical nuclear weapons (or "theater" nuclear weapons), a description
of which illustrates all of the logical complications here. In chapter 5
of his first major book, *Nuclear Weapons and Foreign Policy,* he developed the argument that Western Europe would have to be defended
entirely without the threat of escalation, since SAC would have to be
held in reserve to deter the Soviet intercontinental nuclear forces. In
chapter 6 of the same book, Kissinger then surprised his readers by
advocating theater nuclear forces as a way to accomplish this goal,
arguing that such weapons could be limited in their use and that no
escalation to general all-out war would have to follow when the nuclear
threshold had been crossed. The Kissinger limited-war argument was
found persuasive by many critics of the Eisenhower defense policies in
the late 1950s, but his advocacy of *nuclear* limited war drew much
skepticism.

Kissinger came around to join the other critics of Eisenhower in his
second book, *The Necessity for Choice,* published in 1961, conceding
that any use of nuclear weapons on the battlefield would be hard
to limit; the situation would be all too likely to produce escalation
leading to all-out war.[4] Endorsing preparations for a conventional-
defense limited war, Kissinger thus got into step with the thinking of
President Kennedy and Defense Secretary McNamara, as they for a
time tried to turn away from the deterrence approaches of the Eisenhower years.

In his 1965 book, *The Troubled Partnership*, Kissinger returned to endorsing and advocating the positioning of tactical nuclear weapons, but for diametrically opposite reasoning on their proclivity to escalation.[5] He continued to concede that the risks of escalation to all-out war remained high after any use of theater nuclear weapons, but concluded that this risk was desirable from the viewpoint of Western Europeans and of the United States, precisely because this risk contributed to deterring Soviet aggression in the first place. Having made a reputation for himself by showing the alleged gaps in the reasoning of the deterrence by punishment policy as the protection for Western Europe, Kissinger had thus come around 360 degrees to advocating a continuation of this method of deterrence, reinforced by the coupling link of tactical nuclear weapons deployed in place. Having first argued that these weapons would be valuable solely or primarily for their impact on the outcome of the battle, Kissinger ended up instead stressing their impact on the costliness of battle, costliness for the world, and especially costliness for Moscow.

Why would one assume that theater nuclear weapons are much more likely to come into use, merely because they are deployed in a prospective combat zone, as compared with the missiles and bombers based in the United States, in Great Britain or on-board submarines and other naval vessels offshore? The nuclear warheads in the path of an advancing Soviet tank force are presumably under the lock and key of permissive action links (PAL), designed to make their detonation impossible unless higher authority has ordered their use in combat.

Yet, therein lies the rub for any Soviet officer trying to sell Gorbachev on an invasion of Western Europe. If all the U.S. nuclear warheads were based on-board submarines off the coast or at locations in Britain, a U.S. president could conceivably back away from their use after a Soviet invasion, "chickening out" exactly as Kissinger and others had argued some twenty-five years ago. If the president's veto of the use of such warheads depends rather on the airtight effectiveness of battlefield PAL, however, the Soviet briefer will have greater difficulty in being sure that no U.S. nuclear warheads would come into use, that there would be no crossing of the conventional nuclear firebreak that might lead to an all-out war with Moscow itself being destroyed. Traditionally, field artillerymen all over the world do not let their ammunition be captured by the enemy, but rather go down firing it against the advancing enemy. Could Soviet leaders possibly feel assured that none of the nuclear artillery rounds and short- to medium-range missiles in the path of their advance would come into use? The answer is negative, and deterrence is once again enhanced.

Perhaps the reality is that such theater weapons are really intended by their officers to blunt a Soviet offensive by simply turning it back. Perhaps PAL devices will work so well that no captain of artillery could fire such weapons when a U.S. president did not want him to. But such weapons, as Kissinger belatedly admitted, are probably at least as important for their likely contributions to a chain of events leading up to nuclear attacks on the USSR itself. The winds of Europe blow from west to east, carrying nuclear fallout into the USSR, giving the pilot of a jet fighter-bomber a tailwind if he decides to hit a target a little farther east.

This policy will never be publicly declared in the West, but it can't be ignored in the briefings of the East. The most important word in theater nuclear forces might indeed be *theater*. In all the ways already outlined, alliance defense remains a form of show business.

The Role of the Conventional Balance

The deterrent threat of nuclear retaliation is being reinforced, but is there nothing the United States can do in the meantime to try to reinforce the threat also of conventional defense, the approach that deters by the prospect of denial, the kind of prospect that already so nicely shields Australia against Soviet invasion? Many such avenues should be pursued, as long as the pursuit is quiet and subtle, so that it does not cast doubt on and undermine U.S. willingness to escalate to nuclear weapons when all else fails. The United States surely will never wish to abandon the nuclear retaliatory defense of its alliance partners until it first definitely has another means of protecting them.

In general, therefore, policymakers need to pursue breakthroughs in defensive technology, new antitank guided missiles (ATGM), some new forms of fixed fortifications (with the West German urban sprawl now supplying many of these as a spin-off from the civilian sector), perhaps with a heavier reliance on minefields (if farmland were not so expensive in West Germany).

As stated at the outset, at the core of the problem, for both the West European and South Korean peninsulas about which the United

States is most concerned, is these territories' basic geopolitical vulnerability to an adversary's ability to bring in forces rapidly. Much of this threat is embodied in the many Soviet tanks and other armored vehicles, and the consistent goal of the United States at negotiations such as MBFR (mutual and balanced force reduction) to get Soviet tank totals substantially reduced.

The centrality of the tank threat is easy to forget in the wake of the public excitement in Western Europe and in the United States about the Soviet SS-20 missile. President Reagan's offer to swap the new U.S. ground-launched cruise missile (GLCM) and Pershing II deployments for the elimination of the SS-20 was a good propaganda ploy, especially since the Soviets will lose credibility with the European peace movements as they reject the swap, but it is not a swap consistent with the interests of the United States and its alliance partners by the analysis here.

Consider the two following hypothetical situations. If the Soviets had no tanks and were equipping themselves with SS-20s, would the United States have any great reason for concern and any need for GLCMs, Pershing II and tactical nuclear weapons on its side? The answer is basically no, because the threat of nuclear retaliation from the United States would shield West European cities against the nuclear warheads on these newest Soviet missiles. The same SS-20s could presently hit targets in Japan, Ireland, and Britain, but do not cause any concern there because Soviet tanks cannot roll into those countries; the SS-20 is threatening in the end only as an accessory to the Soviet tank potential. (The SS-20 is basically a failed Soviet intercontinental-range missile, reminding us that the USSR could always aim more warheads at Western Europe simply by retargeting some of the ICBMs now aimed at the United States.)

Conversely, if the Soviet Union had no SS-20s and were still so well equipped with tanks, would the United States have any great reason for concern, and any need for GLCMs, Pershing II and tactical nuclear weapons on its side? Of course, for all the reasons already discussed; the United States would still need to include in the picture the U.S. nuclear retaliation that keeps the Soviets from using their conventional advantage in armored warfare.

If the United States swaps in Europe, it would thus need much more to focus on the swap of tactical nuclear forces for Soviet tanks, ignoring the Soviet tactical nuclear weapons as having only a very indirect relationship to U.S. problems.

Continuing Problems

Yet to show that the extendability issue can be finessed is hardly to dismiss the entire question as merely a troublesome tension for deterrence. The American readiness to use nuclear weapons on behalf of others may be real enough to be deterring, but it can never be certain and might thus nonetheless invite challenge. Probably the worst kind of accident we have to fear is if the other side assumed the United States was bluffing about its nuclear escalation response, and it was indeed not bluffing; a nuclear disaster could result that both sides would have preferred to avoid.

So, more relevant for policy than the issue of "has deterrence worked?" is the question of "can deterrence continue to work?" for the shielding of Western Europe. Could it be, now that the Soviet nuclear force totals have grown to equal or surpass those of the United States, that an extension of nuclear deterrence to shield NATO will no longer be possible?

Such concerns are sometimes linked to a concept of "escalation dominance," as if the presence or absence of such an advantage to the United States and its allies would make all the difference for whether "nuclear umbrella" threats are credible.[6]

Escalation dominance had at least two distinct meanings, which are too often confused. First, even for those advocating a conventional defense for places like Western Europe (that is, advocating "deterrence by denial"), something nuclear will be seen as prerequisite for any such moderated and limited approach: preparing sufficient Western nuclear forces, strategic or in the theater, so that the Soviets never see an advantage for themselves in escalating to the nuclear level. It would be cruelly ironic if NATO forces mounted a stout conventional defense against a Soviet advance, without any nuclear attacks on Magdeburg or Moscow or New York, and the Soviets then reached for their nuclear weapons as a way of salvaging some kind of victory in order to redeem their original investment in the attack.

A second, considerably different, sense of *escalation dominance* also calls for greater Western nuclear force preparations, strategic and in the theater, but with a view less to deterring Soviet nuclear escalation and more to making Western nuclear escalation look credible (because it looked as if the West thought nuclear escalation would pay off in terms of battlefield victory). One of the reasons that a U.S. nuclear response on behalf of a place like West Germany has been credible, despite the arguments about the vulnerability of U.S. cities, has been all along that the United States could become so interested in plausible considerations of counterforce victory that it would not have time to be immobilized by considerations of suffering. Escalation dominance in this second sense means that the United States could be expected to try to snatch victory from the jaws of a conventional defeat by escalating to nuclear weapons if the Soviet tank advance could not be checked otherwise. If it was foolish for Americans to escalate in quest of victory, this would make less difference as long as Americans were known to believe such foolishness.[7] The impact of all this prognostication on Moscow decisionmakers would have to be the understanding that an invasion of the NATO area would lead to nuclear escalation, and thus no invasion would occur.

Escalation dominance in the first sense is sought, as a result, by any U.S. strategists who are convinced of the inutility of nuclear deterrence for shielding Western Europe or South Korea, but who would certainly want to make sure that the Soviets did not themselves elect to escalate to the use of nuclear weapons whenever a successful conventional defense of these places, or some other untoward events from Moscow's point of view, had occurred.

Escalation dominance in the second sense is part of an effort to maintain the credibility of a U.S. first-use of nuclear weapons, not a threat of immediate nuclear escalation, but of something like escalation after a "pause" once a conventional defense had proved impracticable; this is the reasoning behind the murky but possibly still effective policy of "no early first use."

Each of these approaches would thus involve some striving for conventional defensive capabilities to turn back a Soviet tank attack without immediately moving to a use of nuclear weapons that would very possibly become all-out. The first sense of escalation dominance hopes for a total posture of no first use, however, where the second sense of escalation dominance decidedly does not. Each of these approaches might also be endangered if Soviet nuclear stockpiles, theater and strategic, were to grow in size, and if improvements in the U.S. nuclear arsenal were not sufficient to cancel out the impact of this growth.

Pessimists about U.S. protection of its European allies will claim that the erosion of escalation dominance (in the second sense, by which the United States might be viewed as wanting to escalate because of the military advantages in doing so) may take all the credibility and the contribution to deterrence out of U.S. invasion threats.

Yet there have been many other explanations of why the United States would move to the use of nuclear weapons if Western Europe were being overrun besides any suppositions of military advantage that underlie a theory of escalation dominance. Indeed, the logic of escalation dominance has been under attack for more than two decades. Mindless and irrational considerations of impact on the battlefield, of "winning the war that the Russians had started," might indeed persuade a U.S. president to release the tactical and other nuclear weapons earmarked for NATO, rather than accept a conventional defeat. But this would fly in the face of the risk that such nuclear weapons could not be limited to the battlefield, so that Moscow, New York, Leningrad, and Washington would then be destroyed (where otherwise they might have been spared); there has also all along been the risk that such weapons might still not favor the defense and might in the end actually make a Soviet conquest of Western Europe (a Western Europe devastated and radioactive) that much easier.

If U.S. nuclear escalation has been credible, it has not been at any time since 1949 because escalation has made perfect sense for the United States; rather, it has been credible because the traditional focus on the phenomenon of "victory" might still capture the attention and imagination of U.S. leaders, despite all the rational considerations of U.S. national interest working to the contrary, and/or because a Soviet leadership would at least have to take the possibility of such U.S. thinking into account.

Escalation, Credibility, and National Interest

One can think of a variety of reasons why the United States might feel strongly committed to any particular piece of territory in the world, so strongly that it could even, despite the risks to its own safety, be credible in threatening nuclear escalation. The reasons can be both materially selfish and more generously altruistic.

Beginning on the selfish side, the United States might care very much about the natural resources obtainable from a particular region, the oil of the Middle East, for example, or the strategic metals of Southern Africa.

Similarly, the United States can care about the geographic position of a particular territory. In the past, one felt more secure defending one's home in someone else's frontyard or backyard. But if certain areas of the world fall under Moscow's control, it becomes that much easier for the Politburo to direct various kinds of military threats against the United States itself. It is easier to defend France if Germany is still not under Communist rule. It is easier to defend Britain if France has not been occupied. It is also easier to defend the United States if Europe and Central America are not under Moscow's domination.

On the psychological level, having failed to defend a particular area may weaken the defense of other areas, since people will draw the lesson that the United States is not to be counted upon. Giving up on a territory that has been successfully defended in the past, South Korea, for example, might be viewed as a demonstration of declining strength; what the United States was able to do in the past, it is not able to do anymore, and the swing nations of the world tend to take their cue from this kind of precedent.

Finally, there are places that the United States will defend, not because of their raw materials or their geographic position or even because of the dangers of precedent, but simply because Americans identify with the people and would feel deep grief if they were added to the list of peoples under Communist domination. West Berlin might be just such an example of a more general phenomenon. When President Kennedy said, "Ich bin ein Berliner," he was merely adding a city to the more general category of "fifty-first state." Just as the United States is presumably prepared to escalate to nuclear warfare if any of its own fifty states are invaded, it is probably inclined to treat some other portions of the world as almost equally valuable, thereby extending nuclear deterrence, where a less strong identification with others would have made doing so logically impossible.

Not every place in the world can hope to win this kind of identification, of course. Such an American commitment to Somalia seems unlikely, and we know that it did not exist for Vietnam, but it seems just as clear that such a commitment does exist for Canada and for Britain, and probably for much of the world that is democratically governed and on the path of advanced industrial development. It exists for these areas not because of any particular selfish U.S. interest in them, but simply because of the nation's altruistic involvement, the American people's concern for the welfare of the people living there for their own sake.

There is no simple way to translate such explanations of the American commitment in any foreign area into strengths of commitment. It is still not beyond belief that the United States might escalate to the use of nuclear weapons for any of the reasons listed, because the resources of the territory being attacked were too precious, because its physical location posed a threat, because the precedent that would be set in a surrender would be too damaging, or because Americans cared almost as much about the people involved as they care about their own people. If U.S. escalation occurred for any of these reasons, the hope is that the Soviets would never challenge the strength of the U.S. commitment here, and would never have to discover that the United States meant what it had threatened.

It must be remembered, of course, that all such categories of explanation can apply equally well to the Soviet Union, explaining the likelihood that it might escalate to the use of nuclear weapons. The worst fear of all is that the two sides simultaneously might become committed to the same piece of territory, each threatening nuclear escalation if the other did not back off, each guessing that the other was bluffing.

For other corners of the world, it is more probable that the United States could not credibly threaten such escalation, because it could not credibly claim to care so much, for any of the above reasons, about the area being contested. The possibility of limited wars and conventional attacks is greater under these circumstances, because the normal kind of deterrence by denial is never established. Here, conversely, the risk of nuclear war goes down for both sides.

With regard to the belief that the United States might escalate to the use of nuclear weapons in defense of a particular area and/or in retaliation for an attack on that area, four categories describe the status quo situation in the 1980s:

1. In areas that are vulnerable in terms of conventional military capabilities and that (for various reasons) the United States feels strongly enough attached to, such escalation would be credible; the list of areas includes Western Europe, South Korea, and perhaps the Persian Gulf;

2. In areas for which the United States would also feel strong enough attachment to make such escalation credible, but for which no plausible conventional threat exists, "the question never comes up." On this list we would find Great Britain, Australia, Japan, New Zealand, Canada, Ireland, and some others;

    2a. A very special case, again where "the question does not come up," is the continental United States itself. What if the Soviet marines seized Rhode Island? Wouldn't the United States go to nuclear first-use, even if the Soviets had stayed entirely conventional? This example is entirely hypothetical, since the Soviet marines are not capable of invading Rhode Island.

3. Areas that are conventionally threatened, but for which we would not escalate to the use of nuclear weapons (for which we thus have a de facto no first use policy) would include Chad, Thailand, and many other places;

4. Places not conventionally threatened, for which we would also not escalate, would be included although "the question never comes up."

It may well be that categories 3 and 4 take up most of the globe, with category 2 taking up another large area, leaving two or three valuable peninsulas in Eurasia as the real sources of difficulty.

Escalation, Credibility, and the Strategic Balance

We might return now to the credibility of extended nuclear deterrence as it relates to changes in the general strategic situation over time, trying once more to decipher how much the protection of NATO has really depended on escalation dominance or on any other kind of dominance. When examining the stages of comparison between Soviet and U.S. nuclear forces, we might note as many as five:

1. U.S. monopoly, as it existed from 1945 to 1949, with the United States capable of inflicting nuclear devastation on others, and with the Soviet Union (or any other state) incapable of inflicting such destruction in retaliation on the United States;

2. U.S. nuclear "superiority," with the Soviet Union able to deliver nuclear warheads to a fair number of U.S. cities, but with the United States definitely able to inflict far greater destruction on the Soviet Union and very likely to "win" such an all-out war (in terms of having any forces left or ability to wage war at the end);

3. "Parity," in the sense that the force totals on the two sides become so comparable that it is difficult to conclude which is the greater or stronger, and it is similarly difficult to predict whose war-fighting capabilities would survive at the end;

4. Soviet "superiority," with the United States able to deliver nuclear warheads to a fair number of Soviet cities, but with the Soviet Union definitely able to inflict far greater destruction on the United States and very likely to "win" such an all-out war (in terms of having any forces left or ability to wage war at the end);

5. Soviet monopoly, with the Soviet Union capable of inflicting nuclear devastation on the United States, and with the United States incapable of inflicting such destruction in retaliation on the Soviet Union.

A few comments have to be made in looking at this overview. First, despite the seeming logical progression of the stages, there is really nothing about the progression from stage 1 to stages 2, 3, and 4 that could lead anyone in Moscow, or anywhere else, to count on getting to stage 5. Anyone seeing a Soviet monopoly coming is deceived by the apparent symmetry in what has been argued to be a transition from American superiority to parity to Soviet superiority; but one basically "can't get there from here." (It should also be noted that it is indeed very debatable whether "Soviet superiority" is the correct way to describe the current situation, or even the imminent situation.)

Second, in terms of strategic logic, the crucial transition is probably between stage 1 (U.S. monopoly) and the three stages that follow (just as it would be crucial between these three stages and a stage 5, Soviet monopoly). Everything in the world, in terms of the strategic logic of deterrence, depends on whether or not nuclear weapons can be gotten through to Washington and New York (which has been a fact of life since 1949), or can be gotten through to Moscow and Leningrad (which will remain a fact of life for all the future that we can foresee).

If the logical and rational credibility of U.S. extensions of deterrence were to be challenged, it would have to happen on the first transition that plunged the people of the United States into the role of hostages, the transition from U.S. monopoly to U.S. "superiority." As enunciated in NSC-68, and in the writings of Henry Kissinger and Pierre Gallois and countless others, the entire logic of nuclear deterrence is that a nuclear military superiority can not be cashed in on, unless it can be carried through in a manner that shields one's own civilians substantially against attack. The success of extending deterrence has thus come in getting past this logic, not because physical reality gave the United States a continued upper hand, but because of all the psychological ploys listed earlier that made U.S. commitments credible nonetheless.

The U.S. nuclear monopoly in actual practice was used in 1945 to force Tokyo to stop moving its forces forward in China (and indeed to surrender itself to occupation) and in 1946 to force the USSR to withdraw from Iran and to forego any advance into Western Europe. After 1949, however, everything about the use of U.S. nuclear power has depended on something other than monopoly, something taking the vulnerability of New York and other cities into account, something nonetheless working. If it could be carried off after 1949, there is no inherent reason why it cannot be carried off as well after 1989. Unless the Soviets succeed in shielding Moscow and other Soviet cities against U.S. nuclear attack after 1999, moreover, this kind of extension of deterrence, with all its worries and all its problems, should be capable of persisting into the next century or two as well.

Those who would see an important difference among the three middle stages, 2, 3, and 4, "U.S. superiority," "parity," and "Soviet superiority," will claim that Western Europe has been opened to Soviet advances as the nation has moved from stage 2 through 3 to 4. Yet, if this is the case, why was not Eastern Europe wide open to free-world advance when the United States was "superior"? As noted by many authors in the 1950s, even the most rudimentary Soviet capacity for nuclear retaliation was more than enough to keep the United States from offering military assistance to the East Germans or Hungarians, or to others seeking to terminate the imposition of Communist rule on their lands. Conversely, even the most rudimentary U.S. capability for nuclear retaliation may be enough to keep Soviet tanks from rolling farther west.

The practical reality of deterrence is thus that each of the nuclear-equipped sides has a good chance of holding onto what it began the game with, as long as it cares enough about these territories it holds, as long as it would take a major military action by the other side on the order of a tank attack, to change this status quo. If Western Europe were ever to become as prone to guerrilla or terrorist attacks as El Salvador or Vietnam, then the U.S. ability to shield the NATO countries by the threat of nuclear escalation would be terminated, for reasons having next to nothing to do with the overarching nuclear balance or escalation dominance. If Eastern Europe were similarly to become as ripe as Angola and Afghanistan for anti-Soviet guerrilla operations, Moscow would similarly not be able to base its hold on the Warsaw Pact countries on threats of nuclear escalation.

Earlier Anxieties about the Same Issues

Nothing in the discussion to this point is particularly new. As has been mentioned, the debate began immediately after the Soviet atomic-bomb test was detected in 1949 in the NSC-68 document intended to shape policy choices within the U.S. government. The Korean War made the threat of such aggression look all too real only a few months later, and the plan for NATO defense developed at the end of the Truman administration took the form of the Lisbon goals, which called for a military buildup to some ninety-six divisions. [8]

Facing the enormous financial and human costs of such a buildup, the Eisenhower administration shifted instead to what was called the "New Look," and the complicated charade of threatening nuclear retaliation, of pretending to be preparing for repulsing on the battle-field any Soviet advance by using the nuclear-equipped "pentomic" divisions of the U.S. Army. The introduction of tactical nuclear weapons into West Germany with the U.S. "Carte Blanche" exercise created a stir in 1955, as more than three hundred nuclear warheads were hypothetically "detonated" inside West Germany on the first day of the war game. The Social Democrats stated their opposition to the beleaguered Adenauer government on this issue, on the premise that West Germany would be devastated in the process of being defended in an actual war; but within a few years they came around to joining the Christian Democrats in welcoming this link with the United States, as an economical and effective way of deterring any Soviet advance in West Germany. [9]

Showing their own sensitivity to the nuclear escalation threat (and perhaps wishing to eliminate the risks of such escalation and to help pave their way into Western Europe), the Soviets allowed the Communist Polish regime to propose the so-called Rapacki Plan in 1957, calling for a nuclear-free zone including West Germany, East Germany, Poland, and Czechoslovakia, a zone within which no nuclear weapons would be deployed.

In 1961, Secretary McNamara took over the Department of Defense under President John F. Kennedy. He was committed apparently to something of a blend of the Lisbon goals and the Rapacki Plan; obviously wishing to have Western Europe secured by one means or the other, he clearly preferred the means of conventional defense.

While Western European resistance to a conventional defense was condemning this ultimate goal of the McNamara Defense Department to failure, the United States was becoming engrossed in the defense of Vietnam, where no one believed or argued that a nuclear threat could hold back Communist expansion. Conventional force strength deployed in Western Europe hence did not increase toward the end of the 1960s, but rather was thinned out so that the United States could meet the demands of war in Vietnam. These events might have served as evidence to the Politburo that nuclear retaliation would follow after any invasion of Western Europe, because the United States had still failed to prepare for anything else and because (in light of the Vietnam experience) it had soured so much on conventional warfare.

The Kennedy administration had spoken of wanting the ability to fight two and one-half wars simultaneously; but the Nixon administration, which came into office in 1969, announced after a time that it was deliberately scaling down this capacity goal to the ability to fight one war, thus very much matching the old Eisenhower line that what was appropriate and sufficient for general war had to be appropriate and sufficient for smaller wars as well.

More recently, the United States has been developing new anxieties and excitement about its limited war problem for Europe, as the growth of the Soviet nuclear stockpile has apparently once again put life into the scenario outlined by Kissinger. It is alleged that the United States will finally no longer be credible as a power capable of escalating to the use of nuclear weapons in the defense of Western Europe. It is also alleged that the United States will have to come up with something else, a defense by denial rather than a defense by punishment. Several years ago, former Secretary McNamara published an article in *Foreign Affairs,* with McGeorge Bundy, George Kennan, and Gerard Smith as coauthors, openly endorsing a policy that many conjectured he had favored twenty years ago; that is, abandoning the reliance on nuclear weapons as reinforcement for the security of the West European peninsula, as the United States would proclaim a policy of no first use of nuclear weapons and would presumably pull them back out of harm's way.[10]

Current Public Tensions

This reentry of Robert McNamara into a public discussion of defense matters came at a time when considerably greater attention was being devoted to such matters in the United States, in West Germany, and throughout Western Europe (lamentably, there is no way to measure popular attitudes on this subject in South Korea until the military regime in Seoul can be convinced that democracy should be appropriately restored). Much of the alleged concern about nuclear threats in West Germany reflect U.S. plans to deploy new ground-launched cruise missiles and Pershing II ballistic missiles in response to the increased deployment of Soviet SS-20 missiles, a deployment that West German Chancellor Helmut Schmidt pointed to with great alarm in a 1977 address to the annual conference of the International Institute of Strategic Studies.

Yet today's West German anxiety about how GLCMs could destroy Europe is strikingly analogous to the uproar about Carte Blanche a quarter century ago, for what is bad news at first glance can become good news upon reflection by the curious logic that has dominated nuclear strategy ever since 1945. The same factors that make Western Europe a radioactive ruin (along with Eastern Europe and the Soviet Union) make a Soviet attack on Western Europe far less likely.

One could propose the following general interpretation of public attitudes on all nuclear matters—the attitudes in the United States (amid periodic gatherings in Central Park), the attitudes in West Germany, the attitudes all around the alliance:

"We like the way nuclear weapons have affected the world, at least until last night. The total number of wars fought since 1945 has been less than almost any reasonable analyst could have predicted in 1944, with the deterring effect of nuclear weaponry (nuclear weapons being uniquely destructive and uniquely effective in never being used) making all the difference. But we brood about, and hate, the way nuclear weapons might affect the world in the future, any time after tomorrow morning, because the worst that could happen—if calculations go wrong, if deterrence fails, if the net impact of nuclear weapons changes—is the destruction of civilization as we know it. Thus we are against change, against new developments, in this area; we prefer the status quo on nuclear matters, because any and all new ways of handling these weapons could upset the old way that worked."

West Germans are upset by new missile deployments, but would be just as upset by the total withdrawal of U.S. nuclear weapons suggested by the advocates of a conventional defense. Americans get upset about the "war-fighting" talk of the Reagan administration, but get just as upset at the prospect that the Soviets might have used the SALT negotiations to bypass the United States significantly in nuclear weapons strength. A no-first-use or nuclear-free zone arrangement might thus cause as much unhappiness in Europe and as many fears of new trends for the future as are caused by GLCM or Pershing II. And similar unhappiness emerges at the prospect of a proliferation of nuclear weapons to the arsenals of additional countries.

The best rule to follow, therefore, might be simple enough: We ought to seek to "keep nuclear weapons out of the news," to try to allow as few new nuclear developments as possible to emerge for public discussion.

The problem, of course, is that this is more easily said than done, for the ongoing march of military technology makes it inevitable that some new developments will emerge from time to time in nuclear weaponry and in the related delivery systems, generating the kind of "news" that will drive commentators to reopen the discussion on all the choices discussed here.

The following conclusions might be offered regarding the problem of defending the United States' more valuable allies on the peninsulas extending from the Eurasian continent. First, what is old about the problem is probably more important than what is new. Second, people who should know better will continue to reinvent problems as if they were new, problems that have been invented before and solved before. Third, the irrational and timeworn threat of U.S. nuclear escalation can probably still suffice for a long time into the future to shield Western Europe against Soviet attack. The annual Politburo briefing on "windows of Western vulnerability" is probably never as gleeful or upbeat an operation as U.S. policymakers fear.

Notes

1. Pierre Gallois, *The Balance of Terror* (Boston, Mass.: Houghton Mifflin, 1961).

2. Henry A. Kissinger, *Nuclear Weapons and Foreign Policy* (New York: Harper and Row, 1957).

3. For an analysis suggesting that U.S. nuclear escalation is indeed quite credible for deterring attacks on an area as valuable as Western Europe, see Bernard Brodie, *Escalation and the Nuclear Option* (Princeton: Princeton University Press, 1966). See also Thomas C. Schelling, *The Strategy of Conflict* (Cambridge: Harvard University Press, 1960), 182–203.

4. Henry A. Kissinger, *The Necessity for Choice* (New York: Harper and Row, 1961).

5. Henry A. Kissinger, *The Troubled Partnership* (New York: McGraw-Hill, 1965).

6. For a statement along the lines of this argument, see Henry A. Kissinger, "Strategy and the American Alliance," *Survival* 24, no. 5 (September–October 1982):194–200.

7. For a skeptical discussion of whether tactical (theater) nuclear weapons can actually do any of the things they are advertised as being capable of doing, see Robert S. McNamara, "The Military Role of Nuclear Weapons," *Foreign Affairs* 62, no. 1 (Fall 1983):59–80. It remains possible that their unadvertised contribution, of leading to escalation to all-out war, is still a very worthwhile contribution.

8. On NSC-68 and the general initial reaction to the Soviet acquistion of nuclear weapons, see Warner R. Schilling, Paul Y. Hammond, and Glenn H. Snyder, *Strategy, Politics and Defense Budgets* (New York: Columbia University Press, 1962).

9. The interplay of the Eisenhower commitment to theater nuclear forces, and the West German responses, is outlined in Robert E. Osgood, *NATO: The Entangling Alliance* (Chicago: University of Chicago Press, 1962).

10. McGeorge Bundy, George F. Kennan, Robert S. McNamara, and Gerard Smith, "Nuclear Weapons and the Atlantic Alliance," *Foreign Affairs* 60, no. 4 (Spring 1982):753–68.

6

The Tension between Deterrence and Traditional Morality

One way to begin a discussion of deterrence and of its unresolved internal dilemmas would be to recount a repeated experience of this author when asked to come to another campus to deliver a guest lecture (an experience surely matched by those of other college instructors in similar circumstances). Having been asked to cover the topic of deterrence, the visitor is usually unsure how much the students have already heard or read on the subject. As a way of bringing himself up to speed, the lecturer may begin the hour by asking how many of the students came to class "opposed to deterrence." In a room of perhaps some thirty students, three or four in any typical year will raise their hands. The next question is: "If the Politburo leadership did something really obnoxious, like destroying a U.S. city or Paris in a rocket attack, or seizing West Berlin or Hamburg or Frankfurt with conventional forces, how many of you students would oppose a system whereby the United States would then get even by killing very large numbers of ordinary Russian people (people who may well have disapproved of whatever aggressive move the Politburo had just launched, people who would probably never vote for the Communist leadership if they had any choice of alternatives, people who are probably inclined instead to vote Social Democratic or Czarist rather than Communist)?" At this point, some twenty-five or more students raise their hands, indignantly refusing to endorse such a U.S. policy.

The visiting lecturer then dooms himself never to be invited back by pointing out that this may well be what deterrence is all about—threatening the lives of innocent, ordinary Russian people, in order

This chapter appeared as part of a chapter in George Thibault, ed., *The Art and Practice of Military Strategy* (Washington, D.C.: National Defense University Press, 1984).

to dissuade the Politburo leadership from engaging in conventional or nuclear military aggression. The students have simply not been doing their reading. Or, more probably, they have done their reading but have not internalized the fuller moral and political ramifications of what the balance of terror is all about; they have been ready to live with deterrence, but are not ready to think about how it works.

This example illustrates the conflict in the United States between the policy of deterrence and traditional morality. Isn't the very essence of deterrence ("mutual assured destruction") immoral, and isn't it inconsistent with the traditional standards of Western civilization as they have evolved since the Renaissance and inconsistent with whatever standards of warfare that have been developed over the centuries? The United States preserves peace, in the nuclear age, by threatening millions of innocent people, on the expectation (not so badly founded, so far as anyone can tell) that doing so will deter the potentially guilty from initiating wars and aggressions.[1]

The targeting of civilians is of course typically not admitted. If the United States becomes involved in a World War III, killing millions of Russians would be unintended "collateral damage," since military targets were being aimed at, with the damage to civilians simply being unavoidable, given the size of nuclear explosions. Yet the U.S. failure to admit the countervalue intention in its public pronouncements, or even in private discussions of strategy within the government and military, may simply be an evasion and obfuscation designed to head off pangs of guilt and may show how morally reprehensible the entire balance of terror is. Unintended killing of civilians somehow causes less moral anxiety than an intended killing; this attitude is consistent with traditional Western moral thinking. Yet every college student in an international relations course is now being told that the peace of the years since 1945 has depended precisely on the likely destruction of cities and civilian targets in the event of an all-out war; whether this "collateral damage" killing of civilians is "intended" or "unintended," it is required as part of "assured destruction," if an assured second strike is to be meaningful as a deterrent.

One can imagine the howls of indignation if anyone proposed solving any other social problems by such a morally defective approach. Suppose that society wished to reduce the crime rate by arresting the wives and children of accused or convicted criminals whenever the actual culprits escaped apprehension. Would imprisoning or executing the loved ones of the criminal deter crime? Almost surely it would have some of this desirable impact. Would such an indirect approach be acceptable to society? Certainly it would not; virtually everyone would find such an approach totally inconsistent with what we in the West think of as civilization.

It is thus very possible that the most recent wave of disquiet about nuclear deterrence reflects a certain weakening or "moment of truth" about the largely recognized but largely unadmitted nature of nuclear deterrence. The Roman Catholic bishops of the United States may have responded in basically the same way as students in the classroom, reacting with moral revulsion to the details of nuclear deterrence when forced to contemplate them.[2]

The only thing to be said in defense of mutual assured destruction is that it has worked. A 1944 scholar, looking forward to the international relations of the next four decades, but not knowing about the impending introduction of nuclear weapons, would surely have predicted more extensive rounds of armed combat than have actually occurred and more demanding rounds of defense spending. Far more ships would have been sunk on the high seas between 1945 and 1984, far more battles would have been fought across the north German plain, and far less of a West European economic miracle might have occurred.

If we are honest with ourselves, most of us might then admit that we have somewhat welcomed the impact of nuclear weapons—*to date*—even while we dread the possibilities of what life would be like if deterrence failed. Whether we are students in the classroom, or professors, or bishops, or atheists, we might like the way nuclear weapons have worked until last night, but we feel considerable compunction about the way they might work after tomorrow morning. Moreover, we certainly would not like to draw lessons from these weapons' impact since Nagasaki in order to solve problems in any other area of human political arrangements.[3] Perhaps we are now facing an important moment of truth, as a time bomb on the sheer immorality of basic nuclear deterrence has finally gone off. But it is just as possible that this moment of truth will pass and we will all settle back to realize that deterrence, however immoral in mechanism, is morally effective in its end-product—a decreased likelihood of war in general.

Yet there are at least two other possible practical problems in these moral difficulties. First (even if no moment of truth is in store to drive the United States totally away from deterrence), the mere fact that the United States and the Soviets are constantly pointing such deadly instruments at each other's populations may constitute a serious political poison, making real détente and mutual accommodation very much more difficult and strengthening the hands of those within each society who oppose any further communciation or cooperation. In some willy-nilly way, U.S. policymakers hope to achieve a longer-term liberalization of the life-style and political climate in the Soviet Union. Skeptics may wonder whether this can ever be accomplished, given the military impregnability of the Soviet system and the strong vested interests of the Communist establishment. Yet the daily reminder that each side could, in less than an hour, murder millions on the other side surely does not help to create the right atmosphere for liberalization or for any other real improvement in U.S.–Soviet relations.

If the United States hopes to loosen up the Soviet Union, to create a real détente with normalization of relations and a reduction of mutual acrimony and suspicion, it is at least possible that the missiles each side continually aims at each other's cities amount to permanent obstacles to this goal, a political poisoning of the system that is not unrelated to the blatant immorality of this indirect approach to peace.

All of us, on either side of the line, must currently attach a contingency rider to any long-term plans we make, whether it be plans regarding what career field to enter, how many children to have, or where to choose a house or apartment. When contemplating the future, all our problems may look solvable enough, with a sense that "things seem to be working out," but also with a qualifier: "that is, as long as there isn't a nuclear war." Seeing each other as the potential source of the most complete devastation of all normal civilian life, Americans could develop an irreducible hostility toward Russians, and vice versa; this hostility might never go away, as long as mutual assured destruction was the price of peace and freedom.

Second, we are reluctant to admit to others (and to ourselves) that countervalue targeting is critical to deterrence—it is the major assumption, voiced often enough in textbook discussions of what international peace has been all about since 1945, but it is not voiced very often in Washington or Moscow or Omaha. Because of this reluctance, it is possible that the military officers who make plans for and operate the strategic nuclear forces will feel pressed to direct their maximum effort in the direction of counterforce rather than countervalue targeting. If this evasion is simply meant to be morally soothing, disguising the fact that a great deal of countervalue collateral damage will be inflicted in any event, there is no particular problem. If these officers were more industrious and successful in their efforts at achieving accuracy, however, then these efforts might threaten the assured retaliatory forces of the other side, bizarrely reducing the stability of the mutual deterrent system and paradoxically making war more likely. Even the public endorsement of "war fighting" and "war winning" and "counterforce" intentions serves to frighten, irritate, and destabilize, for the other side takes such posturing seriously in a "worst-case analysis."

The Soviet Union is particularly at fault here, never fully endorsing the logic of mutual assured destruction, still telling one and all that (if war comes) its missiles will be aimed at military targets in the United States, with the intention only of shielding the Soviet motherland and reversing the war's military outcome; this sounds like a traditionally moral approach, but is particularly menacing to anyone counting on mutual deterrence. Nevertheless, U.S. statements of strategic philosophy can be faulted on the same count.

Traditional morality, in short, gives exactly the wrong guidance on how to implement mutual deterrence. To ease this problem, the blatantly uncivilized nature of deterrence, we may mislead ourselves into worsening the problem of assuring each side's means to retaliate. The United States could become more moral if it continued to perfect the accuracy of nuclear delivery systems, so that the military could hit military targets more directly, thus reducing the likelihood of hitting innocent civilians; but this approach might compromise the reliability of second-strike retaliatory forces, placing each side in the tense and fearsome situation of "use them or lose them" and as a result making all-out war more likely. It is widely contended that this is a possible result of the enhancement of Soviet missile accuracies, or of shifting from Minuteman to the MX or from Pershing I to Pershing II.

Such improvements in accuracy may be inevitable, as engineers continue to improve upon existing nuclear delivery systems. Such counterforce targeting may also be politically inevitable, as Soviet and U.S. national leaders and military planners continue to pay lip service to more traditional morality, which approves of countermilitary targeting and disapproves of countercivilian strikes. Bombing campaigns to date have always been justified on counterforce grounds, even if the actual intention was to impose countervalue damage, because this made better international propaganda and/or because it made the individual target planners feel better.

It is thus bizarrely possible that we will be able to persuade students in a classroom that mutual assured destruction makes sense (even if it makes civilians the target of nuclear attack), but that the same lesson will not reach the target planners working at Strategic Air Command headquarters in Omaha.

Notes

1. For a quite early view questioning the moral durability of nuclear deterrence, see Fred C. Iklé, "Can Nuclear Deterrence Last Out the Century?" For a reply stating the inevitability of reliance on such deterrence, see Wolfgang Panofsky, "The Mutual Hostage Relationship between America and Russia," *Foreign Affairs* 52, no. 1 (October 1973):109–18.

2. Portions of the bishops' Statement can be found in *Science, Technology and Human Values* 8, no. 3 (Summer 1983):14–35, 39–40. See also Albert Wohlstetter, "Bishops, Statesmen, and Other Strategists on the Bombing of the Innocents," *Commentary* 75, no. 6 (June 1983):15–35.

3. For an extended set of arguments on the moral issues here, see Russell Hardin and John Mearsheimer, eds., "Special Issue on Ethics and Nuclear Deterrence," *Ethics* 95, no. 3 (April 1985).

7

Assessing the Possibilities

What kinds of trends may be associated with nuclear deterrence in the near future, and with the concomitant issues of credibility?

With regard to the survivability of the forces required to maintain the prospect of retaliation in each direction, the United States is worse off than it was in the 1960s and 1970s, but it is surely also better off than it was in the later years of the 1950s. Nothing in today's speculation about a "window of vulnerability" comes close to matching the most fearful U.S. predictions about a possible "missile gap," according to which a Soviet monopoly of ICBMs (intercontinental ballistic missiles) might catch all U.S. bombers on the ground, allowing Moscow to launch a World War III in which victory could be real, in which no significant countervalue retaliation would be inflicted on the USSR. Moving away from multiple-warhead missiles would surely be a step in a better direction, as would emphasizing the survivability of U.S. missiles, rather than enhancing their accuracy so as to make them more effective against the silos sheltering the adversary's missiles.

Aiming missiles accurately is consistent with traditional Western morality, for it allows an honorable targeting approach of aiming only at the enemy's military targets to cripple his ability to fight, rather than at his civilians and his will to fight. But such accuracy and morality is devastatingly inconsistent with the system of mutual deterrence.

One consequence of the world's prolonged ordeal with nuclear deterrence is that the need for assessing the rationality and sense of

This chapter combines portions of a chapter in a book edited by George Thibault, *The Art and Practice of Military Strategy* (Washington, D.C.: National Defense University Press, 1984), and portions of a paper delivered at a conference on "Deterrence in the 1980s," in April 1984 at York University, Toronto, Canada.

responsibility of those people whose fingers are on the nuclear trigger has become increasingly apparent. Each of the powers is moving toward better controls and safeguards in this regard, and the world is accepting the need for curtailing the spread of nuclear weapons to more countries. Every additional country possessing such weapons obviously makes the risk of what might be called "irrational" behavior that much greater. But it is not just nuclear weapons states like the United States and the Soviet Union that have become aware of the dangers of further proliferation; most of the world now quietly accepts the same logic, that deterrence is better left in the hands of a few forces checking and deterring each other.

On the issue of basic morality, public sensitivity about the deterrent reliance on countervalue retaliation is growing, in part because the sheer destructive power of the two major nuclear arsenals continues to grow; but overkill is overkill, such that what was more than enough to deter in the 1970s may not really have gone through any meaningful change as both sides acquire still more in the 1980s. At the least, the redundancy of so much countervalue capability makes a counterforce strike all the less thinkable.

The sheer volume of the retaliatory destruction capability already in place is interestingly illustrated in the conclusions of the nuclear winter study published in 1983.[1] This study argued that all of life on earth might be threatened by the ecological consequences of a major use of even just one of the superpower's arsenals, thus almost concluding that nuclear attacks could be self-deterring, because one suffers unacceptable "second-strike" damage from the collateral effects of one's own first strike (even if not a single nuclear warhead of the other side survives the first attack and is used in retaliation).

This staggering situation can quickly enough be interpreted as appalling. Upon reflection, as with all the other double-edged aspects of nuclear deterrence, it may be calming and reassuring. Who would want to try to exploit the other side's "window of vulnerability" knowing that he would freeze himself and his own population to death in the process of such a "splendid first strike"?

Those who lament the overkill of something like nuclear winter must always remember and be a little on guard against the traditional morality they are bringing to this lament, a morality that is also the source of some questions on the conceptual credibility of deterrence. Such traditional morality is what reinforces the weapons developers who reach for the accuracies that so much threaten mutual deterrence.

We have already discussed the trends alleged to be affecting the problems of whether nuclear deterrence can continue to be extended to shield countries as valuable as those of Western Europe. To respond to the very debatable proposition that a Soviet move into "parity," or beyond "parity" to "superiority," undermines this nuclear umbrella, two very different kinds of proposals have been advanced. One is to abandon all efforts at deterrence by punishment and instead expend substantial energy and money on the enhancement of conventional defenses. This proposal was perhaps the secret aspiration of Secretary of Defense Robert McNamara in the early 1960s. The second approach is to expend funds and energy enhancing the U.S. nuclear stockpile, strategic and theater, to bring the confrontation back toward what could be called "parity" or "U.S. superiority," on the assumption that doing so is somehow necessary to restore the credibility of nuclear escalation in support of Western Europe.

It is of course possible that neither approach is needed. And it is possible, once this burst of intense reflection on the nature and problems of deterrence is past, that we will all conclude once again that the best policy is to leave well enough alone, that "deterrence by punishment" has worked for decades even as things stand now, and that nothing in the current trends is going to change the way it works.

Nuclear Proliferation and Other "Ways Out"

As a way of highlighting the competing natures of the four major problems we have outlined for deterrence, we might try next to review the impact on each of acquisitions of nuclear weapons by other independent nations in what is sometimes called the "horizontal proliferation" of nuclear weapons, but more often simply "proliferation."[2]

Such proliferation probably worsens two of these problems, while perhaps improving one, with the effect on one somewhat debatable. Clearly worsened, as was noted earlier, is the problem of responsible retaliation, as the guarantees of nuclear deterrence against "irrationality" or irresponsibility will always be only as certain as the weakest link. If the fifteenth country to acquire nuclear weapons comes to be governed by a ruler unusual enough to launch a nuclear war on a whim, that country may drag all the other nuclear weapons states, and all the world, into such a holocaust. Similarly, the fourth problem is almost surely compounded and worsened as nuclear weapons spread, as new dyads of countries aim nuclear warheads at each other's cities and thereby deepen the layers of hostility. The alleged hostility between Argentina and Brazil is not really so great at the present. But it could become much deeper and more meaningful if Brazilian nuclear missiles were aimed at Buenos Aires, with Argentine equivalents being aimed at Rio de Janeiro and Brasília.

Our first problem might also be worsened by nuclear proliferation, in that many of the newest "nth" nuclear forces will begin with extraordinarily primitive and vulnerable delivery systems, thus inviting preemptive attacks by neighbors. On the other hand, the spread of additional nuclear weapons forces could substantially complicate, confuse, and discourage any Soviet (or U.S.) plans for a splendid first strike, since (to be meaningfully effective) every last means of nuclear retaliation against the enemy would have to be eliminated in one swoop. Even now, such a strike is complicated in having to take the British, French, and Chinese nuclear forces into account. How much more "splendid" it would have to be to cover another ten separate forces.

The one area for which advocates of nuclear proliferation are usually most able to build a case is that cited by Gallois, the problem of extendability. If U.S. nuclear retaliation on behalf of France, Israel, Taiwan, or South Korea were to be in doubt for any of the reasons listed, there presumably would be less doubt that these countries would use their own nuclear forces when they were about to be attacked and overrun by superior conventional forces.[3]

What is more in doubt, before one is ever persuaded by arguments for horizontal nuclear proliferation, is whether this kind of substitute for extended deterrence is so necessary, given all the other costs of proliferation. As was pointed out earlier, the extendability of nuclear umbrellas raises persistent uncertainties and tensions, but this is not to conclude that no such extendability exists. Nuclear proliferation is thus one "alternative" to deterrence that in the end does not really prove to be such a satisfactory way out. What other alternatives should we consider, given that deterrence will continue to be burdened by tensions and dissatisfactions?

Another such way out that will always draw endorsements is that of disarmament, "beating swords into plowshares," eliminating nuclear and conventional weapons until nothing is left to fight with.[4] This blissful end-state, sometimes labelled General and Complete Disarmament (GCD), still carries the official endorsements of the United States and the Soviet Union, conveyed at UN General Assembly sessions at the beginning of the 1960s; but there are serious doubts about whether anyone realistically expects to reach such a state.

It might be very nice to live in a disarmed world, but the real problem is that getting there, because the last 10 percent of such disarmament might leave each side terribly tempted to hide some weapons away, terribly afraid that the other side was doing so (with the fears stimulating the temptations, and vice versa), all in all making war much more likely than it is today. "Assured second strike" would not be nearly as assured if all the United States had to go on was the Soviets' word that they too were disarming, or if the United States had to rely entirely on the safeguards of the International Atomic Energy Agency (IAEA).

Yet a different alternative, according to some observers a more reliable form of "nuclear disarmament," would mean achieving effective population defense, in a combination of ABM (antiballistic missile) antimissile defense (perhaps based on advanced technologies harnessing lasers or charged-particle beams) and antibomber defense, with a backup of civil defense.

At least two kinds of difficulties, however, are associated with this approach. First, there will always be a real question of whether accomplishing this goal is physically possible, whether a counterinvestment in penetration aids would not repeatedly and easily undo whatever investment had been made in the shielding of cities. Second, there is the same "you can't get there from here" argument outlined for general and complete disarmament; the other side might become extremely nervous if a superpower was about to acquire a perfect ABM system, fearing what that superpower would do with nuclear weapons once its own cities could not be retaliated against.

Just as the world might be a more pleasant place if both sides totally divested themselves of nuclear weapons, it might be that much more pleasant if both sides had ABM plus antibomber protection. But the transition, during which one side was about to become safe and the other side had somewhat longer to wait until it was safe, might be overburdened with risks and temptations of nuclear war, leaving the world far worse off than it was at the beginning.

Another different way out is that of investing in massive conventional defense preparations, such that the United States would no longer have to milk any extended deterrence out of nuclear weapons, thus redressing at least one of the major problems with nuclear deterrence.[5]

A major problem with this kind of approach has rested in the peacetime material and human cost, since more resources would have to be expended and since young men would have to waste many more months of their lives in military service. It is questionable whether the European recoveries, or "economic miracles," after 1948 would have been possible, but for the existence of and reliance on nuclear weapons. Westerners remember the 1950s and 1960s now as an economic "belle époche," with historically unprecedented rates of economic growth and a general prosperity that every American welcomes.

But there is a second difficulty with any total shift to conventional defense. New methods of grouping troops, new maneuver strategies, or new precision-guided munitions (PGM) might soon enough work to make the defenses of NATO stronger, making it possible to blunt any Soviet tank attacks without an escalation to the use of nuclear weapons. Yet if such new approaches to a conventional defense could rule out a Soviet blitzkrieg in one decade, might not the technology and tactics be reversed again in another, as illustrated by the backs and forths of wars in the Middle East? All in all, the character of conventional warfare seems much less predictable and permanent than the basic character of strategic nuclear war. Antitank guided munitions may always be less reliably effective than antipopulation intercontinental ballistic missiles (ICBMs).

Still another way out, equally unlikely of acceptance at the end, is unilateral disarmament, in a unilateral U.S. "dropping out" of the arms race, trusting that foreign behaviors after such a move would be less aggressive than worst-case assumptions would predict, perhaps indeed assuming that the Soviets and others purchased large numbers of weapons only because the United States had such weapons.

Conclusion

We shall never know whether the Soviets would have matched the United States in terminating the arms race, and it has now become too late to try such an experiment for a very simple reason, that is, that more than two countries in the world now possess nuclear arsenals. How would France, China, and Britain respond to the news that the United States had decided to trust the Soviets' good intentions? How would Brazil, Australia, Japan, Israel, and India respond? If the United States were to drop out of the nuclear arms competition, it would not end the competition or the prospect of nuclear war; the burden would simply be transferred to other shoulders, shoulders perhaps less reliable on all the counts we have listed above.

Our search for ways out of nuclear deterrence, in light of its inherent tensions and imperfectly solved problems, thus has circled back to where it began several pages ago, with nuclear proliferation. Perhaps we have missed a good alternative as we went around the circle, but more likely we have not. The world must try to overcome its moral and practical problems on nuclear deterrence, for the simplest of arguments: that there is currently nothing better.

Notes

1. Carl Sagan, "Nuclear War and Climatic Catastrophe," *Foreign Affairs* 62, no. 2 (Winter 1983–84):257–92.

2. For an overview of the nuclear proliferation problem, see Lewis A. Dunn, *Controlling the Bomb* (New Haven: Yale University Press, 1982).

3. On the argument for nuclear weapons as a means of safeguarding national security for states lacking sure patrons, see Robert E. Harkavy, "The Pariah State Syndrome," *Orbis* 21, no. 3 (Fall 1977):623–49.

4. For a very thoughtful analysis of positive possibilities of disarmament, see David C. Gompert, Michael Mandelbaum, Richard L. Garwin, and John H. Barton, *Nuclear Weapons and World Politics* (New York: McGraw-Hill, 1977), especially the section by John Barton, pp. 151–211.

5. Perhaps now the most widely cited argument for a conventional defense for Europe is offered in McGeorge Bundy, George F. Kennan, Robert S. McNamara, and Gerard K. Smith, "Nuclear Weapons and the Atlantic Alliance," *Foreign Affairs* 60, no. 4 (Spring 1982):753–69. For a West German response, see Karl Kaiser, Georg Leber, Alois Mertes and Franz-Josef Schulze, "Nuclear Weapons and the Preservation of Peace," *Foreign Affairs* 60, no. 5 (Summer 1982):1157–70. See also Bernard W. Rogers, "The Atlantic Alliance: Prescriptions for a Difficult Decade," *Foreign Affairs* 60, no. 5 (Summer 1982):1145–56.

8

Nuclear Winter: Bad News, No News, or Good News?

he general argument of this chapter can be stated fairly suc-
cinctly. The conclusions of the "Nuclear Winter" study are
widely regarded as bad news for mankind, as something to
which a human being should react with depression and revulsion, and
perhaps with some mobilization toward changing a very bad status
quo. Yet are these conclusions really news? If anyone is startled by the
predictions of how bad a thermonuclear war would be, the real surprise might lie in the fact that so many of us have avoided digesting
such pessimistic conclusions since 1952, or 1945, or indeed since
1918. And is the news so bad, or might one not view it instead as the
final sealing of a necessary deterrent bargain between the superpowers?

Absolute Weapons or Merely Weapons?

A description of the degree of destruction that might be inflicted on the
planet Earth in any war expending the nuclear arsenals of the United
States and the Soviet Union is horrendous enough to be shocking, even
if none of it were to be new. At the extreme, the analysis presented
in 1983[1] suggests that retaliation by the victim would almost be unnecessary for the attacker to be punished (or perhaps for him to be
deterred), since the atmospheric changes caused by a nuclear attack
could affect the entire hemisphere, lowering temperatures enough to
cause massive famines, even in the country that had launched the
attack.

This chapter is essentially the paper delivered at a conference at the University of
Maryland in September 1984 on "Nuclear Deterrence: New Threats and New Oppor-
tunities"; it will appear in the conference proceedings, to be published by Pergamon
Press, edited by Catherine Kelleher, Frank Kerr, and George Quester.

In a rounding of yet another corner, we may finally come to grips with what is really not such a new question, for it has been around since the introduction of nuclear weapons, or perhaps since the introduction of aerial means of delivery for ordinary weapons: whether war will now be unbearable for the winners as well as for the losers.

The possibility has been raised numerous times that the "winners" would envy the dead, or would be dead, or would at least see no significant advantage for themselves as compared with the "losers" who had just been driven from the field. The predominance of the countervalue impact of modern weaponry might well cancel out the importance of whatever could be achieved through counterforce applications of such weaponry. Yet such predictions have also been repeatedly rebutted, because the physical situation was perhaps not so surely capable of taking the meaning out of victory, and/or because there has all along been a counterchorus extolling the continuing appropriateness and opportunities for counterforce targeting.

Is the bomb big enough? That is the question. Is it big enough to cancel out any interest in who has bombs left at the end of a war, and who is about to run out of them, that is, in who has won the war and who has lost it?

We have here a debate that has over decades placed two sets of nuclear war analysts into a dialogue and contest with each other, at the very least in a challenge of two burdens of proof. As an outstanding example of resignation and adjustment to the countervalue impact, we can read the writings of Bernard Brodie, beginning with his contributions to the aptly titled 1946 book, *The Absolute Weapon*.[2] As examples of the opposing bias, we might note the other major book published in 1946, William L. Borden's *There Will Be No Time*,[3] and, a decade or so later, Albert Wohlstetter's famous *Foreign Affairs* article, "The Delicate Balance of Terror."[4]

The first form of this debate on the nuclear issue pertained, of course, to the fission bomb dropped on Hiroshima and Nagasaki (the original atomic bomb, or A-bomb), which was dramatically announced to the world with its use against the first of these two unfortunate Japanese cities; the very possibility of fusion thermonuclear bombs (the hydrogen bomb, or H-bomb) was still only the most theoretical of possibilities in 1945 and 1946.

Was the atomic bomb big enough to make anyone exposed to its attack lose interest in victory? Bernard Brodie thought so, at least at the time he was writing his portions of *The Absolute Weapon*:

> If the aggressor state must fear retaliation, it will know that even if it
> is the victor it will suffer a degree of physical destruction incompar-
> ably greater than that suffered by any defeated nation of history,
> incomparably greater, that is, than that suffered by Germany in the
> recent war. Under those circumstances no victory, even if guaranteed
> in advance—which it never is—would be worth the price. The threat
> of retaliation does not have to be 100 per cent certain; it is sufficient
> if there is a good chance of it, or if there is belief that there is a good
> chance of it. The prediction is more important than the fact.[5]

Yet there were still more than enough analysts ready to question
the destructive power of this earliest of nuclear weapons. The public
response to the test conducted against ships at the Bikini Atoll in 1946
indeed indicated that most observers were more surprised, in this
second look, by how limited the impact of such explosives seemed to
be, rather than by how destructive they were.[6] The world memorial-
ized the Bikini test by naming a swimsuit for it, a mark of how deep an
impression was made by the countervalue capabilities that had just
been demonstrated.

In his last speech to Parliament, in 1955, Winston Churchill suggested that the A-bomb had not been enough of a deterrent to be ultimate, but that the H-bomb was, that the crucial threshold therefore
had not been crossed until 1952 and after, when the thermonuclear
weapons were at last perfected and deployed. He put it this way:

> There is an immense gulf between the atomic and the hydrogen
> bomb. The atomic bomb, with all its terrors, did not carry us outside
> the scope of human control or manageable events in thought or
> action, in peace or war. But when Mr. Sterling Cole, the Chairman
> of the United States Congressional Committee, gave out a year ago—
> 17 February 1954—the first comprehensive review of the hydrogen
> bomb, the entire foundation of human affairs was revolutionized,
> and mankind placed in a situation both measureless and laden with
> doom.[7]

Yet anyone who has seen movies of the Hiroshima survivors or has
read accounts of the attacks on Hiroshima and Nagasaki might indeed
conclude that Brodie was correct in his first guess and that Churchill's
discrimination between two distinct levels of nuclear destruction was
indeed wrong and irrelevant. If Hitler or the Japanese had possessed
only such atomic bombs and the means of delivering them to the cities

of the United States, would the United States not have had to settle for less than forcing occupation armies into Tokyo and Berlin? Would not the winner in any future war, even if fought with the nuclear weapons of only 1946, nonetheless have felt that the suffering was unbearable, such that the prosecution or initiation of such a war would have been deterred from the outset?

Forerunners Crying Wolf

How could any school of analysis have persuaded itself to delay its perception of an ultimate event in this matter? The tendency to continue stressing the military applications of weapons (with the latest in nuclear weapons only being part of the "war-fighting" package) is in part to be explained by the memory of some faulty predictions of such destructiveness in the past.

While some would question whether the atomic bomb is an unignorable weapon, this author is convinced that the world would have effective nuclear deterrence today even if the next stage of thermonuclear weaponry had proven impossible. Yet, as Brodie well understood, this was not the first instance of an argument for such absolute status. The years between World Wars I and II had seen some parallel predictions advanced about how much destruction would be inflicted in the air attacks of any future war, inflicted by a combination of dynamite, incendiaries, and poison gas. Extrapolating from the last air attacks of World War I, such analyses anticipated the major destruction of urban centers, the breakdown of fire-fighting services, the swamping of medical services, and the killing of tens of thousands of people through the combination of blast, fire, and deadly gases. All in all, the predictions developed by the British and Allied air staffs at the end of 1918, the predictions exploited by writers like Giulio Douhet and J.F.C. Fuller (and by a number of other analysts who captured a little less public attention) amounted to the atomic bomb, if not the hydrogen bomb; they predicted a disaster for all mankind, a disaster that would be replicated in retaliation inflicted, as the losing air force took revenge for the assaults of the winning air force, a disaster that might even (à la nuclear winter) drag down the winning side without any explicit retaliation.

In his *Command of the Air,* Douhet makes clear that each side's air force will be able to elude the other. He describes the very high levels of destruction that each air force will be able to impose on the other side's cities and industrial base on the military pretext of crippling the enemy's ability to fight, but with enormous damage to the values of civilization in any event.

> Here is what would be likely to happen to the center of the city within a radius of about 250 meters: Within a few minutes some 20 tons of high-explosive, incendiary, and gas bombs would rain down. First would come explosions, then fires, then deadly gases floating on the surface and preventing any approach to the stricken area. As the hours passed and night advanced, the fires would spread while the poison gas paralyzed all life. By the following day the life of the city would be suspended; and if it happened to be a junction on some important artery of communication traffic would be suspended.
>
> What could happen to a single city in a single day could also happen to ten, twenty, fifty cities. And, since news travels fast, even without telegraph, telephone, or radio, what, I ask you, would be the effect upon civilians of other cities, not yet stricken but equally subject to bombing attacks? What civil or military authority could keep order, public services functioning, and production going under such a threat? And even if a semblance of order was maintained and some work done, would not the sight of a single enemy plane be enough to stampede the population into panic? In short, normal life would be impossible in this constant nightmare of imminent death and destruction. And if on the second day another ten, twenty, or fifty cities were bombed, who could keep all those lost, panic-stricken people from fleeing to the open countryside to escape this terror from the air?
>
> A complete breakdown of the social structure cannot but take place in a country subjected to this kind of merciless pounding from the air. The time would soon come when, to put an end to horror and suffering, the people themselves, driven by the instinct of self-preservation, would rise up and demand an end to the war—this before their army and navy had time to mobilize at all![8]

The Douhet analysis, like that of Borden, which followed some two decades later, describes each air force as being automatically in a race to inflict this destruction on the other side's home area first, once a crisis had evolved into an actual war. The unanswered question, given the physical premises of capability outlined so clearly by Douhet, is why each side would not have held back this enormous destructive capability of its air force, on the basis of the warning that is now so much a part of the pattern of mutual deterrence, of mutual no first use of nuclear weapons between two sides that have them: "We won't as long as you don't, but we will attack your cities directly after you attack our cities."

Such predictions of the nature of air attack, whether or not the shift to an ultimate countervalue role had been perceived, proved to be overstated for the actual workings of the bombings of World War II. Based on such predictions, the British civil authorities had prepared seven times as many hospital beds as were actually ever needed during the worst of the 1940 German Blitz or afterwards with the retaliatory raids of the German V-1 and V-2 bombs. Expectations of widespread panic among the urban masses of London and other cities, based on definite outbreaks of such panic during World War I in the face of very minor zeppelin and airplane assault, were not realized.

German cities were hit much harder than those of Britain had been, and Japanese cities were to be exposed to serious air attack even before the introduction of the atomic bomb; for example, a single night's firebomb attack on Tokyo took some one hundred thousand lives, more than were lost at either Hiroshima or Nagasaki. The Tokyo firestorm, like those over Hamburg and Dresden earlier in World War II, seemingly matched the predictions of the interwar analysts, but Hitler did not surrender, and the Japanese did not surrender until the attacks on Hiroshima and Nagasaki, closely coupled with the Soviet declaration of war on Japan in August 1945.

Having heard the forecasters of aerial attack in effect "cry wolf" on the particular point of whether civilian populations and governments would be able to stand up to such horrendous air attack, post–World War II analysts were understandably on their guard against a premature concession of ultimate deterrence impact. As has been noted, the atomic bombs had not inflicted the deadliest blows of World War II, unless one wished to consider the radiation aftereffects, which were still badly understood at Hiroshima and at Bikini, and were thus almost surely underrated. In the minds of many air-war planners and of much of the public, the big difference between the two forms of assault might only have been that Tokyo required some three hundred B-29s for the attack, while Hiroshima required just one B-29, somewhat modified and reinforced.

But at least the nuclear attacks had led to a Japanese surrender, while the conventional bombing raids had not. The Japanese surrender in August 1945 was of course startlingly good news for most Americans, as sudden and unexpected as the announcement of all of the Manhattan Project. In the national glee about not having to duplicate the Normandy landings on the Japanese home islands and not having to fight World War II into 1946, 1947, and 1948, it was in fact remarkable that any authors or readers could settle down to sort out the fuller strategic implications of what had occurred. The Brodie-edited volume and the Borden book were written during months when all the authors would have expected the war to drag on for some time, amid fanatical Japanese resistence in the continuing conventional war.

After the Japanese surrender, some analysts concluded that Japan might have been about to surrender in any event, merely because of the major countervalue suffering being experienced in the conventional bombings and in the U.S. naval blockade of the Japanese home islands.[9] The case has been made many times that it was politically or militarily unnecessary to introduce the use of nuclear weapons on Japanese cities and that it was therefore morally very inappropriate.

As has been mentioned earlier, the general drift of this argument is difficult to sort out. Why would Japan have surrendered? Would the surrender have come simply because its army and navy were convinced that they were militarily defeated, and so ended the contest when they saw no point in pursuing it any longer? The behavior of the Japanese in the hopeless defense of various islands in 1943 and 1944 certainly did not suggest that they would cut their losses as soon as a military defeat was inevitable. Or would the emperor and other civilian authorities have intervened because the sheer burden of the blockade and the bombings on the quality of Japanese civilian life was too much to bear, in other words because of the countervalue rather than counterforce impacts of the use of U.S. weapons? If this was the case, that the surrender was being extracted by torturing the Japanese civilian population (much as the Allied naval blockade had tortured the German home front in 1917 and 1918), rather than by defeating the Japanese military, then the moral distinction between conventional and nuclear weapons is hardly so clear.

In any event, much of this discussion, in the pleasant but sudden aftermath of the end of World War II, could be viewed as an argument that nuclear weapons were not so significantly different from the weapons that had already been in use, as in any case defeat was closing in on Japan.

Hopes for Civil Defense

Some continuing treatment of the nuclear weapon as "just another weapon," to be analyzed for its contribution to military victory, thus stems from premature forecasts that something like mutual assured destruction was at hand, forecasts that were in effect disproven in the massive bombing campaigns of World War II.

Related to this treatment is the confidence sometimes professed by civil-defense authorities on either side, who cite the rapid recovery of Germany after the destruction of Hamburg and other cities and even a rapid resumption of railroad service through Hiroshima. Given that civil-defense officials everywhere have to avoid admitting the hopelessess of their task, their citing the German example might seem like a commendable extraction of some encouragement from historical wartime instances, as well as from the patterns of community help and community recovery after such peacetime disasters as earthquakes, hurricanes, or tornadoes.

Yet earthquakes obviously never affect an entire country at once, and neither do storms. The bombings of Hamburg and Dresden occurred on nights when the rest of Germany more or less escaped attack, and the analogous situation applies to the atomic bombings of Hiroshima and Nagasaki. Whether German or Japanese civil-defense authorities could have provided as much help to bombing victims if there had been no undamaged hinterland is much more in doubt. The worst case for the future involves simultaneous thermonuclear attacks on a great number of locations in the United States or the Soviet Union. Even a simultaneous attack with Hiroshima-sized atomic bombs, carried through by fifty bombers striking fifty cities on the same night, would have to be a greater problem for civil-defense authorities by a quantum jump, perhaps so much greater a problem that it would amount to unbearable countervalue punishment, and thus be (as Brodie had suggested in 1946) the absolute weapon.[10]

Since the world has never experienced a thermonuclear war, one can hardly expect experts on the subject ever to agree on how horrible it would be. Some margins of error have to be established, although the best guess has often been that the margin for error has to be greater, perhaps even open-ended, on the high side of the scale of destruction, while optimistic possibilities of "less destruction than we might have expected" will still be only marginal good news.

There was one such wave of relatively more optimistic analysis at the beginning of the 1960s, as Herman Kahn's *On Thermonuclear War*[11] captured great public attention for its discussion of the possibilities of civil defense and as a large amount of research was commissioned by the U.S. government on the applications of civil defense to recovery after an all-out nuclear war. While such studies defined most of the difficulties that would burden any contemporary civil-defense effort, as compared with the German, Japanese, and British efforts during World War II, they typically (and not surprisingly, since such research presupposes at least a little optimism) concluded that human life would not be ended in such a war, that "the survivors would not envy the dead," in Herman Kahn's statement of the question, and that some acceptable recovery was possible—if only the proper advance preparations had been made.

The federal government's interest in commissioning such research peaked in the first years of the Kennedy administration, coupled with discussions of investment in a civil-defense shelter program; less research on the possibilities of surviving a World War III was to emerge thereafter. Another, smaller, peak of such analysis surfaced at the beginning of the Reagan administration, which (alleging that the Soviets were making extensive civil-defense preparations for a nuclear war) talked of responding in kind.[12] The opinions of T.K. Jones, that we would all survive if we only invested in such elementary preparations as buying shovels to use in converting our basements into shelters against radioactive fallout, drew substantial mockery from the Democratic opposition.[13]

Looking back on the optimism offered by the analysis of the early 1960s it is easy to fault it as sounding too good to be true. And moreover, the changes that have occurred in the strategic arsenals since the 1960s upset very much of what could have been considered hopeful in the earlier picture.

To repeat, all the successes of civil-defense preparation in the past involved disasters affecting only a city or two, with all the other cities of the country then being mobilized to come to the aid of those that had been stricken. The problem of a thermonuclear war, in 1962 just as in 1984, was rather that many cities might be struck with the same disasters in a single day, with radioactive fallout threatening those who had survived the initial explosions or rendering ill those who had not found a shelter in time. The ensuing breakdown of economic exchange, political discipline, and elementary social functions simply have no precedent in history. The incidence of the bubonic plague (the Black Death) in fourteenth-century Europe is perhaps the closest approximation (with civil-defense authorities in the United States reportedly subsidizing the study of Latin, so that the experiences of the Plague might be researched more extensively for whatever lessons or insights might be offered), but even the Plague did not hit Europe in a single day.

Making the situation much worse than it was in 1962, moreover, is the expansion of nuclear arsenals on both sides since then, especially the expansion of capacities for holding nuclear strikes in reserve, for prolonging the war. Almost all of whatever optimism could be mustered ("compared to what?" the question always has to be) was premised on an early end to the nuclear exchange (perhaps all the missiles would be fired as part of some quick "spasm war"), whereupon one could begin to apply and implement the plans one had made for a recovery. But if nuclear warheads are going to be detonated in the second, third, sixth, and tenth weeks of a war, renewing the rounds of radioactive fallout, it is not so clear how anyone will be able to leave the fallout shelters to begin providing for the necessities of life.

There are surely imaginable varieties of "nuclear war" that would allow life to go on. If nuclear warheads were used only for antisubmarine warfare (ASW), for example, Americans' home lives might not be disturbed at all. There are other conceivable nuclear targeting approaches for the United States and the Soviet Union that would inflict far less than the maximum destruction. Yet the collateral effects for most of such "limited nuclear options" quickly become much more serious in magnitude, and the accompanying risk of escalation to an all-out effort (all-out in counterforce terms, or countervalue terms, or both) is great.

We know for certain that humanity can survive repeated rounds of conventional war. We have no real way of knowing whether or not humanity can meaningfully survive a war once it becomes nuclear, in particular when such a nuclear war rises from the conventional/nuclear firebreak to move toward its maximum. The Nuclear Winter study may suggest this possibility in a new and interesting way, but the common sense of many reasonable people might have directed them to the same conclusion decades ago.

Traditional Morality and
Traditional Military Professionalism

Why concentrate on counterforce when it can never be effective enough to blunt the enemy's countervalue options for retaliation? Why aim for victory, when the defeated enemy can still always punish your people in ways that make that victory totally joyless? This is the question tormenting us throughout this chapter, with nuclear winter perhaps (perhaps not) being the final part of the argument, but the reader will recall that some earlier stages in the development of destructive military technology were once considered candidates for the "final page."

Some other, more intellectual and philosophical, factors have also helped to make it difficult for commentators like Borden and for analysts inside the military to accept the "ultimate weapon" assured-retaliation argument. Concentrating on counterforce is the traditional approach of the professional soldier, sailor, or airman. It involves holding back the opposing military forces and defeating them, so that they cannot impose any damage on one's own cities and civilians. Until the airplane (and the submarine) made it possible for suffering to be imposed on civilians by crossing over or under the front lines, this concentration on counterforce was a very plausible way to state and simplify the goals of warfare, and it was an approach consistent with higher morality. Where possible, the soldier aimed at the uniformed warriors of the other side, avoiding unnecessary destruction of their civilians, but defeating the troops so that they could not impose suffering on the soldier's own civilians.

Even apart from any moral advantages of such a traditional emphasis on counterforce targeting, it is a bit much to expect professionals to shed the basic assumptions of their craft in some sudden revolution. The burden of proof is always on the new way of looking at things, as compared with the old; one can call this inertia, or simply common sense. For instance, Douhet, despite his description of what amounted to an absolute countervalue capability, assumed that air forces in an all-out war would race past each other, trying to win a military victory.

William Borden's continued adherence to this view can be seen in the very title of his book, *There Will Be No Time,* and in his parallel picture of how air forces would race to preempt each other.

But the trend of a genuine atomic war, waged with nuclear explosives previously mass-produced on a scale comparable to the air fleets existing in 1939, might be clear in the first exchange of blows. It would simply be a question of whose long-range weapons struck home faster and in greater quantity.[14]

The interpretation of nuclear weapons as "another weapon" stems in part from old ideas that for many minds have not been displaced by new ideas. Another part of the appeal of this older view comes from its closer conformity to traditional Western morality. Such a counterforce approach continues to sound and feel more moral, even after Hiroshima and Nagasaki, even into the 1980s. It amounts to the kind of targeting philosophy that is not indictable for war-crimes trials. It lets the individual military officer feel as good on Sunday morning as on any other day of the week.

The mutual assured destruction message is that the only purpose of modern strategic weapons is to be aimed at civilians, and thus they should prevent themselves from coming into use. The lag in public and professional acceptance of this idea might stem from normal inertia, as old thinking is slow to be replaced by new, and (as mentioned earlier) by some real doubts as to whether the frightfulness of these weapons is sufficient to carry out this function of deterrence. But the lag might also emerge because the new message is so blatantly immoral, while the old strategic truth, that one should try to defeat the enemy's military forces rather than aiming directly and deliberately at his civilians, at least still has some moral tone to it.

Shifting to another layer of motivation, it has often been charged that the military services (in the USSR, as well as in the United States) join in the bureaucratic politics game of seeking larger budgets and larger allocations of manpower and equipment.[15] An emphasis on the counterforce role will justify a larger defense budget than would a simple resignation to, and acceptance of, the "finite deterrence" countervalue role. One not only stresses one's own counterforce options in this kind of approach, but also worries a great deal about the enemy's counterforce options, in a series of "bomber gaps" and "missile gaps" and "windows of vulnerability." As was always the case, stressing the capabilities of one's opposite number is a subtle way of impressing the taxpayers and civilian leadership with the potential of one's own specialty. Navies generally remind the public of the threats posed by the adversary's navy. Armies speak of the threat of the hostile army. And nuclear-equipped air forces speak of being targeted by, as well as targeting, the enemy's nuclear-equipped bomber and missile forces.

Some of the skepticism about the absolute nature of nuclear weapons could thus hardly be labelled as optimism from the U.S. standpoint. If the Soviets could organize their own civil defense effectively enough and could direct their own new nuclear forces in a counterforce strike at the forces of the United States, might they not be tempted to do so?

Albert Wohlstetter directed a Rand Corporation study of U.S. Air Force basing in the 1950s, which concluded that the chance of this prospect becoming a reality was not out of the question. Presenting the general lines of the argument in his "Delicate Balance of Terror," Wohlstetter showed how nuclear weapons might still plausibly come into use as had other weapons in a move to win a war:

> What can be said, then, as to whether general war is unlikely? Would not a general thermonuclear war mean "extinction" for the aggressor as well as the defender? "Extinction" is a state that badly needs analysis. Russian casualties in World War II were more than 20,000,000. Yet Russia recovered extremely well from this catastrophe. There are several quite plausible circumstances in the future when the Russians might be quite confident of being able to limit damage to considerably less than this number—if they make sensible strategic choices and we do not. On the other hand, the risks of not striking might at some juncture appear very great to the Soviets, involving, for example, disastrous defeat in peripheral war, loss of key satellites with danger of revolt spreading—possibly to Russia itself—or fear of an attack by ourselves. Then, striking first, by surprise, would be the sensible choice for them, and from their point of view the smaller risk.[16]

U.S. security depended on the Soviets' being convinced that atomic retaliation was unacceptable, but Wohlstetter did not see as being so assured, at least until substantial changes were made in the way that U.S. bombers were deployed on their bases, and then perhaps when nuclear missiles, based in underground silos or on board submarines, had come along to supplement the retaliatory capacities of these bombers.

Wohlstetter's analysis attracted a great deal of attention at the end of the 1950s, and it illustrates the major hurdles that the advocates of mutual assured destruction have had to overcome. In retrospect, skeptics have questioned whether the U.S. Strategic Air Command was ever as vulnerable to a Soviet first strike as Wohlstetter and his Rand colleagues had suggested. Similar skeptics would today question whether the United States has fallen into any window of vulnerability. Addressing the more general influence of Wohlstetter's argument, Bernard Brodie responded in 1978:

> For similar reasons, I must add before leaving the Wohlstetter article that I could never accept the implications of his title—that the balance of terror between the Soviet Union and the United States ever has been or ever could be "delicate." My reasons have to do mostly with human inhibitions against taking monumental risks or doing things which are universally detested, except under motivations far more compelling than those suggested by Wohlstetter in his article.[17]

MAD and Some Critics

The advocate of a simple reliance on countervalue retaliation, on mutual assured destruction, would resent any emphasis on counterforce if it could be effective, for doing so might panic each side into feeling that its retaliatory capabilities were not assured, so that it thus had to be constantly on guard against the other's surprise attack. The most serious resentment would otherwise have to be directed only at the money wasted in expenditures on the extra missiles that would be redundant to the countervalue mission, as well as insufficient for a meaningful counterforce mission. (Counterforce, to repeat, could only be meaningful if it severely reduced and blunted the other side's second-strike countervalue capability.)

A few analysts of a finite deterrence persuasion will also purport to be shocked by the extent of the overkill, the redundancy of targeting cities like Moscow many times, amid a threat to all of the USSR's population and all of the human race. Such an expression of shock would express solidarity with those critics of U.S. defense preparations who simply oppose most or all of the expenditure on nuclear weapons, or on all weapons. Yet to be shocked about overkill is hardly consistent with the logic of the "finite deterrence" endorsement of mutual deterrence and of mutual assured destruction. Unless the extra U.S. warheads really posed a threat to Soviet missile silos, the redundant threat to Soviet city dwellers only confirms what mutual deterrence requires, that the cost to the superpower of launching a nuclear war would be unacceptable.

The arguments offered in criticism of the nuclear stockpile size cut both ways: "What does it gain us to be able to kill the same Russians seven times, instead of only once?" "What is lost in being able to kill them seven times, if they are sure to be killed at least once?"

When someone professes to be startled by the countervalue threat posed by contemporary nuclear arsenals, therefore, one must await the sentences that will follow, for the speaker is all too likely to plunge ahead on one or the other of two very different paths. Perhaps he will endorse a need for freezes and substantial disarmament. Perhaps he will instead endorse a need for new approaches to targeting, on morally traditional approaches to war fighting rather than mass homicide.

The debate on the implications of the awesomeness of nuclear weapons has thus continued to take interesting twists and turns through the 1970s and into the 1980s. Fred C. Iklé published an article in 1973 titled "Can Nuclear Deterrence Last Out the Century?" somewhat farsightedly sketching out the moral crisis that has now captured a wider attention.

> Our arms-control experts and military planners insulate themselves from the potential implications of their labors by layers of dehumanizing abstractions and bland metaphors. Thus, "assured destruction" fails to indicate what is to be destroyed; but then "assured genocide" would reveal the truth too starkly. The common phrase, "deterring a potential aggressor," conveys a false simplicity about the processes that might lead to a nuclear attack, as if we had to worry only about some ambitious despot who sits calculating whether or not to start a nuclear war. A moral perversity lies hidden behind the standard formula: in the event this "aggressor" attacks, we must "retaliate by knocking out *his* cities." Tomas de Torquemada, who burned 10,000 heretics at the stake, could claim principles more humane than our nuclear strategy; for his tribunals found all his victims guilty of having knowingly committed mortal sin.
>
> The jargon of American strategic analysis works like a narcotic. It dulls our sense of moral outrage about the tragic confrontation of nuclear arsenals, primed and constantly perfected to unleash widespread genocide. It fosters the current smug complacence regarding the soundness and stability of mutual deterrence. It blinds us to the fact that our method for preventing nuclear war rests on a form of warfare universally condemned since the Dark Ages—the mass killing of hostages.

Indeed, our nuclear strategy is supposed to work the better, the larger the number of hostages that would pay with their lives should the strategy fail. This view has become so ingrained that the number of hostages who could be killed through a "second strike" by either superpower is often used as a measure of the "stability" of deterrence. Our very motive behind the recent treaty curbing the deployment of missile defenses is to keep this number reliably high.[18]

Iklé's argument, working outward from a discussion of the sheer magnitude of the destruction such weapons could inflict, was that the world would surely sooner or later demand a switch to some other approach to preserving peace and/or to fighting a war if it came. The world would have to move away from any deliberate or inadvertant ("collateral") pattern of countervalue targeting, because the punishment posed here was too severe, because the world's moral structure could not stand the strain and hypocrisy of basing peace on a threat to all of civilization. Counterforce targeting would become meaningful again, in the image of Iklé and others, not because the countervalue impact of nuclear war could be shrugged off, but because it would have to be avoided. Harnessing new delivery technologies to more accurate delivery of weapons would be the only morally acceptable way to face the future.

The Iklé article produced a response by Wolfgang Panofsky, who argued that the vulnerability of life that Iklé had so graphically outlined was indeed inevitable, and perhaps in some sense desirable *faute de mieux*, in that the two sides to the superpower confrontation should sit back to a standoff of deterrence more or less like what Brodie's 1946 book had outlined.

> Naturally the present situation is far from ideal. We cannot be relieved of moral responsibility for having permitted a situation to develop in which large segments of the population of both West and East can in fact be sacrificed at the will of political leaders; neither is the situation free from acute danger in case of failure of mutual deterrence. Iklé aptly criticizes the mutual-hostage relationship which these policies imply by eloquently recalling that the threat of the killing of civilians has been condemned as immoral in the codes of both ancient and modern warfare, and by also pointing out the fragility of "stability through deterrence," for example in scenarios of accident and unauthorized nuclear attack.

Yet how can we do better? The critics seem to imply that the mutual-hostage relationship between the populations of the United States and the Soviet Union is a consequence of policy, and would therefore be subject to change if such a policy were modified. Yet this relationship is a matter of physical fact and is thus grossly insensitive to any change in strategic policy.[19]

If Panofsky's article is to be read as a response to Iklé, might it not also be read just as well as the response to Carl Sagan's piece on nuclear winter some ten years later? Perhaps it is a mistake to take our startled responses to the full measure of nuclear overkill as any sign about whether the status quo of policies is to be overturned. Perhaps we should indeed heave a sigh of relief at all the additional complications for civil defense and postwar recovery that continue to be uncovered, for each of these complications simply amounts to one more reinforcement of strategic stability and deterrence, one more argument against anyone's wishing to grasp for a sneak-attack nuclear victory or fearing that the other side was contemplating such a move.

As a sign that he had not been convinced by the Panofsky response, Iklé, after becoming Director of the Arms Control and Disarmament Agency, delivered an address in 1974 outlining in stark terms the surprising magnitude of destruction that could be anticipated in any nuclear war. He noted how virtually every test of thermonuclear weapons (testing before the ban was ratified in 1963) had produced surprises on the high side of the spectrum, effects more dangerous to all of human life than had been anticipated, effects upsetting any hopes for civil defense or rapid recovery. Anyone thinking that the predictions of global damage offered in the Nuclear Winter study are somehow unique and unprecedented would do well to read Iklé's address, offered a decade earlier.

Instead of the dozens of atomic bombs that frightened us so much in the late 1940s we are now confronted with many thousands of nuclear weapons.

This story, I am sure, you were all aware of. But for those of you who have not followed this macabre branch of science closely, I have important news: We are not only unable to express the human meaning of nuclear war—the only meaning that matters—we are also unable to express the full range of physical effects of nuclear warfare, let alone to calculate these effects.

Why is this so? Because the damage from nuclear explosions to the fabric of nature and the sphere of living things cascades from one effect to another in ways too complex for our scientists to predict. Indeed, the more we know, the more we know how little we know. Several accidents and chance discoveries permitted us to catch a new glimpse of this nether world over the past 20 years. At least half a dozen such discoveries seem worth recalling.[20]

And anyone thinking that disarmament was the only conclusion that could be reached after such gloomy premises had been established should note how Iklé and others had reached very different conclusions, in advocating war-fighting postures and preparations for fighting with less escalation.

Similarly, President Reagan's "Star Wars" Strategic Defense Initiative may simply have been a political move intended to undercut the kind of moral objections to nuclear deterrence exemplified in the U.S. Roman Catholic Bishops' Statement, as well as the shock of the possibilities of nuclear winter, all of these attitudes being linked to popular momentum for the "nuclear freeze" movement. Conversely, the initiative may instead reflect some genuine abhorrence for the worst of what nuclear war could inflict on the United States and in part nostalgia for the days when the United States could have completely escaped H-bomb and A-bomb attack in any war.

It is thus abnormal for anyone to spell out the likely character of a thermonuclear war and simply leave it at that, telling us that we need to be content with the status quo, to accept a structure of mutual assured destruction, or mutual deterrence, and to leave well enough alone. Detail on nuclear war amounts to startling detail, and the startling nature of the factual premise normally drives its recounter to advocate something different from the status quo. Yet are the alternatives to be disarmament or the MX? And is there an alternative that we can really, upon deliberation, find preferable to what we have?

The same galvanizing shock that drove Iklé in 1973 to become an advocate of new nuclear "war-fighting" options was to drive the authors of the TTAPS nuclear winter study in a different direction.

Nuclear Winter

Carl Sagan's *Foreign Affairs* article, which presented a summary of the TTAPS report, has been viewed as offering a very startling change in the physical basis of what is considered the nature of nuclear deterrence. The article puts forward some policy recommendations that one would very much want to endorse. But it also offers some larger policy conclusions that may be much more problematic and questionable.

The important physical finding is, of course, what has been labelled "nuclear winter," the prediction that a unilateral nuclear strike by either of the two superpowers (and perhaps even by one of the other nuclear weapons states) would put so much soot into the atmosphere that the launching nation would also suffer horrible punishments, as a cooling of the atmosphere produced substantial famine all over the Northern Hemisphere, or perhaps all over the globe. In effect, "deterrence takes care of itself," as the victim does not need to retaliate, does not have to worry about maintaining a second-strike retaliatory capability; the imposition of a first strike on someone else is very likely to generate its own natural second strike.

Some of the policy conclusions the Sagan article puts forward are old and are merely renewed or reinforced by the nuclear winter conclusions. There is a commendable emphasis on deMIRVing missile forces and on otherwise removing whatever illusory gains might stampede a side into launching its missiles on an apparent warning of the other side's attack, or any other hurried preemptive firing policy.

Some other agreeable recommendations are quite new (triggered specifically by the nuclear winter finding), and most important is that these findings be publicized so that no U.S. or Soviet military or political leader can escape having this news. In Sagan's own words, we have perhaps stumbled onto a doomsday machine, and nothing is worse than having such a weapon without the other side's knowing about it (incidentally the central plot of Stanley Kubrik's script for *Dr. Strangelove*).

If the leaders do not know how automatically their own societies will be punished, regardless of apparent windows of opportunity or windows of vulnerability, they might ignorantly bring such punishment down on all of us. If they understand the inescapable linkages, however, they might be that much less likely to see any opportunity for launching a nuclear sneak attack, or to fear such an attack by the other side, and this might take a fair amount of tension out of the confrontation.

It is here that one begins to feel some disagreement with Sagan's other conclusions. If nuclear winter is as likely as the study quite convincingly suggests, why not accept it as a positive reality? Policymakers have preached mutual assured destruction as a moderating and stabilizing physical reality for several decades now, and this new study is hardly the first to conclude that the destruction for all parties in a nuclear war is likely to be unacceptably severe. The tension of the U.S.–Soviet competition has not emerged so much because of the likelihood of this reality, but because some analysts on each side of the line keep suggesting the opposite, that destruction will not be assured, that civil defense can make the difference, and so forth.

Sagan's calculations on the real potential of the existing nuclear stockpiles might thus be very good news, confirming once and for all that destruction is mutually assured, so assured that it will be Soviet missiles that wind up having punished Soviet society, even if no U.S. missiles survive a sneak attack, and vice versa.

Sagan's policy suggestion fits well with the world's intuition that disarmament is good, but it hardly squares with other parts of his argument. For example, if U.S. policymakers follow his advice to lower nuclear arsenals below the threshold of nuclear winter, do they not thereby simply reinvigorate those who see opportunities for a nuclear first strike and/or claim to fear such a perception of opportunity on the other side?

If all the temptations and worries of a first strike, posed by MIRVs, enhanced accuracies, and short times-to-target, could be eliminated first (a very big "if," given the onward march of missile technology), we might more readily conclude that a substantial reduction of forces would be in order, with a more meaningful sigh of relief that nothing like nuclear winter could occur as the inadvertent result of an attack (that is, Russians would never starve because of what Soviet missiles had done to U.S. cities, although they might still suffer because of what U.S. missiles were doing in retaliation—the more normal form of mutual deterrence). But what if these temptations cannot be eliminated?

In a bizarre way the Nuclear Winter study only at first glance undermines the logic of those worried about the adequacy of U.S. nuclear retaliatory forces. Instead of making the question pointless, the study dignifies the question of temptation, by answering with a resounding reassurance that the retaliation will be adequate—as long as the two nuclear stockpiles remain so large. Deterrence is assured, not because the Soviets never wanted war or because war is always pointless, but because the Soviets will starve if they apply a thermonuclear torch to U.S. cities. This is a reassurance of deterrence, a reassurance that the Soviets will not begin a nuclear war, which is altogether satisfying and convincing. But where the argument goes from here is not so clear.

The study suggests that weapons like the Pershing II and the MX are redundant. Critics have for a longer time noted aspects of the MX that are quite undesirable (the extreme accuracy, the multiple warheads) even without the new information about nuclear winter, although there are other aspects of the MX that might be desirable (the lesser exposure to an incoming missile attack). Yet if the United States does not need the MX, does it not still need to stay above the threshold, threatening future generations to keep this one alive?

Bad News, No News, or Good News?

This entire discussion has thus become an extraordinarily optimistic interpretation of nuclear winter. What is indeed so new about the study that no one would have intuitively anticipated nuclear winter before? One "new" conclusion is that deterrent retaliation almost takes care of itself, in such a way that the attacker is punished by the impact of his own missiles, even if no one else's missiles can escape the counterforce first strike to hit back on second strike. All in all, this news might almost be regarded as welcome rather than bad news, given how much concern has been devoted to the survivability of second-strike forces. The "window of vulnerability" ceases to be a "window of opportunity" for anyone, if the soot from the fires that are ignited by a missile attack will impose freezing conditions and starvation on the side that "got away with" a "splendid first strike."

A different kind of news is that the Southern Hemisphere, and the underdeveloped nations in general, will suffer along with the two superpowers in any all-out nuclear war. Not only will civilization and the future of human life be threatened within the USSR and the United States, but across the entire globe. There are at least two kinds of logic that might lead us to be more appalled at this aspect of the news.

First, the superpowers are perhaps thus imposing an inevitable punishment on the "innocent," rather than merely on the guilty developers and possessors of thermonuclear weapons, contradicting the most elementary notions of rightness and justice.

Second, we are for the first time facing the possibility of the destruction of *all* human life, and not just life in the advanced industrial states. Perhaps there is some damage threshold before which the normal casualties of a U.S.–Soviet nuclear war, dragging down Europe as well, would not yet be viewed as so total a disaster; a global aftermath that disrupts the ecology and nutrition of Central Africa as well is qualitatively more of a disaster, perhaps unacceptable where the earlier prospect was less so.

But it is not so difficult to turn the moral tables on both such arguments. First, is it really so sure that Brazil or Zaire, Vietnam or Honduras, will have been so innocent when the cosmic accounting of the blame for a nuclear war has to be assessed? Predicting how such a war would have erupted in the first place is very difficult, relating to some very intricate chains of political troubles that could lead up to it. Sweden, Costa Rica, Switzerland, and New Zealand are likely to be innocent, but who else is sure to escape indictment? Second, reacting to the prospective *global* ecological calamity outlined in the Sagan article, many of us would believe that even a much more confined thermonuclear war is already an unacceptable disaster, morally so bad that nothing could meaningfully be worse.

The ultimate moral response thus remains as it was, that assured destruction even if it be labelled MAD (mutual assured destruction), is contingently acceptable precisely because it deters itself from happening. Knowing how bad a nuclear war would be keeps national leaders from crossing the line into such a war. If the damage of a thermonuclear war were ever to become plausibly close to acceptable, if ideas of "limited nuclear war" were given too much credence, if the defenses of populations came to be rated as effective, or if the nuclear arsenals of the powers were to be substantially reduced, then this barrier to war might be in trouble, even where rulers were "rational" in all normal senses of the word.

There may thus be nothing immoral or impractical in suggesting that we do only one important thing about the prospect of nuclear winter: specifically, that we make certain that everyone knows about it. We must make certain that Soviet analysts, spokesmen, and responsible government leaders are induced to comment on this prospect and signify an awareness of it. And we must do the same for those U.S. officials who match Soviet posturing by not yet stating the meaninglessness of "victory" in a nuclear war.

Notes

1. Carl Sagan, "Nuclear War and Climatic Catastrophe," *Foreign Affairs* 62, no. 2 (Winter 1983–84):257–92. See also R.P. Turco, O.B. Toon, T.P. Ackerman, J.B. Pollack, and Carl Sagan, "Nuclear Winter: Global Consequences of Multiple Nuclear Explosions," *Science* 222, no. 4630 (23 December 1983):1283–92.

2. Bernard Brodie, ed., *The Absolute Weapon* (New York: Harcourt Brace, 1946).

3. William L. Borden, *There Will Be No Time* (New York: Macmillan, 1946).

4. Albert Wohlstetter, "The Delicate Balance of Terror," *Foreign Affairs* 37, no. 2 (January 1959):211–34.

5. Brodie, *The Absolute Weapon,* 74.

6. For a reference to the public's interpretation of the 1946 Bikini test, see Gregg Herken, *The Winning Weapon* (New York: Alfred A. Knopf, 1980), 224–26.

7. House of Commons Debates, 1 March 1955.

8. Giulio Douhet, *The Command of the Air* (New York: Coward-McCann, 1941), 58.

9. On the Japanese deliberations leading to the surrender, see Herbert Feis, *The Atomic Bomb and the End of World War II* (Princeton: Princeton University Press, 1966); and Robert Butow, *Japan's Decision to Surrender* (Stanford, Calif.: Stanford University Press, 1954).

10. The difficulties of contemporary civil defense are outlined in United States Congress, Office of Technology Assessment, *The Effects of Nuclear War* (Washington: U.S. Government Printing Office, 1979), chapter 3.

11. Herman Kahn, *On Thermonuclear War* (Princeton: Princeton University Press, 1960).

12. For an overview of the evolution of American civil-defense plans, see Allan M. Winkler, "A 40-Year History of Civil Defense," *Bulletin of the Atomic Scientists* 40, no. 6 (June–July 1984):16–22.

13. A critical interpretation of the ideas and influence of T.K. Jones and other civil-defense advocates is provided in Robert Scheer, *With Enough Shovels* (New York: Random House, 1982).

14. Borden, *There Will Be No Time,* 84.

15. For a good example of this kind of "bureaucratic politics" analysis of the motivation of military professionals, see Morton H. Halperin, *Bureaucratic Politics and Foreign Policy* (Washington, D.C.: Brookings Institution, 1974).

16. Wohlstetter, "The Delicate Balance of Terror," 222.

17. Bernard Brodie, "The Development of Nuclear Strategy," *International Security* 2, no. 4 (Spring 1978):69.

18. Fred C. Iklé, "Can Nuclear Deterrence Last Out the Century?" *Foreign Affairs* 51, no. 2 (January 1973):267–85.

19. Wolfgang Panofsky, "The Mutual Hostage Relationship between America and Russia," *Foreign Affairs* 52, no. 1 (October 1973):109–18.

20. Fred C. Iklé, "Nuclear Disarmament without Secrecy," *Department of State Bulletin* (30 September 1974):454–58.

9
Traditional and Soviet Military Doctrine: Tendencies and Dangers

The point of this chapter is to discuss what may be a very natural tendency in U.S. and Soviet military analysis (perhaps in every nation's military analysis) and at the same time a very misleading or dangerous tendency. Military officers, out of simple pride in doing their duty and out of a sense of morality shared with their countrymen, may focus too much on defeating their opponents in battle, an outlook that may threaten any political accommodations or détente, even increasing the risk of "a war nobody wanted." The chapter will begin by describing some general sources of this outlook, with reference to instances in which it has been overcome in the United States, and will end by discussing the Soviet failure to document any overriding of this tendency, causing some serious damage for the entire U.S.–Soviet relationship.

The Traditional Counterforce Tendency

The tendency to concentrate on one's opposite number as the prime target is displayed very clearly in the writings of Alfred Thayer Mahan on naval policy and of Giulio Douhet with regard to air force operations, but it shows up in writings on all the service branches. The writings of Mahan serve as a stellar example, because the clarity of Mahan's writings captured so much broad attention around the globe. Mahan's view of what had been natural for the Royal Navy in its best years and what would have to be natural for the U.S. Navy as a suc-

George H. Quester, "Traditional and Soviet Military Doctrine: Tendencies and Dangers," from Douglas MacLean, ed., *The Security Gamble,* Maryland Studies in Public Policy (Totowa, N.J.: Rowan and Allanheld, 1984), 28–49.

cessor was nothing less than capturing the dominance of the sea by driving other fleets from it. Alternative uses of naval power, for example, simply harassing the merchant operations of the dominant sea power, were viewed as insufficiently ambitious by Mahan, as attempting to apply naval power without having first consolidated a hold on enough of it.

> So far we have been viewing the effect of a purely cruising warfare, not based upon powerful squadrons, only upon that particular part of the enemy's strength against which it is theoretically directed— upon his commerce and general wealth; upon the sinews of war. The evidence seems to show that even for its own special ends such a mode of war is inconclusive, worrying but not deadly; it might almost be said that it causes needless suffering. . . .
>
> . . . It is not the taking of individual ships or convoys, be they few or many, that strikes down the money power of a nation; it is the possession of that overbearing power on the sea which drives the enemy's flag from it, or allows it to appear only as a fugitive; and which, by controlling the great common, closes the highways by which commerce moves to and from the enemy's shores.[1]

Strategists of aerial combat have been similarly inclined to debunk any plans that do not place high priority on first sweeping an enemy's air force from the sky.

We today often view the overhead means of delivery, by airplane or by ballistic missile, as enshrining the countervalue capabilities of mutual assured destruction (MAD), by which either side can always inflict retaliatory destruction on the other, regardless of who wins the exchanges of combat and by which such retaliatory threats deter either side from ever launching such combat. Nuclear weapons constitute the necessary destructive effect on such means of delivery today, but the predictions of analysts between the two world wars imputed similar levels of destructiveness by the use of simple poison gas or dynamite.

Yet while the premises of assured destruction seemed (prematurely) to have been established, both Douhet and Fuller in their strategic advice drifted again toward the counterforce approach, destroying the enemy's air force and his ability to wage war, rather than toward the countervalue approach, inflicting painful destruction for its own sake, to dissuade the enemy from wanting to continue the war (or to deter an enemy from ever deciding to begin a war).

For example, Douhet:

To have command of the air means to be in a position to prevent the enemy from flying while retaining the ability to fly oneself. . . .

. . . A nation which has command of the air is in a position to protect its own territory from enemy aerial attack and even to put a halt to the enemy's auxiliary actions in support of his land and sea operations, leaving him powerless to do much of anything.[2]

Such a stress on counterforce attack, directed at the same service on the opposite side, may come out clearest and strongest for navies and for air forces, although it is also to be found historically in analyses of ground operations. The clarity of the field on which combat is conducted at sea or in the air lends itself to this approach. Only partly coincidental, these are the means most involved today in the delivery of nuclear weapons to the enemy's homeland, a coincidence (as we shall discuss a little later), that can cause the United States some considerable anxiety.

Clausewitz's *On War* can be interpreted in numerous and conflicting ways, amid a debate about whether Clausewitz is to be seen as the apostle of total war or whether this message is overshadowed by his basic premise that war is the continuation of politics by other means. The two could be reconciled, of course, by seeing Clausewitz as an interpreter of the French Revolution and the Napoleonic period, with all of politics being much more "total" now, and with war (as the continuation of politics) therefore also being much more total.

Clausewitz at one point translates this idea very specifically into an enjoinder that the aim in warfare is to disarm the enemy. One could hardly phrase the concept of counterforce more clearly than this, as Clausewitz's words will seem intuitively true for the majority of military men.

I have already said that the aim of warfare is to disarm the enemy and it is time to show that, at least in theory, this is bound to be so. . . . So long as I have not overthrown my opponent I am bound to fear he may overthrow me. Thus I am not in control: he dictates to me as much as I dictate to him.[3]

When all of Clausewitz's complications are taken into account, the emphasis on total war is diminished, of course, and with it the emphasis on disarming the armed forces of the other side. Clausewitz importantly stresses the political object of war, which could stop short of a victory that had stripped the other side of its armed forces. He notes the importance of the defense as a periodic explainer of lulls in warfare:

> The third determinant, which acts like a rachet-wheel, occasionally stopping the works completely, is the greater strength of the defensive. A may not feel strong enough to attack B, which does not, however, mean that B is strong enough to attack A. The additional strength of the defensive is not only lost when the offensive is assumed but is transferred to the opponent. Expressed in algebraic terms, the difference between A + B and A − B equals 2 B. It therefore happens that both sides at the same time not only feel too weak for an offensive, but that they really are too weak.[4]

Yet, as on a number of other points, Clausewitz's reader is left at the end with no clear signal that he should renounce the disarmament of his enemy. Here (and perhaps only here) could one achieve something meaningful and lasting by the energies invested in a war.

To test how far this emphasis on the disarming of one's opposite number goes back into history, we can turn to the writings of Sun Tzu, generally thought to have put his thoughts to paper between 400 and 300 BC, well before, obviously, any of the writings of military strategists in the West.

> Invincibility lies in the defense; the possibility of victory in the attack.
>
> One defends when his strength is inadequate; he attacks when it is abundant.[5]

Why does one have to go to the offense, once one's strength is again adequate? Why is the attack necessary for any meaningful sense of victory? Because victory entails getting rid of the enemy's menace, by disarming him.

How would such a stress in strategic purpose affect operational distinctions? At sea, it has often been connected to whether a navy follows the maxim of "never divide the fleet." If the object of one navy must simply be to concentrate on sinking the other navy, then it makes sense to keep the fleet together, for the mathematics of fire-exchange ratios, as theorized by F.W. Lanchester in the Lanchester Square Law, suggest that the greatest counterforce impact will be achieved this way. If other functions are instead given greater priority at times, for example, supporting landing forces ashore, protecting one's coast, or harrassing an enemy's coasts, then very different deployment patterns are ordained and even differing ship designs.

In air warfare, a stress on winning control of the air presumably suggests that more resources be assigned to air-superiority fighters (such as the F-15), while a commitment to earlier use of air platforms would dictate a greater investment in fighter-bombers, planes sacrificing some potential for air-to-air combat in order to gain a greater potential for air-to-ground combat (such as the F-16).

As a nontrivial illustration of how such a bias toward counterforce affects procurement decisions, accuracy for intercontinental ballistic missiles (ICBMs) or for various forms of ground-launched, sea-launched, or air-launched cruise missiles (GLCMs, SLCMs, ALCMs) is hardly necessary if the target were mainly to be the urban population concentrations of the other side. Such accuracies become much more desirable when the target is the missile forces of the other side—the enemy missiles presumably aimed at U.S. urban populations or at U.S. missiles—or even when the target becomes some other portion of the enemy's military potential.

It is just as "natural" for the strategic nuclear forces of either side to aim at the strategic nuclear forces of the opponent, as it was "natural" earlier for navies to aim at each other, or for air forces to aim at each other. It has been correspondingly regarded as unnatural and evil for such missiles to be aimed at innocent civilians. Yet, in an important and bizarre point, to which we shall return, peace may now depend on civilians' being the target and on the military's natural inclination toward counterforce targeting being overcome and renounced.

Sources of the Counterforce Tendency

We shall now attempt to outline some possible explanations for this bias of the professional military toward the counterforce role. A few of the explanations offered may portray the military officer as self-serving, much as the "bureaucratic politics" literature paints all government workers as selfish, but a larger part of the problem stems instead from the officer's deeper desire to render service for the public, for the ultimate consumer of whatever a military force produces.

The tendency toward counterforce operations, toward trying to win "command of the sea" or "command of the air" or "full control over the ground," will be very understandable and recognizable upon reflection to all who have ever been afflicted with the "Protestant ethic" or similar goads toward hard work and success. It basically strikes one and all as natural, because it amounts to putting first things first, to capitalizing before consuming, to taking care of the means to happiness first, and then applying these means to final consumption needs. "Erst die Arbeit, und dann das Spiel," goes an old German saying, drumming diligence into young children. "First the work, and then the play." "First earn yourself a million dollars or two, and then buy yourself a yacht."

A navy therefore feels comfortable and, more importantly, virtuous in first sinking the opposing navy, and *only then* beginning to assist sister services, to harass enemy merchant shipping, to convoy its own merchant shipping, or to attack enemy coastlines and defend its own coastlines. An air force should first shoot the other air force out of the sky, and then (having established the position of air dominance) turn to assisting forces on the ground or attacking enemy industry and shielding its own rear areas.

Military force is of course to be related to political and civilian uses. Clausewitz's aphorism about war being a continuation of politics is nowhere denied here, for every commander realizes that his ultimate reason for trying to dominate the seas, air, or ground appears with the political uses of that domination. Yet the distinction between preparation and use that carries over from the world of ordinary civilian endeavor implants a substantive psychological block here. One feels more virtuous in postponing considerations of use, of accentuating the accumulation of politically usable military power without yet having used it. Thinking about how one will spend one's income can get in the way of earning it. Becoming diverted by other uses of naval power can get in the way of acquiring that naval power. Even assisting the army is something that a navy feels justified (and responsible) in sliding back on the schedule, as compared with sinking the opposing navy.

We are not arguing that the ultimate uses of military power are ever fully forgotten. Rather, a more subtle bias is generated toward overemphasizing the counterforce role of military power. Just as some businessmen become so intent on acquiring money that they and their wives become incapable of enjoying spending it, so the stress on defeating the enemy in combat is given too much weight.

The dominant motive behind the bias outlined here may thus come in this sense of capitalization, the puritan feeling that it is noble to husband capability and round out capability, after which, in due time, capability will be used. When there are no more enemy ships to be sunk, no more enemy aircraft to be shot down, then one can with no trepidation turn to applying sea power or air power to more practical uses.

A second reason for the stress on counterforce reverts to traditional standards of nobility and morality. The enemy of the same cut of uniform is fair game. Civilians are not. For navies to get into anything beyond attacking opposing navies is thus to wander onto a slippery slope, whereby noncombatants come to be the target. The most honorable note of military training anywhere is that the only legitimate target will be people in uniform on the other side.

American academics specializing in the study of international relations since the introduction of nuclear weapons are largely reconciled to a kind of reasoning whereby it is desirable that civilians be the target of the retaliatory forces on each side, as part of what Donald Brennan meant to criticize when he labelled it MAD—mutual assured destruction—an acronym that has been adopted by those who accept such mutual deterrence, the so-called Madvocates. Such academics usually have no difficulty persuading their students in any semester-length course that there is no practical alternative to such mutual targeting of nonmilitary "countervalue" targets if peace is to be assured, since a shift toward aiming at "counterforce" military targets would indeed be very destabilizing and threatening to peace.

Yet, these academics and their students, together with a fair number of policymakers in United States administrations in the 1960s, amount to a very small community, as compared with the vast majority of Americans who may still be appalled whenever they are forced to think about the idea of deliberate targeting of civilians. Sunday sermons would be very quick to attack this policy as the height of immorality and so would newspaper editorials, thus reinforcing a signal that the military has received all along from its civilian constituency, that it is more noble to go counterforce than countervalue, more noble to attack ships, airplanes, and soldiers than to attack civilians.

No one has ever been tried for war crimes for shooting at or bombing military targets. If the German U-boat campaign of World War I had been directed only at British warships, rather than at civilian-registry merchantmen, the United States public would never have become aroused to enter the war on Britan's side. All of the U.S. bombing raids in World War II, including even the nuclear bombing of Hiroshima, were rationalized as somehow directed at military targets.

The morality of counterforce efforts, and the immorality of countervalue campaigns, is thus part of the general public attitude in the United States, and around the world, not excluding the Soviet Union. Soviet enunciations of military doctrine have always taken world opinion into account, trying to exploit such opinion, but even somewhat internalizing it. Soviet statements on possible nuclear war always pretend that exclusively military targets will be struck at, a message as frightening as it is moral, a message creating important problems to which we shall return.

A third motive for the counterforce emphasis is a little less noble, being part of the bureaucratic politics mechanisms whereby services promote themselves within their domestic decision-making processes against competitors fighting for budgetary allocations. For example, to stress the threat of the opposing navy is normally to convince one's citizens of the value in general of a navy. To stress the threat of the enemy's tank forces is to pull compliments and appropriations toward one's own tank forces. To place high priority on the shooting down of the enemy air force is to promote one's own air force.

A fourth kind of motive blends aspects of those already listed. When a navy is freed to do battle against the opposing navy, rather than being held close to shore to support the infantry with artillery fire, it is freer to "do its own thing," to carry through a project all of its own. There may be a higher feeling of purity and accomplishment in this (which is something like the extensions from the Protestant ethic noted at the outset), or there may be more gratification in executing a campaign without having to coordinate with or take instructions from a sister service (which is closer to the idea of parochial bureaucratic self-indulgence). An analogy is the business executive who enjoys running his own company, who derives gratification not only from capitalizing his firm into the millions of dollars, but also from being allowed to maintain his own way of doing things, working within a field he knows best. Sailors around the world respect other sailors. Sailors prefer to conduct their combat against other sailors.

This brings us to a fifth and last psychological reinforcement for the military's inclination toward counterforce. Disarming an enemy tends to involve taking the offensive, rather than waiting for the enemy to attack. The history of strategic analysis has its enthusiasts for the defense, but very few, for the more memorable writers are always those discussing more ambitious strategic goals. Trusting in the defense means forswearing a "command of the sea" or "command of the air," forswearing "disarming the enemy," and since 1940 it is most typically labelled a "Maginot mentality."

Can one aspire to high rank being an expert on pill boxes or concrete fortifications? The bias of the military is that defensively oriented technology is noninnovative, "sit-still," status-quo-oriented, while offensive technology is very innovative, constantly on the move, constantly replacing old systems with new systems.

There are indeed some respectable alternatives to the goal of a counterforce disarming of the enemy. The highest calling of the Swiss Army (a very respectable fighting force, by all estimates) is not to "disarm the enemy," but rather to repulse the enemy and to impose the lesson that he ought not to try again to conquer the Swiss in their redoubts. Cynics would say that this is simply what the Swiss have to limit themselves to, because of their small size; a larger Switzerland could eliminate the Austrian, French, Italian, German, and Russian menaces once and for all, stripping away their arms.

Yet more than size is at work here. The Swiss mentality is one of "leave us alone and we'll leave you alone." Switzerland does not get invaded, but it does not stampede anyone else into useless wars either. If size limitations are all that have kept Swiss officers from taking Clausewitz too seriously (with classical geographic limitations keeping the Swiss from getting very fond of Mahan), there might still be some other good reasons to welcome the Swiss model, to pose it as an alternative model of role and self-esteem for the military profession.

Are there signs of such counterforce thinking on the civilian side of foreign policy decision making and analysis? We have been suggesting all along that a correct approach to the strategic problem should often be more a combination of consumption and investment, rather than just a heavy stress on investment. Mahan aside, navies often contribute more when they concentrate less on the sinking of the opposite navy. "All work and no play makes Jack a dull boy," "All counterforce and no derivative service," for the bulk of a war, may be less than optimal service in the national interest.

Among civilian analysts of foreign policy, one sometimes sees an approximation of the same misleading biases in a stress on "vital interest." Nations have interests; that is, they have preferences by which one outcome is preferable to another. But what do we mean then by *vital* interests"? Presumably this term refers to certain results that have much higher priority than others, to certain accomplishments that should be assured first, before any attention is assigned to other matters, to certain foreign policy goals upon which the attainment of other goals will depend. Once again, a sense of paramount responsibility causes some things to look very much like capitalization, while others are relegated to the status of consumption goods and indulgence. The elevation of some attainments to the level of "vital' can become a shorthand by which too much attention is assigned to them.

This attitude sometimes translates into a simple and straightforward version of a "realpolitik" or "power politics" approach to the analysis of foreign policy, whereby it is contended or implied that a nation should naturally always choose the policies that increase its national power, never instead being guided by considerations of ideology or moral values.

Yet the inherent criticism of such a "realistic" approach is that Americans, Russians, Chinese, or anyone else may care about more than power (the prior "capital goods" of international influence), caring also or instead about the uses and applications of such power (the "consumption goods" in this realm). The advocates of a realpolitik approach are always on prudentially firm ground when they remind others that it is no good to have values without having some power with which to implement and support them. Yet they move along to an idea logically much less supportable when they begin to suggest that power is the end in itself rather than simply a means to an end. The drift of such analysis illustrates how the mentality that seems morally to support counterforce reasoning can have an appeal for civilians as well as the military.

Alternative Military Professional Emphases

Are there any exceptions to this military bias toward "doing battle with the opposite number"? Of course there are, because common sense dictates that certain weapons and the vested interest of the people trained for those weapons will sometimes preclude doing counterforce battle of this kind.

Submarine warfare until recently was of this nature. Submarines have been useful for many things, but had not typically been very effective against other submarines. A broader counterforce notion, akin to the reasoning of Mahan, would of course have directed the submarines against the surface fleet of the opposing navy, and some of the German U-boats of two world wars and some of the U.S. submarines of World War II were deployed with this target in mind. Yet the primary target in all three of these submarine campaigns became much more of a *guerre de course,* an assault on the merchant shipping of the enemy, coming close to victory in the two German attempts, very much contributing to victory in the U.S. assault on a Japanese shipping. The U.S. submarines of World War II went mainly after merchantmen and did not concentrate on sinking the Japanese fleet. The rest of the U.S. Navy, in particular the aircraft carriers, indeed concentrated on sinking the Japanese Navy, but the whole of the U.S. naval effort (submarines being a very significant part of it) comes out much more balanced in this regard, delivering victory in the process.

Some other forms of military equipment are very clearly earmarked to counter something other than their opposite number. Antiaircraft guns have been aimed at enemy aircraft, not at the antiaircraft guns of the other side. Antisubmarine warfare (ASW) was until recently carried out mainly from surface vehicles and aircraft and was surely not pledged to sweep the enemy's ASW from the seas. Minesweepers try to undo the work of the enemy's minelayers, while minelayers work to undo the work of the enemy's minesweepers.

When the target on the other side is military in any sense, the officers involved can still thus rally around the banner of counterforce. Mines may sink an enemy battleship just as readily as they might sink a merchantman. Yet the odds are overwhelming that mines and submarines will find more merchant than warship targets, so that effective use of these tools requires that Mahan be paid lip service at best, that no particular concentration on the counterforce role be attempted. Submarines and minelayers thus begin *using* naval power right from the beginning of the war, rather than simply capitalizing and expanding upon naval power. If the mere investment in such types of ships and equipment thus pulls officers away from an excessive fascination with the counterforce role, the obverse relationship is probably also a reality. Navies taking Mahan seriously have tended to underinvest in minelayers and submarines.

At least three critical questions must always be asked about placing such a strong emphasis on defeating the opposite military force.

First, can the defeat be accomplished, or will attempts be prone to failure, as more of one's own force is used up on the counterforce attack than is taken out of the enemy force?

Second, are one's priorities in a war so important that other functions should really be postponed until the grand accumulation of capital in a counterforce campaign is finally accomplished? To return to our homely analogy, shouldn't the man who wants to accumulate a million dollars still consider taking vacations and spending some of his money, even when he is only part of the way to his goal of goals? Shouldn't one divert energies even earlier to helping sister services and to attacking or shielding civilian targets?

Third, might not a focus on the counterforce destruction of an enemy's ability to fight be threatening and destabilizing, making wars more likely? The logic of why counterforce preparations are destabilizing is now familiar, even if it is uncongenial to all of the normal professional military. When either side has the ability to disarm the other's military, it will be tempted to do so, lest it lose this ability later on, lest the other side attain it afterward. Wars will happen that would not otherwise have happened. If both sides believe they have the ability to disarm the other side, victory may simply go to whoever strikes first, with the result that each side will race to strike in crisis, shooting first and asking questions later, producing a war that neither side may have wanted. This is often thought to be the way that World War I began. It is also feared to be the way a World War III could begin.

Any reasonable strategist will have to consider whether his country will win a war, if it happens, and whether he can reduce the costs of the war to his country, if the war happens. But he will also have to consider the impact of any deployments and strategies on the likelihood of war. To stampede an adversary into a war unwanted by either side is not good strategy, even if the stampede is caused by what looked optimal as the way to fight the war once it had been begun.

The clearest deviation from the instinctive military inclination toward doing battle with opposite numbers thus comes in the nuclear age, with weapons that for a time looked as if they could play almost no counterforce role, but would have to be countervalue in nature. The submarine-based missiles of the original Polaris force had to be aimed at civilians and so did the landbased U.S. Air Force missiles, since they were so deficient in accuracy that they could only be aimed at Soviet cities. Since Soviet military command posts have tended to remain in cities and since Soviet industry (also located in cities) is crucial to maintaining military force, such weapons could still be rationalized as countermilitary rather than countercivilian, but most strategic reasoning identified them as weapons of revenge, rather than as weapons for attaining dominance.

Yet the attitudes described here are those of low enthusiasm in both services for these totally countervalue roles, as compared with the rest of the Navy and as compared with the manned bombers of the U.S. Air Force. More seriously, we must note the enthusiasm of each of these services for the enhancements of accuracy that became possible in the 1970s, accuracies that once again allow generals, admirals, colonels, and Navy captains to contemplate doing battle with their opposites, rather than with civilians. What is seemingly responsible or noble can become very dangerous, as the natural instinct toward counterforce here threatens the stability of the strategic balance.

To give an example, the tendency to seek to disarm the opposite military force is just as natural as the individual's desire to save for the future. The Keynesian paradox was that this virtue of prudential saving could be bad for the economy in the net total, when not enough investment opportunities were present to soak up all savings at full employment. The paradox of arms control is that too keen an interest in winning wars, if they happen, may make wars more likely.

It is no easier to suppress the pride military strategists take in the counterforce role than it is to suppress the instincts of stewardship and productivity that are at the root of working and saving for the future. Sweeping the enemy from the seas, skies, or battlefield is neat and clean, it is replete with possibilities for further exploitation afterwards and for political rewards.

The best that we might hope for may rather be that the military officers under the sway of this kind of imperative will become somewhat more aware of it, perhaps so that they can discount it. At other decision-making levels, these tendencies will have to be counteracted where they threaten to pull the country into dangerously unstable confrontations with adversaries probably afflicted with similar tendencies.

The Obtuseness of Soviet Strategic Pronouncements

Americans can certainly agree that détente is in trouble, even if they will disagree about whose fault it is. Critics of the Reagan administration and of the latter half of the Carter administration would argue that the United States has needlessly returned to Cold War rhetoric and has needlessly chosen to direct substantial new investments into weaponry. The "hawks" are having their day with the election of Ronald Reagan, and their very name suggests that the United States is to blame for a "hawkish" new turn in foreign policy.

Yet would the hawks be nearly as persuasive if the Soviets had done all they could to ease tension, to prove the continued possibility and value of détente? The Soviets have never made some important moves in this regard, some of them at the level of concrete weapons procurements, others even more importantly at the level of declaratory statements of military strategy planning.

The Soviets have indeed substantially modernized their military forces since 1970 in strategic nuclear forces as well as in the forces configured for conventional war, and part of the problem stems simply from such force augmentations. Where once the more dovish U.S. analyst of arms matters might have predicted that the USSR would only elect to match the United States in totals of ICBMs and of submarine-launched ballistic missiles (SLBMs), the Soviets produced both of these kinds of strategic nuclear missiles in quantity in the 1970s, ultimately exceeding the United States in the totals frozen at a status quo in SALT I. The Soviets have also very much modernized and expanded their conventional ground force capability, thus continuing to expose Western Europe to the possibility of a Soviet ground invasion.

The picture of Soviet blame, in terms only of procurements, is far from clear, however. These comparisons of missile totals tend to omit the strategic nuclear bomber, with which the Soviets did not match the United States, and they also leave out the French and British strategic nuclear forces, and U.S. theater nuclear forces based forward in Western Europe, all of which could inflict considerable damage as well on the Soviet Union.

The United States did not add to its total of missile launchers in the 1970s, but it did add substantially to the total of nuclear warheads that could be delivered to Soviet targets, by developing multiple warheads for the missiles it possessed, this coming initially in reaction to Soviet preparations for antiballistic missile defense, a population-defense system that the Soviets abandoned at about the time they signed a treaty with the United States forbidding most deployments of ABMs. The United States then held advantages for most of the 1970s because of its lead in MIRV (multiple independently targeted reintry vehicle) technology. New problems were slated to arise in the 1980s when the Soviets caught up with the United States in MIRV technology and when they could apply this technology to the larger numbers of missiles they had already acquired, missiles which had generally been greater in size and carrying capacity than those of the United States.

Given this confusing picture of the ins and outs, or possible actions and reactions, it will be contended here that it is not Soviet *procurements* that are most to blame for fueling renewed rounds of the arms race in the 1980s, but rather some aspects of the style of Soviet strategic *pronouncements,* aspects very much in the counterforce tradition that this chapter has been describing. Still tied too much to the older moral tradition of what the military's purpose should be in war—to protect one's own homeland and civilians, by destroying the enemy's military forces—Soviet statements of strategic doctrine are provocative.

One could easily enough write out the script of what U.S. policymakers would like the Soviet leadership to admit about nuclear war, for it is the duplicate of what some U.S. strategists and arms controllers have been writing for more than two decades. The Soviets should admit that the retaliation of nuclear war will be so horrible in both directions as to make victory immaterial, and they should, even before this, admit that they are better off if the United States has assured means of inflicting such retaliation.

Since the facts of a future nuclear war are generally clear and stark enough with regard to the gross levels of destruction that would occur, there is every reason to believe that Soviet analysts see the entire picture just as Americans have seen it.[6] The problem is that Soviet statements of their perceptions have not gone the entire distance of discussing these realities. As a result, it has been possible for U.S. analysts of a "hawkish" persuasion to argue that the Soviet leaders are not aware of the same realities as U.S. leaders are, are not as intimidated by these new realities, and are not guided by the same general formulations about the nature and priorities of nuclear war and peace.[7]

Two major concessions have thus not yet been made in the Soviet discussion of nuclear strategic reality, even while the Soviet commentary is now close enough so that a hope for this final rounding out of the picture is not to be abandoned. First, as was noted quite lucidly by the late Donald Brennan in a published exchange with Raymond Garthoff, the Soviets have not yet duplicated the extreme reasonableness one finds in the Western side, in describing it as desirable that the

United States have a second-strike retaliatory capability.[8] Indeed, the Soviet commentary often stipulates that such a capability now exists on both sides, as the inevitable result of developing the technology of mass destruction. For the moment, this commentary concedes that the best efforts of the Soviet military forces could not ward off such destruction. But it implies that such forces should continue trying to terminate this retaliatory threat against the Soviet population, to achieve success at some time in the future.

What is most lacking is an expression of feeling that each side should want the other to have this retaliatory countervalue capability, should restrain its own counterforce capabilities so as to avoid threatening this capability, and should even hope for the other side to develop this capability. Such, after all, was the conclusion of Oskar Morgenstern in a book that was part of the U.S. arms control literature at the end of the 1950s, *The Question of National Defense.* Morgenstern concluded thus:

> Russia's position is therefore in no way different from ours; she needs a deterrent force and she needs it in as invulnerable a form as possible. This is how she will build her force. She will use those forms of invulnerability best suited to her geography, her economic capabilitiec and the weapons systems she has chosen. It is immaterial at the moment what this choice actually is.
>
> An invulnerable deterrent force on each side makes any attack by either one less likely since the ordinary means of surprise fail. Surprise is, as we saw, the greatest inducement and temptation to stage an attack—when all other conditions are favorable—provided the attacked country has a vulnerable retaliatory force.
>
> *There is a second principal: In view of modern technology of speedy weapons delivery from any point on earth to any other, it is in the interest of the United States for Russia to have an invulnerable retaliatory force and vice versa. . . .*
>
> . . . We recall the extraordinary and steadily increasing danger of misinterpreting natural phenomena of the most varied kind as signs of an attack. Again, if the enemy with a vulnerable force does conclude falsely, even if only once, that he is being attacked and if we are in the ballistic missile age of nonrecallable action, a world catastrophe cannot be avoided.
>
> We do not want to live under conditions so precarious. We want to protect ourselves against accidents and errors where these have consequences of the magnitude of an all-out thermonuclear war.[9]

The second very much related Soviet doctrinal concession which also has not yet quite been delivered, is an acknowledgment that there is no point in trying to win (or to avoid losing) a nuclear war even if the other side has begun the attack. Soviet statements forswearing an interest in victory have all too often become an assurance that the Soviet Union would never strike first and would never begin such a war, thus shifting the discussion to suggesting that the West is more likely to be the aggressor in such a war. Left vague is whether the alleged guilt of the United States, in having been the aggressor, would then justify a Soviet effort to do the utmost to repel this attack.

A really forthcoming Soviet statement (again the duplicate of what many Americans have said) would say that no matter who started a nuclear war, there would still be no point in trying to snatch victory away from the enemy and bring it home instead, that victory is as meaningless for the innocent in such a war as it is for the guilty, that the only point of nuclear weaponry would be to inflict retaliation, pure and simple.

There was a time when Soviet statements on nuclear war caused much more worry to foreigners, because such statements seemed to question whether such war would be very painful at all. If the Soviets did not anticipate the destructiveness of such a war, could they be deterred by its prospect, deterred from any conventional invasion of Western Europe, or deterred from trying to conquer the United States and the world by some sort of nuclear sneak attack? When Stalin (and later, Mao) made such statements, they were probably engaged in a colossal bluff, pretending to be indifferent to the power of nuclear weaponry when they had none themselves. Fearful commentators on Soviet strategy still detect strains of this kind of Soviet bluff ("Are we so sure the Soviets are bluffing, that they are not seriously indifferent to the destruction of Moscow and other cities?"), especially when Communist leaders seem to be laying heavy stress on civil-defense measures, including shelter for themselves, but also some evacuation or shelter for the more valuable elements of the working population. Skeptics are inclined to question the utility of Soviet civil-defense preparations, since they have never been fully rehearsed and since a thermonuclear attack would in any event tax the utility of even the best-run and most carefully prepared civil-defense arrangements.

In any event, the major complaint one would have to make about Soviet obtuseness in public statements about nuclear war would no longer be directed precisely to this matter.[10] There is no shortage now of published Soviet statements indeed admitting that nuclear war would be a disaster, with such statements appearing ever since the death of Stalin, often illustrated and elaborated in great detail. The Soviets concede that they would suffer badly, would lose a great deal, in any nuclear war, just as all the world would lose. They concede, "realistically," that there is assured destruction under present conditions and that such assured destruction is indeed mutual.

The problem is no longer that Soviet statements do not admit the likelihood of such a countervalue impact. Rather it is that, like many other commentators around the globe, the Soviets will not bring themselves to admit a desirability of such countervalue impact.

What protects people, whether it be ABM or civil defense or an elegantly executed counterforce military strike, is bad for the world now, because it makes war more likely. Such has been the new conventional wisdom of U.S. professional strategists during the 1960s and 1970s, contrary to the older and more straightforward military wisdom that directed weapons at an enemy's forces and not at his people. But this is not yet the accepted and enunciated conventional wisdom expressed by Soviet authorities. Is it somehow impossible for the Soviet leadership to make so sweeping an acknowledgment of the logic of mutual assured destruction (MAD)? Some would say that the United States is simply asking too much of the Soviets here. How could the leaders of the Communist world ever state so baldly that it was *desirable*—not just inevitable, but desirable—that the sick and wicked capitalist world be able to rain retaliatory destruction down on the Soviet bloc in the event of World War III? Those in the capitalist world can barely bring themselves to make such a statement of desirability about Communist retaliatory capability, and the West is much less constrained and ideologically uniform in what its theorists put forward.

An important point in this entire discussion is indeed that only *some* U.S. analysts have endorsed the full logical premises of MAD, by which the United States should favor retaliatory capabilities in the hands of its adversary and by which the United States should become totally indifferent to victory in nuclear war; other U.S. analysts reject such premises. Another important point is that Americans are withdrawing from accepting MAD precisely because no Soviet statements have as yet fully endorsed these premises.

If it were politically and ideologically impossible for the Soviet leadership to advocate U.S. retaliatory capabilities, it might similarly be impossible for these leaders to shrug off all considerations of victory and defeat if a nuclear war were ever to occur. Soviet leaders stress that their forces are not intended or designed to attack, but are designed to *defend*. Yet to prepare to defend, by the curious logic of nuclear deterrence, is more menacing than to prepare to retaliate, and the result again means stopping short of fully acknowledging the pointlessness of defending, or of doing anything else to alter the outcome of a nuclear war.

Soviet spokesmen, with many U.S. military officers nodding their heads in agreement, would say that MAD might be an objective situation (that is, unavoidable for the moment), but cannot be a military strategy (cannot be something that is deliberately chosen). No one can ask a Soviet officer to stop trying to blunt the military power of an enemy, to give up, if war comes, trying to shield the Soviet motherland against attack. Is this not what Soviet cadets (or the cadets of the U.S. service academies) are taught to devote their lives to from the very day of their taking the oath?

How can a Soviet leadership which so emphasizes the moral superiority of "socialism" over capitalism not pledge itself to the defense of socialism in the event of war? How can the U.S. leadership avoid matching this pledge, given its own moral feelings about Western democracy as compared with Communist dictatorship?

Nevertheless, everyone has to compromise his own ideology a little as part of coming to terms with the realities of the threats of nuclear war. The Soviets have backed off from other ideological tenets in the past as part of a recognition of military realities demanded by their own military professionals, and as part of the arms control dialogue with the United States. It should not be impossible for the Soviets to take the last remaining steps to state that they see the grim realities that the West does, with all the far-reaching ramifications of these realities. It is likely that the Soviets have been held back less by ideology than by an insufficient awareness of how much damage they do, within the U.S. strategic debate, by sticking to formulas that have become outmoded by the nature of nuclear war.

Because the Soviets, despite their many claims about never wanting to begin a war, continue to show interest in "defending their homeland," in who would win "the war the capitalists had started," they strengthen the case in the United States who accuse the Kremlin of being callous about nuclear war, of being so indifferent to the potential destruction of such a war as to maintain an interest in winning it. The Soviets have been portrayed, not unconvincingly, as having a picture of nuclear war different from that held in the West, while American advocates of avoiding nuclear war-fighting planning are accused of naive ethnocentrism, of projecting onto the Soviets a resignation to deterrence that is a simple reflection of American feelings, a resignation for there is no documentary support. So, because of the lack of a few key sentences or paragraphs of Soviet description of strategic reality, the Western analysts who favor increased spending on preparations for nuclear war are thus given substantial reinforcement for their arguments.

Defenders of such Soviet clinging to outmoded concepts of strategy will note that this traditionalism is hardly lacking in the military thinking of the West, and is indeed now being wholeheartedly endorsed by the Reagan administration, as it was even earlier by the Carter and Nixon administrations. Has not the United States repeatedly made plans for counterforce "warfighting" use of nuclear weapons, aiming at "military targets" all over the Soviet Union, rather than (as the academic analysts supposed or proposed) merely targeting nuclear weapons against Soviet cities as a straightforward deterrent? In a chain ranging from Sunday sermon to newspaper editorial to the writings of a military planner, is there not a great deal of American feeling that nuclear weapons should be used (if war comes) to win victories, rather than to kill millions of innocent Russian people, to strike at military targets rather than at Russian cities?

U.S. military planners and strategic analysts have indeed never been unanimous in endorsing mutual assured destruction. Yet the most important point to be made here is that MAD did win a significant following in the United States, a following that has now diminished in large part because the Soviets did not sufficiently enunciate their own acceptance of it. Despite all U.S. pretensions of accuracy, military targeting, and counterforce intention in the past (a pretense very much required by the background of U.S. and world moral feelings already described), the reality of U.S. nuclear war planning for many of the years since 1950 has been more fully consistent with MAD.

The U.S. strategists believing in MAD know that it is *good* to direct nuclear warheads at the enemy's people and to leave one's own people exposed to enemy nuclear attack, and that it is *bad* to deviate into counterforce targeting and designing protection for one's own people. The press and the clergy, backed by centuries of tradition, teach just the opposite as to which is good and which is bad. Facing these opposite injunctions, U.S. military officers have had to pretend to be finding military targets, even when they were aiming to punish civilians, a pattern of necessary hypocrisy that existed already during World War II in the bombings of Dresden, Cologne, Tokyo, and Hiroshima. It would be a mistake to overrate the sincerity of the countermilitary (counterforce) motive here, just as it would unfortunately be a dangerous mistake in the future to underrate it. Today's hypocrisy about "counterforce intentions" could become tomorrow's sincere accomplishment, with (God forbid) a first-strike possibility then emerging to bait the world into a war.

The nearest to a full endorsement of MAD by the U.S. government probably was attained in the later years of Robert McNamara's term as Secretary of Defense. Some muting of the endorsement was still inevitable, for it would always have been politically awkward for a U.S. official to state quite explicitly that the United States looked forward to an assured vulnerability of U.S. cities to Soviet attack. Nonetheless, one heard statements of concern around the Pentagon even in the early 1960s that the Soviets were moving too slowly toward getting their land-based ICBM and submarine-based missile forces into the shape required for an assured second-strike deterrent, the kind of survivable second-strike force that would presumably eliminate all nervousness in Moscow about a U.S. preventive-war attack.

It must be noted that Secretary McNamara in 1962 himself went through a phase of traditional counterforce emphasis, as can be seen in his celebrated Ann Arbor speech proposing the "no-cities" doctrine, by which (in the event of Soviet agressions against Europe) the nuclear force of the United States would be directed only at military targets around the Soviet Union, but would not strike at population centers unless U.S. population centers had been struck. This stress on military targeting, like more recent ventures, such as President Carter's Presidential Directive 59, might or might not have included attempts to strip the Soviets of strategic nuclear capability. One version of "military targeting" spares Soviet cities—but also spares Soviet capabilities for striking at U.S. cities, to avoid putting Moscow into a nervous "use them or lose them" situation. Another, of course, quite "naturally" includes Soviet missile silos in the category of "military targets."

McNamara's short-lived enthusiasm for this kind of use for nuclear weapons was probably intended to cash in on the continuing

U.S. advantages in nuclear force strength at the beginning of the 1960s, and thus to balance supposed continuing Soviet advantages in conventional strength deployable into Europe. Within a few years, however, McNamara proved much more willing to resign himself to an approach that acknowledged Soviet needs for an assured second-strike force, matching and balancing the same kind of posture for the United States.

Considerations of elegant counterforce war, in the planning and procurement of U.S. strategic forces, declined in importance to less ambitious considerations of "damage limitation" and then further to a maintenance of "assured destruction" vis-à-vis the Soviet Union. McNamara's own collection of excerpts from his posture statements and other public papers, published in 1968 as *The Essence of Security*, contains no reference at all anymore even to a "damage limitation" counterforce role for U.S. strategic forces (that is, to the traditional role of all military forces) and instead includes discussion of *mutual* assured destruction that is not substantially different from the arguments earlier of Morgenstern:

> We do not possess first-strike capability against the Soviet Union for precisely the same reason that they do not possess it against us. Quite simply, we have both built up our second-strike capability—in effect, retaliatory power— to the point that a first-strike capability on either side has become unattainable.
>
> There is, of course, no way by which the United States could have prevented the Soviet Union from acquiring its present second-strike capability, short of a massive preemptive first strike in the 1950s. The fact is, then, that neither the Soviet Union nor the United States can attack the other without being destroyed in retaliation; nor can either of us attain a first-strike capability in the foreseeable future. Further, both the Soviet Union and the United States now possess an actual and credible second-strike capability against one another, and it is precisely this mutual capability that provides us both with the strongest possible motive to avoid a nuclear war.[11]

When options of more traditional uses of nuclear weapons surfaced again with Defense Secretary James Schlesinger in Richard Nixon's presidency, Desmond Ball aptly labelled the entire venture as a case of "déjà vu." The explanation for what then happened, from Schlesinger to the plans for the MX to PD-59 to the Reagan views on protracted nuclear war, would amount to a long and complicated story, with the emergence of enhanced accuracies playing an important role (if we can choose so easily among targets, why not exploit the choice?), with the desire of some U.S. defense managers for expanded projects playing another role, but with Soviet doctrinal statements also being terribly important, if nothing else for giving argumentive ammunition to the hawkish U.S. advocates of new strategies and new weapons systems.

President Reagan's sudden March 1983 endorsement of hopes for a future space-based laser ABM system amounted only to the most explicit statement of the U.S. government's drift away from commitment to mutual assured destruction, a drift rationalized by many arguments of very uneven persuasiveness and rationalized at all stages by the contention that Soviet strategic doctrine had never itself accepted MAD.

Some Hopes for Soviet Accommodation

The Soviets are not so obtuse, it has been contended here, as to have missed much of what U.S. strategists so readily perceive about the nature of any future nuclear war. They are also not so obtuse as to miss completely the impact their facade of obtuseness has made on the U.S. strategic debate in the last years of the Carter administration and in the time since Ronald Reagan was elected president. It is from this awareness that any hope may emerge that the strategic dialogue necessary for a mutual recognition of mutual assured destruction will finally be completed.

The Soviets have only a few more crucial steps to take. Footnoted by a frank acknowledgment that hawkish U.S. commentators had fastened on shortcomings in earlier Soviet doctrine, several of these Soviet logical concessions began to emerge in 1981, in Leonid Brezhnev's last year. The outside world of military analysts will watch now to see whether such a process of strategic convergence can be continued and completed under the regime of Mikhail Gorbachev, succeeding after the interims of Andropov and Chernenko.

Gorbachev has begun by showing signs of wanting to hew to a number of new courses, at least for Soviet domestic policy. He perhaps will also want to call a spade a spade with regard to nuclear deterrence. Nevertheless there will still be powerful forces in the Soviet Union intent on retaining some of the obtuseness of the older postures, still touting the virtues of seeking victory after the capitalists have allegedly begun a World War III, still asserting that their highest duty would be to strike the weapons from the hands of the capitalist enemy and to protect the motherland against any and all forms of destruction. Such strategies do not only produce higher defense budgets in the West; they also no doubt enhance such defense spending in the Soviet Union, perhaps in response to the augmentations provoked in the West.

One can illustrate the more hopeful trend, but also its limitations to date, with several news releases from the Soviet side late in 1981, at the beginning of Brezhnev's final year in office. The releases included a highly publicized "press conference" with questions posed by *Pravda* to the Communist leader for his answer[12] and a widely distributed follow-up booklet, entitled *The Threat to Europe*. Aware of the importance U.S. and other Western strategic analysts had been attaching to the Soviet failure to renounce all interest in war-fighting options or in the difference between victory and defeat in a nuclear war, the Soviet statements in this booklet stressed repeatedly that the USSR would never initiate a nuclear war, would never launch a preemptive or preventive type of attack.

> Soviet military doctrine is of a purely defensive nature. "We never had and never will have any strategic doctrine other than a defensive one," says the declaration of the Warsaw Treaty states of 15 May 1980. It does not admit of either a first or pre-emptive strike or of any "lightning" invasion of Western Europe. In so doing it follows definite political, ethical and military principles. There is no aggressive element in Soviet military doctrine because the Soviet Union has no political, economic, social or military aims in Europe or anywhere else that it intends to secure by armed force.[13]

While never unwelcome, this kind of Soviet pledge is also never fully satisfying, since aggressors in this century have rarely admitted that they had begun a war. Hitler's advance on Warsaw came after the Poles had allegedly attacked Germany, and Kim Il Sung's push toward Pusan in 1950 came after a Communist claim that South Korea had attacked North Korea. If the Soviets were never to launch an attack on the United States during the alleged "window of vulnerability," Moscow would surely claim that the capitalist world had begun the war.

Much more necessary, much more forthcoming, would be Soviet statements suggesting that, even if the USSR were heroically defending itself against a capitalist U.S. aggression, victory would be meaningless; that is, that even where Moscow still claimed the legitimacy of self-defense, it would not translate this argument into the prerogative of looking for a "victory." The Soviet *Threat to Europe* pamphlet came closer to making this kind of statement than have Soviet statements in the past, at least by indirection, as when it quoted a retired U.S. admiral of liberal persuasion who had (like many Americans) noted the same pointlessness of victory:

> In this sense, we see eye to eye with Rear Admiral Gene La Rocque, Director of the US Centre for Defense Information, who says neither side could eventually consider itself a victor in the event of a major nuclear war between the USSR and the USA. More than a hundred million people would perish on either side, and up to three-quarters of the two countries' economic potentials would be destroyed.[14]

The *Threat to Europe* booklet is then more forthcoming than the Soviet leader it quotes, again neatly displaying the tensions and gaps that have been discussed here. After conceding Western dissatisfactions with Soviet doctrine, the booklet itself concedes that there will be no victor in a nuclear war:

> QUESTION. *Can a nuclear war be considered winnable?*
> ANSWER. Western political and military writers contend that Soviet military doctrine is based exclusively on the belief that a world nuclear war can be won. But that is a simplistic and distorted view of our approach. In fact, the Soviet Union holds that nuclear war would be a universal disaster, and that it would most probably mean the end of civilisation. It may lead to the destruction of all humankind. There may be no victor in such a war, and it can solve no political problems. As Leonid Brezhnev pointed out in his reply to a *Pravda* correspondent on 21 October 1981, "anyone who starts a nuclear war in the hope of winning it has thereby decided to commit suicide. Whatever strength the attacker may have and whatever method of starting a nuclear war he may choose, he will not achieve his aims. Retaliation is unavoidable. That is our essential point of view."[15]

But the Brezhnev quote cited immediately thereafter says only that "anyone who starts a nuclear war" will have committed suicide. Since the Soviet view of events and history is always that the United States will be the initiator of a war, this statement amounts to less of a concession, since the USSR "defensively" will be imposing unavoidable retaliation, with such "retaliation" in the past often enough amounting to a pursuit of "victory."

These Soviet statements are interestingly forthcoming in noting that adequate concessions have not always been offered in the past; that is, that some change of the professed Soviet strategic doctrine must be called for, as part of taking the steam out of the arms race.

> Q. Why then do Soviet theoretical works on military strategy of, say, the early 60's refer to offensive action, to building up a military advantage? Doesn't this prove that Soviet military strategy reposes on these principles even today?
>
> A. No. it proves no such thing. Soviet military strategy is neither immutable nor everlasting. It changes with the changing world. The same happens in the United States, where the strategy of flexible response and thereupon that of realistic deterrence replaced a doctrine of massive retaliation. Soviet theoretical works of the early 60's reflected the views of their time. And it was a time when the United States commanded a considerable nuclear-missile advantage, when it threatened the Soviet Union with massive nuclear strikes and declared that a nuclear war against the USSR was winnable.[16]

Still missing, of course, is the fullest acknowledgment of mutual assured destruction, a statement that it is actually in the Soviet interest to have the United States assured of a capability of attacking and destroying Soviet cities. Will the Soviets ever publish an analysis like that of Morgenstern or of McNamara? When they do, we will at last be able to lay to rest the myth that the Soviet leadership does not understand how bad nuclear war is; we will also be able to lay to rest the military tradition that the professional soldier must first and foremost try to put his opposite number out of business.

Some Conclusions

What should be the more general conclusions here? First, a counterforce emphasis on striking at the enemy's military forces rather than at any other targets, especially purely civilian targets, has deep roots in the past for Americans, and for Russians, and for virtually all the military forces of the world, because of all the natural explanations cited.

Second, such an emphasis is totally outmoded, and is indeed dangerous in the light of the development since 1945 of weapons with the potential for retaliatory mass destruction, the weapons upon which world peace has largely depended since the 1950s, the weapons that one side might use if an adversary seemed about to be able to eliminate them in some kind of counterforce attack. What must be avoided for the future are any confrontations of weaponry, and confrontations of strategic philosophy, which put either side into a "use them or lose them" situation, with regard to such weapons of mass destruction.

Third, the Soviets have done less than their share of acknowledging this shift in reality, causing some in the United States to worry that Moscow does not see this reality and causing others to question whether this is indeed reality. Americans have changed their minds repeatedly about accepting the need for both sides to have assured second-strike means of inflicting retaliatory destruction. The United States is moving away from such acknowledgment for the moment, partly because of a Soviet obtuseness that seems to impose on the West all the burdens and disadvantages of facing up to this new reality. Any movement away from the new reality, back toward the old traditional emphasis on disarming the opposing air force or navy, and so forth, is undesirable. Any failure to acknowledge the new reality is similarly undesirable.

Fourth, there is hope that the Soviets can be brought around to accepting the realities and desirabilities of mutual assured destruction. If their failure to accept MAD in their public statements explains some of the recent U.S. commitments to weapons like the MX and Pershing II, Moscow is now encountering the price of its own disingenuousness. One hopes that the Soviets can muster up a franker discussion of the nature of nuclear deterrence before this price becomes too high.

Notes

1. Alfred Thayer Mahan, *The Influence of Sea Power upon History: 1660–1783,* (1890; reprint, New York: Hill and Wang, 1957), 119, 121.

2. Giulio Douhet, *The Command of the Air* (New York: Coward–McCann, 1942), 24–25.

3. Carl von Clausewitz, *On War,* ed. and trans. Michael Howard and Peter Paret (Princeton: Princeton University Press, 1976), 77.

4. Ibid, 217–218.

5. Sun Tzu, *The Art of War,* trans. Samuel B. Griffith (London: Oxford University Press, 1963), 85.

6. For what this author regards as very balanced views on Soviet thinking, see Dimitri K. Simes, "Deterrence and Coercion in Soviet Policy," *International Security* 5, no. 3 (Winter 1980–81):80–103; Robert Jervis, "Deterrence and Perception," *International Security* 7, no. 3 (Winter 1982–83):3–30; Donald W. Hanson, "Is Soviet Strategic Doctrine Superior?" *International Security* 7, no. 3 (Winter 1982–83):61–83; Stanley Sienkiewicz, "SALT and Soviet Nuclear Doctrine," *International Security* 2, no. 4 (Spring 1978):84–100; John Erickson, "The Soviet View of Deterrence: A General Survey," *Survival 24, no. 6 (November–*December 1982):242–51; and Richard Ned Lebow, "Misconceptions in American Strategic Assessment," *Political Science Quarterly* 97, no. 2 (Summer 1982):187–206.

7. For an illustration of this kind of interpretation of Soviet strategic thinking, see Richard B. Foster, "On Prolonged Nuclear War," *International Security Review* 6, no. 4 (Winter 1981–82):497–518. See also Richard Pipes, "Why the Soviet Union Thinks It Could Fight and Win a Nuclear War," *Commentary* 64, no. 7 (July 1977):21–24; Edward L. Rowny, "The Soviets Are Still Russians," *Survey* 25, no. 2 (Spring 1980):1–9; and Francis P. Hoeber and Amoretta M. Hoeber, "The Soviet View of Deterrence: Who Whom?" *Survey* 25, no. 2 (Spring 1980):17–24.

8. See Donald G. Brennan, "Commentary," *International Security* 3, no. 3 (Winter 1978–79):193–98. Brennan was responding to Raymond L. Garthoff, "Mutual Deterrence and Strategic Arms Limitation in Soviet Policy," *International Security* 3, no. 1 (Summer 1978):112–47, later version reprinted in *Strategic Review* 10, no. 4 (Fall 1982):36–51. See also Richard Pipes, "Soviet Strategic Doctrine: Another View," *Strategic Review* 10, no. 4 (Fall 1982):52–58.

9. Oskar Morgenstern, *The Question of National Defense* New York: Random House, 1959), 75, 76.

10. See Raymond L. Garthoff, "The Death of Stalin and the Birth of Mutual Deterrence," *Survey* 25, no. 2 (Spring 1980):10–16.

11. Robert McNamara, *The Essence of Security* (New York: Harper and Row, 1968), 35–36.

12. As reported in the *New York Times,* 4 November 1981, p. A6.

13. Soviet Committee for European Security and Cooperation, and Scientific Research Council on Peace and Disarmament, *The Threat to Europe* (Moscow: Progress Publishers, 1981), 10–11.

14. Ibid. 9.

15. Ibid.

16. Ibid, 11.

10
Ethnic Targeting: A Bad Idea Whose Time Has Come

The intention of this chapter is quite straightforward. It is to pull to the surface "a bad idea whose time has come" and thus contribute perhaps to containing it. Among the advisors and supporters of Ronald Reagan, and earlier in the Carter administration, and even in the public literature of the last several years, we have seen discussions of a use of nuclear missile accuracy that may get the United States into a great deal of trouble, discussions of an aiming of such missiles specifically at some ethnic groups within the Soviet Union, while seeking to spare others.

The United States will surely have a physical capability to discriminate on such ethnic grounds. Ballistic missiles such as the MX will offer accuracies much greater than any the United States possessed in the past. Even better accuracies will be offered by the new cruise missiles that are to be added to the U.S. arsenal in the 1980s.

Such extreme accuracies have long been worrisome to arms controllers, because they might threaten the survivability of the opposing side's strategic forces and thus in some crisis panic it into "a war nobody wanted." Advocates of the new accurate missile systems have accordingly acknowledged this particular risk and have suggested deployment modes and policy pronouncements to avoid it.

Yet the question has become whether such extreme accuracies can be put to any other use, more beneficially reinforcing U.S. deterrence, while not threatening the USSR with a U.S. first-strike; it is in one of these other suggested uses for such accuracies that we now confront a subject more worrying.

George H. Quester, "Ethnic Targeting: A Bad Idea Whose Time Has Come," *Journal of Strategic Studies* 5, no. 2 (June 1982):228–35. Reprinted with permission.

Ethnic Targeting

The logical basis for a U.S. ethnic-targeting strategy is not so difficult to spell out. The Soviet leaders are presumed to be concerned mainly (or only) about power. They would launch a war if they could thereby enhance their power, but will abstain from aggression whenever the prospect is rather that such aggression would lead to a rebuff constricting Kremlin power.

To deter Soviet attack, the United States must thus aim its forces so that it in the end would take power away from prospective aggressors, so that they will choose to abstain from aggression. Destroying their tanks is one way to do this and destroying their factories (or their leadership's bomb shelters) is another, but what if neither would suffice to ensure that aggression would be a net loss in terms of the Kremlin's power lust?

The proposals advanced for targeting new missiles thus shift to ethnic considerations. The Soviet Union is in many ways a continuation of the old Russian Empire, especially in the way that Great Russians continue to dominate the non-Russian nationalities in the day-to-day exercise of political power. Power (to repeat) is what the Soviet leadership is assumed to crave; ethnic bias is an important tool in that holding of power, just as it has been in the past.

Why not then convey the message to the Kremlin's Great Russian oligarchy that any future nuclear war would kill mostly their ethnic kinsmen, while tending to spare the non-Russians, so that the ethnic balance would be tipped to undermine this oligarchy's grip on its domain? Looking ahead to any such war, the Kremlin would encounter an early and stark version of the demographic change that is already in the cards on the basis of birthrates alone—relatively fewer Great Russians, relatively more Uzbeks and Kazakhs.

The accuracies of new missiles allow the practice of such a targeting option that even would have been thinkable in the old days, but smaller warheads can be used and can be aimed more precisely. One could, for example, leave relatively untouched the older cities of the Baltic Republics of Latvia, Lithuania, and Estonia (in which the local nationalities still tend to predominate), while systematically destroying the newer suburbs inhabited more heavily by Great Russians. One could exempt the Asiatic sections, while hitting European Russia. One could exempt the Ukraine and White Russia, while directing most of the attack at the Great Russian nationality from which the Politburo leadership itself has been drawn, the nationality that allegedly is a primary agent of this leadership's grip on power.

Colin Gray hints at such a strategy in his 1979 article entitled "The Case for a Theory of Victory":

> More to the point perhaps, identification of the demise of the Soviet state as the maximum ambition for our military activity, encourages us to attempt to seek out points of high leverage within that system. For examples, we begin to take serious policy note of the facts that:
> —The Soviet peoples as a whole have no self-evident affection for, as opposed to toleration of, their political system or their individual political leaders.
> —The Soviet Union, quite literally, is a colonial empire—loved by none of its non Great Russian minority peoples.[1]

Considerably more explicit is Richard B. Foster in a 1978 report of the Stanford Research Institute:

> The Great Russian nation is Slavic, with a history of Pan-Slavism. Great Russia is the centre of gravity of the USSR empire. The "liberation" element of a U.S. political targeting concept is in part concerned with breaking up the Soviet empire. In this concept the non-Russian republics in the USSR as well as Eastern European nations would be spared collateral damage insofar as possible with very careful targeting of military forces and bases.[2]

Equally explicit is the suggestion by Bernard Albert in a 1976 *Orbis* article titled "Constructive Counterpower":

> The purpose of the suggested attack would not be to stimulate a popular revolt, but only to encourage the local communist leadership to refrain from active cooperation with the central government in its own self-interest. In return, the United States would attack only the Soviet control apparatus and refrain from any destruction of Ukrainian values. An attack structured to damage Great Russia but not the nationality states poses an extreme threat to the central leadership, for should the war be protracted, the Ukraine might emerge as the strongest post-conflict state.[3]

The Carter administration's changes in targeting doctrine, leaked to the press in the summer of 1980, involved only a partial move in this direction. The list of targets facilitated by the new accuracies and options, as installed in Presidential Directive 59, apparently included Soviet military forces, the factories key to any early Soviet economic recovery, and the concrete bomb shelters reserved for the Soviet leadership.[4] The list was justified using arguments very much like those noted above, that the Soviet leadership will have to be deterred in kind, deterred by the prospects of defeat, rather than by the simple punishment of all of its people.

The Presidential Directive issued by Carter thus did not venture into the more dangerous terrain of ethnic targeting, but the risk of such a move is all too great, because the power-oriented perception of Soviet motivations applies, because the enhanced accuracies of new missiles also make ethnic targeting an "option." The rumblings about this kind of option are to be heard now in Washington, and, as has been noted, such suggestions are not impossible to find in print.

At times the expectation of greater casualties among Great Russians is merely extrapolated from the fact that most Soviet missile silos are located in the Russian Soviet Federated Socialist Republic (RSFSR), so that U.S. warheads directed at silos (to keep them from being reloaded to fire additional rounds at the United States) would inevitably impose additional collateral damage on the people around them. But if the ethnic differential in Soviet casualties in a nuclear war were thus more incidental than deliberate, it might still be a mistake for U.S. planners to be welcoming it.

The Inevitable Minimum

As with the "strategy" that is attached to any other weapons system, doubts may arise about how seriously to take such discussions. As greater accuracies accrue as the simple fruits of technology, could we merely be seeing the justification of such new capabilities by their project managers? Do policymakers have to find a use for accuracy, in both the cruise missile and the MX, because the taxpayer might otherwise decide that his money was being wasted (or because these accurate missiles might otherwise be seen as nothing but a counterforce instrument directed at Soviet missile silos, that is, as unambiguously menacing and destabilizing)?

But it could just as well be that these are serious and worthwhile targeting options, approaches strategists would have wanted to consider a long time ago if only the means had been there to exercise such fine choice with such high accuracy. Most Americans might indeed prefer to punish only a portion of the adversary's population, rather than punishing all of it, if only the guilty could be distinguished from the innocent. Those who take Soviet strategic pronouncements very seriously might similarly decide that the United States in fact has a deterrence gap if it continues to rely only on the blunderbuss approaches of mutual assured destruction. What if the Soviets are serious (rather than just bluffing) when they state that they care more about other things than about the destruction of their cities?

It must be noted that some of such ethnic discrimination in targeting is natural and inevitable and has been in effect all through the nuclear age. When speaking of the 'assured destruction' of the Soviet Union and its cities, were U.S. strategists determined also to assure the destruction of Budapest (the heroes of 1956) or Prague (the heroes of 1968) or Warsaw (the kinsmen of the pope and of many Americans)? Of course not. Viewing Eastern Europe as a set of captive nations involuntarily under the control of Moscow, the United States might have felt driven to use some nuclear warheads against troop concentrations and related targets within these nations, but would have genuinely tried to avoid imposing collateral damage on the civilians surrounding such targets. The mutual assured destruction targeting philosophy would conversely indeed have welcomed such collateral damage within the Soviet Union and would have moved directly to striking at the hearts of cities.

Exempting Poland, Hungary, and Czechoslovakia from attack, to exempt Lithuania, Latvia, and Estonia might only be a small step, since the U.S. government has never legally recognized the incorporation of these countries into the USSR, since these also are, therefore, "captive nations." But this is the beginning of a slippery slope, for the differentiation of these three "Soviet Socialist Republics," along with the Eastern European "independent states" of the Warsaw Pact, could then slide into further differentiation in favor of other SSRs. Since these "republics" are demarcated on ethnic grounds, the precedent and invitation for ethnic targeting is already in place.

(As a historical aside, the U.S. Army Air Force did practice some amount of ethnic discrimination in targeting during World War II. Prague was never bombed, while Dresden was flattened.)

If the average American can thus discriminate between a Pole and a Russian or a Latvian and a Russian, the next step might be for him to discriminate between an Uzbek (if he has ever heard of an Uzbek) and a Russian, or an Ukrainian and a Russian. These people too can arguably be thought of as living in captive nations, governed against their ethnic or ideological preferences. These nations can also be seen as the power possessions of the Great Russian imperialists, people whose demographic expansion vis-à-vis the Great Russians would threaten the very power the Muscovites are alleged to crave.

The suggestions of ethnic targeting put forward recently are thus not so novel or strange or without precedent. It is precisely because they have some logical precedent and some plausible logic that they are in danger of winning a wider acceptance and a wider declaration and application. Yet the general point of this article is that such thinking should be reined in and contained, that its further elaboration and extension would hurt, rather than help, U.S. interests.

The Costs

What are the likely costs for the United States of any continued slide into the logic of ethnic targeting? There are costs in world image and in possible Soviet retaliation.

We are in fact discussing genocide as a substitute for massive retaliation. Even if genocide were indeed to produce fewer fatalities than old-fashioned massive retaliation, its sheer cold-blooded deliberation is likely to offend the moral sensitivities of much of the world, of our allies as well as of the neutrals.

As a retaliation against Soviet aggression, it would be one thing if U.S. missiles could be so pinpointed as to kill only 1000 or so of the most guilty Soviet leaders (or even the 140,000 Communist leaders sometimes suggested now as another target for U.S. pinpoint accuracy). If very few innocent other Russians were killed, the world might come to see such U.S. military planning as just and morally appropriate, somewhat analogous to the execution of Nazi leaders after the Nuremburg trial.

But aiming at millions of Great Russians, only because of their ethnicity (because they are given preferential treatment in promotions to positions of power in the USSR and thus may serve as part of the conspiracy that holds onto such power), would strike Europeans as behavior more typical of the defendants than of the prosecution at Nuremburg. It is genocide to choose to kill, or not to kill, simply on the basis of the likely language of the victim, rather than hitting him incidentally as part of the general assault on the nation.

A second kind of cost in any such U.S. trend is that the Soviets will also have accurate missiles and could soon enough contemplate some ethnic targeting of their own. Indeed, one might have expected some such Soviet target choice to have been made already, just as a similar choice was somewhat inevitable in the U.S. comparisons of Moscow and Prague.

Soviet propaganda has always depicted black and Spanish-speaking Americans as downtrodden groups, as victims of the capitalist system. Could Soviet missiles (especially the newer ones, which will be so much more accurate) in any future war really be targeted without some consideration of these factors? The Soviet Union might well offer Mexico neutrality and exemption from attack in any World War III in exchange for whatever benefits Mexico might deliver in the postwar recovery period. Would it not make sense to offer the Mexican government some similar exemption for the ethnic Mexicans within the United States, many of whom are indeed legally still nationals of Mexico?

Just as in U.S. planning, some of such Soviet thinking has to be inevitable. Yet the tone of international politics will be considerably worsened if such thinking is elevated and amplified on both sides. Will Soviet discussion take place in the future on how nuclear warheads are carefully aimed at Scarsdale and not at Harlem, at the San Fernando Valley and not at the Spanish-speaking sections of East Los Angeles? The world thinks of such scenarios as sick, but sicknesses have been contagious in the past.

The Sources: Missile Accuracy and Soviet Doctrine

If one wished to identify the root causes of this line of reasoning, it would be a mistake to direct criticisms at individual strategic analysts reaching logical conclusions here. Rather, the sources of the difficulty are in the technology of high missile accuracy and (even more) in the gamesmanship of the Soviet strategic adversary.

It is always necessary to aim at targets about which the Soviet leadership is certain to care, for deterrence otherwise cannot be assumed. Many Americans might have assumed that the mere destruction of the cities of the USSR would suffice as a deterrent, but the classic difficulty is that Soviet pronouncements still pretend to be intent on victory in any future war (although always claiming that it would be the capitalist countries that had started such a war). Political power would be theirs in the end, as a matter of victory and conquest, and it is never admitted that the destruction of Moscow and Leningrad would be too great a price for this, that their destruction would have made all of this a net loss for the Soviets.

Soviet obtuseness thus keeps alive the debate about what is an adequate deterrent for shielding North America and Western Europe. If the Soviets will not clearly admit that they regard the normal costs of a nuclear war as outweighing any prospects of military victory and political power, then some analysts will naturally conclude that more deterrent is needed. Most particularly, such U.S. strategists conclude that the deterrent must come in the very same measure and category as the presumable goals of any Soviet aggression in the first place.

Thus we cannot assume that a minus in category A will outweigh the Soviet prospects of gain in category B. Rather, to be sure of deterring Soviet attack, it is argued that the United States must apply its forces to inflict a minus in category B itself. Since it is power that the Communist leaders would be seeking rather than the welfare of the Soviet population, U.S. strategists must apply the accuracies of new U.S. missiles in order to make it likely that any aggression on their part would lead to a *loss* rather than gain in power. And here, of course, is the premise for ethnic targeting.

Some Conclusions

Mutual assured destruction is surely already "sick," in that the two nuclear superpowers have deterred each other from initiating wars by the threat of killing millions of each other's people. Yet the philosophy of ethnic targeting will strike most observers as sicker, forcing those who are aimed at, in either country, to resent the ethnicity of those who are exempted from punishment. How are the Great Russians of the USSR to respond to the U.S. policy of sparing Lithuanians from attack? Should they program a few warheads of their own against this republic, just to restore the demographic balance that the U.S. attack had upset? Are differing ethnic groups in the United States going to attack each other, to deny the USSR any ultimate say in who survives and who dies in a thermonuclear war?

The advantage of mutual assured destruction was that it still typically pretended to inflict "collateral damage," or "bonus damage," as part of a necessarily blunderbuss attack on the enemy's war-fighting ability. While many academic strategists long ago concluded that the real objective of any nuclear force was precisely mass homicide, the official statements of each side never had to admit this, but could always still pretend that military targets were being aimed at, with civilians suffering only incidentally in the process. Countries were thus to be attacked all at once, sharing in the miseries of this prospect together.

The choices offered by new guidance systems perhaps made it inevitable that such hypocrisy would end. If the United States now has to admit that it will be killing people because it wants to (since such killings could have been avoided by pinpointing military targets), the nation also now gets drawn into discussions of who it wants to kill.

The accuracies of new ballistic and cruise missile systems surely are the basic source of the problem here. Where the CEP (Circular Error Probable—the circle around the intended target within which half of one's warheads will fall) was once more like a half-mile, in the future it promises to be in the hundreds of feet. Such accuracy poses a counter-force threat of first-strike attack, since a warhead falling this close to an underground silo is very likely to destroy the missile inside that silo. It also poses all the other options, and other problems, we are discussing here.

What was true for U.S. nuclear targeting must thus be true for the Soviet side as well. The ability to aim nuclear warheads so precisely inevitably raises the question of how such an ability to discriminate will be used. The greatest fear currently, of course, is that the new accuracies of Soviet missiles may be directed at the land-based missile silos of the Minuteman and Titan (and then also at the silos of the MX). As part of making the scenario for such a partial Soviet counter-force strike plausible (the U.S. submarine-based missile force would presumably still escape attack), it is sometimes projected that the Soviets would carefully aim to avoid, as much as possible, imposing casualties on American civilians. Such a "surgically clean" use of nuclear warheads is one use to which the Soviet capabilities might be put. Another use, however, would be to try to kill some Americans while leaving others alive.

It does not take a particularly destructive imagination to come up with many of these uses, for simple technological development of today's superb accuracies would almost inevitably pull imaginations in this direction, in speculations about what the adversary might do and about what one's own forces can do. The ability to stamp out *all* of such speculation is simply not there. The task is rather to contain such speculation lest it somehow take on a life of its own, markedly poisoning all possibilities of détente between the superpowers, perhaps greatly weakening the U.S. image abroad.

Rather than differentiating among the USSR's nationalities, a more typical American attitude in the past was that Great Russians resented Soviet dictatorship just as much as did Ukrainians or Moldavians, that these all were people to be identified with (and indeed liberated, if this could ever be accomplished without a recourse to the devastation of war). A genuine Marxist analysis would similarly not have differentiated among the ethnic groups of the United States, but would rather look forward to giving all of them, black and white alike, the benefits of "socialism." It would be healthier for the balance between the two superpowers if targeting analysis were held back at this less discriminating level. It would be healthier also for the image and interests of the United States.

Notes

1. Colin S. Gray, "Nuclear Strategy: The Case for a Theory of Victory," *International Security* 4, no. 1 (Summer 1979):68.

2. Richard B. Foster, *The Soviet Concept of National Entity Survival* (Arlington, Va.: SRI International, 1978), 62.

3. Bernard S. Albert, "Constructive Counterpower," *Orbis* 19, no. 2 (Summer 1976):362.

4. William Beecher, "U.S. Drafts New N-war Strategy vs. Soviets," *Boston Globe,* 27 July 1980, p. 1; and Richard Burt, "New Nuclear Strategy: An Inevitable Shift," *New York Times,* 7 August 1980, p. 3.

11
Accelerated Warfare versus Constant-Speed Human Beings: A Threat to Peace?

The War of 1812 was ended by a peace treaty signed at Ghent on Christmas Eve, 1814. Yet the last battle of the war was fought at New Orleans two weeks later in January of 1815, as Andrew Jackson's motley collection of soldiers and frontiersmen beat off General Packenham's seasoned veterans of the Peninsula Campaign against Napoleon. The news that a peace had been negotiated could simply not reach either side in enough time to head off this one last battle.[1]

C.S. Forester's fictional Capt. Horatio Hornblower underwent an embarrassing experience (this must have had many real-life equivalents) when he was despatched to the Pacific on a mission off the west coast of Central America.[2] Having been given his orders when Spain was still officially an ally of Napoleon, he with great skill and enterprise sank an important Spanish ship; he was then to discover, upon being reached by the next despatch boat, that Spain had in the meantime switched sides to become a British ally against Napoleon, and Hornblower's career may have been damaged because of his having been so unlucky as to sink a ship for the wrong side.

If in the past slowness of communication sometimes tragically caused it to take months to stop a war or to notify a warship that someone had changed sides, it also might ("happily"?) have sometimes taken the same months to start a war, that is, to notify the two sides out in the field that they should begin shooting at each other. The satirical French antiwar film, *Black and White in Color,* depicts such a situation as late as 1915, as the border between a French African and a

German African colony only very late receives the news that the mother countries are at war. This situation is easy enough to imagine before the widespread use of radios but is virtually impossible to imagine today.

Wars can thus begin, or they can end. Alliances can switch in the middle of wars; that is, war can end between one pair of players and begin between another pair. Which way would one wish to instruct his remote forces to lean, given the risk that news might be slow in coming from home? If one distant outpost received its despatches before the other, it would hold the advantage in a "news from home gap," knowing before anyone else that a war was on, or off, or that alliances had shifted. Under such conditions, should one instruct distant forces "when in doubt, shoot"? But so simple a compensation for the slowness of message delivery would not have worked, for frontier outposts might then have been constantly at war, even when the European mother countries were at peace. And, as the Hornblower example illustrates, the follow-on question in a multipower world would have been "shoot at whom?" since tomorrow's possible enemy could also have been tomorrow's possible ally.

The reader should not conclude, of course, that communications and weapons impact have in every situation been slow in the past. For the commander immediately on the scene, the process of battlefield C^{3}I (command, control, communication, and intelligence) might already have been immediate and "real-time" in 1805, deducting only for the garblings and distortions that emerged in the "fog of war." The duration of some of the most important battles of history has also not been prolonged, with Trafalgar consuming perhaps six hours and Waterloo eight or nine.[3]

Whatever drawbacks and moderation were imposed by slow communications in an earlier time were instead the result of the enormous geographic extension of imperial activity, as the British, Dutch, Portuguese, Spanish, and French fleets circled the globe, once Columbus had so conclusively demonstrated that the world was not flat. One could always make up for the slowness of communication by delegating authority (just as one can make up today for an overtaxing of central decision-making capacity), but such delegations of authority always also risked a loss of imperial cohesion. Would one really wish to trust Captain Hornblower to decide which nation's ships to attack in the Pacific or to trust colonial governors whether they should be at war with their neighbors?

Such historical slowness of communication seems bizarre today, when the risk is rather that messages will flow with enormous rapidity, in enormous volume. Today, one indeed often speculates about real-time surveillance of the battlefield, as commanders on each side will not have to *wait* for reports, but can watch their forces being deployed and being destroyed. Since communications are arriving with great rapidity, answers and orders will perhaps have to be rendered with equal rapidity, placing a very different strain on the Horatio Hornblowers of the future.

Much of what will be discussed in this chapter stems from this enormous change in the speed of communications. The changing strains this will impose on human decisionmakers will be explored, as will the basic logic of time-urgency and time-constraints involved. If communications were *too slow* for optimal decision making at the beginning of the nineteenth century, are they in some sense *too rapid* today? How could communications ever be too rapid to be desirable for human purposes, civilian or military? Was there some point in time, in between, when we would therefore have rated the pace of communications as "just right"? Or if things have never been "just right," could we nonetheless note some "least bad" time between 1800 and the present, a time when the balance of communications capability and a matching human decision-rendering capability was "the best we have seen"? Despite the apparent symmetry, are there some problems in speed of communications very different from those arising from slowness of communications?

Despite the obvious drawbacks of the slow communications processes that prevailed before the development of radio and before the undersea cables were placed, there existed at least one advantage as compared with today's problems, the problems to which we will wish to assign the bulk of the discussion.

When it could take as long as thirty days to get a message to a distant unit of one's military forces, one would never be in quite such a rush to compose and despatch the message. However important it might be that an unnecessary battle be avoided, that the wrong foreign outpost not be attacked, or that an offensive campaign be begun, the fact that months would be consumed in delivering the critical message inevitably inclined the drafter of the message to take a few minutes more in composing it, in considering its wisdom, in reflecting one more time on the appropriateness of the action being ordered.

Compared with the present, the slowness of 1800 thus had the spinoff advantage that the opportunity cost seemed affordably low for a little bit more of reflection and contemplation, for a little less anxiety and panic.

Speed versus Slowness

The initial temptation is thus to conclude that "communications used to be too slow for human purposes; today they are too rapid," but this formulation is quite incomplete in its logic, for the problems of rapid communication are very different from those of slow communication, since the stress is placed on very different parts of the decision-making process. We will have to sort out the logic of a number of measures of speed, and then sort out how these different aspects of the problem interlock.

First of all, we must deal with speed of communications, as has already been discussed in the preceding examples.

We must then deal with speed of weapons impact. Some weapons work almost instantaneously; there is no discernable or usable time-gap between the firing of a bullet and the hitting of the target; this was true in 1800 just as it is today. Other weapons are important for the varying times they consume in getting to their targets, because of the time-lags thus offered for decision making and adjustment, and even for recall or aborting of the action, on either side. Cruise missiles are important because they take longer to reach their targets than do ballistic missiles. Could it be a blessing that they take longer? Could it be that the "superior" (speedier) technology is not so straightforwardly better for the purposes we wish to serve?

We must then connect these measures of speed with speed of decision. We will have to differentiate speeds of decision to shoot, and decisions not to shoot. We will have to sort communications intended to initiate action, and those intended to cancel an action, to terminate an action, or to forbid a military action. At points we may also wander into philosophies of "fail-safe" and "burden of proof," as we wonder whether to predispose any military units in one direction or the other, while minds scramble furiously to reach a decision.

The "last chance to shoot," for fear that the enemy is about to begin shooting, must thus be importantly different from "the last chance to stop the shooting," in terms of the impact we can anticipate and in terms of the kinds of logic and psychology the two situations impose on those making the decisions.

"Haste Makes Waste"

The possibility of overloading foreign-policy decision making, when the sheer urgency of decisions cannot be met by the human beings involved, is not so hypothetical. We have in this century seen several crisis situations in which policies had to be formulated in too great haste to produce satisfaction afterwards, precisely because the interaction of military potential on two sides placed a premium on preemption and rapid action.

A surprise attack cannot per se be blamed on excessively compressed decision time. The attacker can prepare his treacherous attack at leisure, while the unsuspecting victim presumably is feeling far less stress and strain than might be appropriate. But the *prospect* of the possibility of a surprise attack indeed places a great strain on the decisionmaker, exactly the kind of communications overload we are considering here. The choice is over and over again "to mobilize or not to mobilize," "to strike first or to wait and take the chance of being struck," "to preempt lest one be preempted—but perhaps thereby to plunge the world into a war nobody wanted." Mobilization schemes thus put everyone very much on the qui vive, alerted lest the other side mobilize first, lest he attack when one's own side has not yet completed its mobilization. Other "offensive" weapons systems similarly add tension to the policy process, because they favor whoever takes the initiative, whoever lunges forward in a crisis, over whoever has elected to sit still and wait. (If there is any real meaning to "defensive" systems, it would be the reverse, describing weapons that in battle reward whoever chooses to wait and sit still, whoever lets the other side do the attacking.)

The outbreak of World War I is thus plausibly an illustration of presumed offensive advantages affecting the ground force deployments on both sides, with Germany and Austria versus France and Russia feeling locked in a sort of game-theoretical "prisoners' dilemma" situation, in which each side felt that it had to mobilize lest the other side mobilize its reserves, each then feeling that it had to strike before the other had its mobilization completed.[4]

The information reaching Berlin, or Paris or St. Petersburg, was at all points fragmented and uncertain regarding what the other side was doing. Had there been more time to sort it out, had considerations of future war possibilities not placed so much urgency on the decision process, the evidence might well have lent itself to more reassuring interpretations. Because the kaiser and his opposite numbers could not allow themselves a more leisurely analysis of the evidence, however, they were plunged into a hurried process that produced a self-confirming prediction of war and four years of grievous damage to European civilization.

The 1967 war between Egypt and Israel had very similar characteristics, since each side believed that victory might go to whoever got its fighter-bombers into the air first over the other side's airfields, and as a more leisurely analysis of the mixed evidence about adversary intentions became no longer affordable. The result this time was a very short war, with a major Israeli victory, but not the kind of victory that solved Israel's long-term security problems. Very plausibly "a war neither side wanted," it was at least not as prolonged and costly as World War I had been, but it again demonstrates some of the worries we must entertain about the human ability to render decisions in step with an accelerated impact of weapons.

The 1973 Yom Kippur Egyptian surprise attack illustrates the opposite coin of the dilemmas we have been examining. Facing ambiguous evidence about Egyptian plans and the obvious costs of launching a preemptive attack when there might be nothing to preempt, Israel commanders waited longer than they should have, in concluding that an Egyptian attack was actually under way. Any analyst afterward would have to view the Israeli losses suffered thereby as one more warning against waiting too long in ambiguous situations, especially against waiting too long in those military atmospheres in which offensive capabilities exist, when whoever strikes gains some advantage thereby, while waiting in place entails something of a price.

Such real-life examples serve to warn us of a host of future possibilities. As long as each side remains heavily equipped with tanks on the NATO Central Front, or in Korea, or in the Middle East, there may be a continual temptation to strike first in a crisis, with greater burdens thus being imposed on whoever has to make the decision about war or peace. Whenever heavy reliance is placed on reserves or on last-minute deployments from rear areas, a similar kind of pressure for rapid analysis and rapid decision will emerge.

Israel and its Arab neighbors are of course inherently and inevitably plagued by this dependence on mobilization systems, as the Israeli army in wartime includes the majority of its military-age male population, while it must include far fewer in peacetime. NATO's dependence on reserves similarly may increase the tension during a future crisis. "To mobilize or not to mobilize" is a terribly difficult decision to reach and is always a time-urgent decision. Forces in being, forces already in place, by contrast reduce the decision-urgency of the crisis substantially.

Analogous to mobilization decisions, in terms of the burden they place on the communications of a government, is the movement of troops from rear areas by air. Americans are understandably proud of the technological elegance of the arrangements by which troops in North America can be flown on short notice to West Germany: "A division in North Carolina is as good as a division in West Germany."

Yet, by the command, control, and communication (C^3) considerations we are addressing here, a division in place is preferable to a division ready to be moved on short notice into place. An act of moving the troops would logically come only because the Warsaw Pact was moving its troops, but it would also be seen by that Warsaw Pact as a signal that *they* should be moving their troops. The risk of beginning a self-confirming plunge into war would grow, balanced against the risk of being caught by the enemy's surprise attack.

Similar kinds of decision-overload can occur with deployments of troops by the same C-5 aircraft outside of Europe, as "rapid deployment forces" race to beat their opposite numbers into the Persian Gulf or some corner of Africa or Asia. The time-urgent question, on both sides, will again and again be, "Are they moving? Might they beat us?" World War I began as a race to get additional troops up to the Franco-German frontiers. Some other war might be begun as a race to get troops into Kuwait or Tunisia.

Similar kinds of urgency pertain of course to nuclear war scenarios. The decision process for submarine-based ballistic missiles (SLBM) remains nonurgent, almost the model for what one could hope in decisions on everything else that is military. The command and control process for land based ICBMs similarly used to allow for a more leisurely contemplation of choices, with a more careful examination of what the adversary might be up to; but the increased accuracies of ICBMs and cruise missiles—combined with the addition of multiple warheads—may make speed quite significant again for this part of nuclear war, just as it has been all along for the bomber forces, the third leg of the strategic nuclear force "triad."

The enhanced accuracies of missiles now offer nuclear targeters a much wider array of options, allowing for greater discretion in what is hit on the other side and what is not. But, by rendering vulnerable the kinds of missiles that used to be secure under layers of concrete, the same accuracies of missiles have introduced the very kinds of urgency we are condemning here, an urgency that someday may overstrain the decision-making capabilities of the national leaders on each side.

At the extreme, the national leaderships themselves will become the time-urgent target, as the president of the United States must race from the White House to his National Emergency Airborne Command Post (NEACP) aircraft, trying to escape missiles being fired from the Soviet submarines that have moved in close to the Atlantic coast, and thereafter having to evade additional Soviet missile warheads seeking to catch him wherever his aircraft has moved to. What kind of digestion of information, what kind of orderly and sensible response to incoming data, could be expected of a U.S. president, or a Soviet leader, who was being subjected in effect to a major assassination effort in the earliest rounds of a World War III?

Returning to the subject of conventional war, the simple speedup of electronic communications creates more of the kind of opportunities that become burdens. Electronic detection of oncoming enemy aircraft or of advancing enemy armored columns will offer a long series of time-urgent targets, urgent in the sense that they can be destroyed if, and only if, they are immediately fired upon, while the intelligence data is still current and live. Any desire to wait for a visual confirmation of the enemy approach (to check whether it is indeed an enemy approach, or to digest the implications of the approach more fully), will simply cause that side to lose the advantage offered by speedy electronic intelligence gathering. "Shoot first, and ask questions later" becomes all the more attractive, with all the costs and risks this rule has always brought with it.

We look forward to real-time surveillance of battlefields in the future, as the commanders on each side will have a relatively fog-free view of their own troops and the enemy's and thus will be caught less often by surprise. Data about the progress of the armed confrontation will thus move very rapidly, at the speed of electricity and light; the pity is that weapons and troops will be moving rapidly also, albeit not as rapidly. Rather than being able to contemplate the chessboard at leisure, we may be playing a game of chess in which each side is free to keep moving its pieces while the other thinks about its move.

Each of these developments thus places a greater strain on the decision-making process, as signals arrive at a faster pace and must be answered at a faster pace. Each of these developments of course results from the enhancement of weapons systems, as what the military buys for itself for 1980 is more effective in combat than what it purchased in 1960. Whatever the strains on the command and control arrangements, the United States could probably count on beating an enemy relying on 1960 equipment if the United States deploys that of the 1980s; the reverse would also be true.

The question of combat effectiveness, of who will win a war, must thus often be balanced against considerations of time-urgency and commandability, considerations of stability and arms control, considerations of the likelihood of war and the likelihood of escalation. As each side moves from single-warhead missiles to multiple-warhead missiles, from poor accuracies on such missiles to very good accuracies, it presumably deploys more effective weapons; but these are also weapons that much more reward those taking the initiative and making the first strike, and thus place a strain on the decision process on each side. As each side moves to rapid-deployment capabilities for its conventional ground forces, it similarly acquires a capacity for intervention and combat that would have been undreamed of in the past, but that makes it harder to render cool decisions in a crisis.

The choices are not always so tough, of course. There will be periods of technological development in which the next rounds of possible improvements in weaponry are stabilizing, enhancing one's ability to win a war if it comes, but at the same time reducing the incentive on either side to strike first, generally strengthening the defensive, and offering rewards for waiting and sitting still in a crisis. The development of new antitank guided missiles (ATGM) may be an example of this, a weapon of the 1980s outclassing the tanks of the 1960s, but also stabilizing the confrontation by suggesting that each side wait in a crisis, rather than lunging forward.

Weapons and "Prisoners' Dilemma"

The impact of this communications and decision-urgency on the likelihood of warfare changes, quite independently of the degree of political conflict between the sides. Parties that hate each other deeply may still avoid war when the weapons are defensively oriented, when either side would make a fool of itself by moving forward. Parties that dislike each other only slightly might, conversely, plunge into war when the basic tilt is toward the offensive, when whoever moves forward collects great advantages thereby.

We might all thus welcome any swing toward the stabilizing defensive. Yet, as often as not, the logical next step in improving one's military capability will be offense- rather than defense-oriented, and hence will be destabilizing rather than stabilizing. By simply coming into existence, therefore, such new rounds of weapons increase their chances of being used.

Students of military history sometimes scoff at the idea of weapons bringing themselves into use, and there are indeed some more trivial versions of such an accusation that are easier to reject. Do generals and prime ministers often put a weapon into use simply because they are fascinated by the new toy and want to play with it? War is a more serious business than this, and it slanders the men who have made military decisions to accuse them of such a mindless employment of the weapons they have procured. Do the same generals and prime ministers sometimes employ a weapon merely to prove to their legislatures and their general publics that the weapon was a wise investment, that it was not a pointless squandering of tax revenues? This charge may have more bite to it, for the weapon that never comes into practical and effective use is much more likely to be indicted afterwards as a boondoggle and a poor investment, reflecting badly on the judgment of the decisionmakers. Yet even this kind of real concern for the image and professional reputation of military decisionmakers does not account for any great part of our fears of war here. Most legislatures and most publics by now are able to understand that the best of all weapons may be those that serve by never having to be used.

The real worry about weapons bringing themselves into use—about weapons that by their very existence increase the likelihood of war, even without any increase in political hostility between the sides—stems from the command and control burdens we have been discussing throughout this chapter. Weapons that place a premium on striking first come close to plunging the two sides in a political crisis into a game-theoretical "prisoners' dilemma" situation. The conflict is actually not quite prisoners' dilemma, a situation that is altogether too simple in its decision rules, according to which each side *must* strike the other under all circumstances. Rather the conflict looks to each side as if it *might* be prisoners' dilemma. Here, each side would prefer not to attack the other, as long as the other is not attacking, but each side would prefer to attack if the other side had an attack underway. This situation places a tremendous burden on the decisionmakers on each side, since they must continually watch for signals of the other's movements for fear of being preempted by the speed of the other side's treacherous attack, but also for fear of misreading the adversary—of "responding" when there was no attack coming.

Such can be the continual tension of a crisis between peace and war. And, during a limited war, such can be the continual tension as each side contemplates the advantages and the costs of escalation, waiting to see whether the other side is about to escalate its use of weapons, and so on.

Speeding Up Human Beings?

Crises have arisen often enough in the past, and limited wars have been fought in the past. In most of such situations, the decisionmakers had more time to sort out their impressions of the adversary's behavior and felt less urgency about responding. Although there were years in which central authorities were handicapped by a slowness of communications to their own forces, the opposite—rapidity of military weapons effects and military communications—was not the problem.

When speed, rather than slowness, became the problem, as at the outbreak of World War I, the decision process did not bear up so well under the strain. To sound the basic theme of this chapter, the speed of communications has been enormously increased, and the speed of weaponry has been correspondingly increased, but there is little evidence that much progress has been made in accelerating the speed of reliably weighing alternatives by human beings. How much has been added to technology that could make Ronald Reagan function any more quickly than Napoleon, or Frederick the Great, or Julius Caesar?

How indeed could one hope to achieve a speedup here? In a generation that has relied heavily on drugs for getting through daily life, one could envisage the development of "pep pills" and "rationality pills," analogous to the "uppers" and "downers" that seem so much abused today. Some blend of tranquilizer and "pep pill" might presumably have been designed as optimal for inducing faster and still reliable decision-making performance by presidents and generals. Yet most of us would be skeptical about any such reliance on drugs, having noted the unpredictability of the impact of such foreign substances on the performance of people in everyday life. Short of prescribing a cup of coffee for the decisionmaker (but not too much coffee, lest he be made too irritable by the caffeine), we would generally be given these days to prescribing as little medicinal reinforcement as possible. We have become somewhat more skeptical about the wisdom of any reliance on medicine and drugs, retreating to "nature's way," but thereby renouncing whatever passed for progress on this front since the time of Frederick the Great (Frederick presumably had access to coffee).

Moving away from medicinal solutions, what about the application of electronics and computational techniques to speed up human decisions? A great deal can be done here, in rapid digestion of data and in presenting stimulating graphical displays of the choices, problems, and opportunities to be extracted from the data.

To interface between such electronic expediters of decisions and the continuing human makers of decisions will probably have to be mostly visual, with some reliance also on audio signals. Some valuable research thus needs to be done on the kinds of video and audio displays that shorten the time-lags involved, given that there are no other ways of making the connection between data and user. The choices are between digital and analog displays, between black-and-white or color displays, two-dimensional or three-dimensional displays, between use of words or use of warning signals on the audio.[5] There may indeed be a need to subdivide kinds of personalities and kinds of leaders by their receptiveness to different modes of interface here, perhaps even varying by time of day and degree of fatigue or stress.

One cannot yet really imagine moving beyond this point to any direct wiring of a computer to the human decisionmaker, however, in having electrical charges reach his brain in the reverse of an electroencephalograph. Our inherent reliance on sight and sound will slow down the decision process to something still comparable to that of Napoleon. But what if the worldwide battlefield is being swept by weapons and reported by signals far more rapid than those of the Napoleonic wars?

As another way of speeding the necessary human responses in crisis situations, we could of course apply a very old approach: organizing exercises and maneuvers to train leaders for the environment they will be facing if a real war breaks out. While it is always difficult to make the simulation realistic enough, and dangerous to trust any conclusions extracted from such a simulation, something is indeed gained from the experience as a training exercise. The most serious difficulty usually comes in getting national leaders to free the time to take part in such simulations, so that any training goals will actually be achieved.

Apart from exercises and simulations, we can also design other training programs to accelerate high-quality decision processes for any future war situations, analogous to the training any pilot receives for future cockpit emergencies. The analogy is quite instructive. Flying an airplane today surely calls for more rapid responses in emergency situations than did flying an airplane in the 1940s. Computers and visual displays have been used to speed up pilot responses, while drugs are something no air force or airline would rely upon. Training programs, however, are very heavily relied upon.

Our task would thus be to devise a training curriculum for future war leaders in an age of high-speed communications, comparable in its relevance and effectiveness to the training received by pilots of jet aircraft. Yet it may be much more difficult to design such a curriculum for the statesman than for the pilot.

The extreme of preplanning for rapid-decision war situations comes, of course, with contingency planning, with fully orchestrated and prearranged war plans, of which the Schlieffen Plan may be the most famous (or notorious) example. Such elaborate prearrangements (what are called standard operating procedures in other contexts) have the advantage of cutting thought and response time in high-urgency situations, but this comes at a cost in flexibility and adaptability.

Some theorists of cognitive processes might answer that ordinary human responses to choice situations also only amount to prearranged contingency planning, with the difference being that a human mind can hold on file many more distinct contingencies and variations of response than could ever be committed to paper in the manner of traditional war plans. If speed of formulation and response is the problem for future weapons confrontation, the answer is simply to store more such prepared responses, more elaborated war plans and contingency plans, in someone's mind, so that they do not have to be laboriously developed and reassembled when the crisis hits.

If too few humans are capable of such storage in their memory banks, the next step might be to turn not to paper as in the Schlieffen Plan, but to computers. A theorist of cognitive processes might indeed see no qualitative difference between the computer and the mind of a human decisionmaker; the human decisionmaker (to date) has simply been capable of storing a larger array of options, while the computer (already) has proven itself faster at disgorging an option.

Will the time come when strategists trust preprogrammed computers to respond to all the signals of a "real-time communications" battlefield, the signals of adversary intention and deployment, the signals of enemy weapons-use and weapons impact? Will the imminent urgency of decisions and the inability to speed up the human mind sufficiently in response lead strategists to so drastic a step, as all of warfare becomes preprogrammed? The humanist would of course regard this as the ultimate in depravity. And even the strategist will have qualms, if only because computer error has become too much a part of his daily routine.

Slowing Down War

We thus encounter a dead end in any efforts to speed up the ability to respond in a war, so the other choice we must explore is how to slow down warfare, how to reduce the urgency of the decisions demanded of each side. Excessive urgency in decisions can produce undesirable results. And (in a non-zero-sum world) such excessive urgency on one side can also hurt the other.

Let us stress that there is no human need to slow communications or movements down to the pace of 1814. When each side had to distrust its communications ability too much, it sometimes had to give an order to "fight until directed to stop," with the case of the cease-fire order taking more than a month to reach New Orleans.

One can think of only a few examples, for future wars, of communications being too slow for the human purposes we wished to serve. In the Napoleonic age, poor Captain Hornblower might have been sitting in the Pacific beyond the reach of communications speedy enough to switch him away from the target at which he had originally been directed. When first despatching him, the Admiralty knew it was running such a risk, but it preferred to send him out as a nonrecallable missile, rather than having no impact in the Pacific at all.

Similar choices of course have to be made whenever one fires a nonrecallable ballistic or cruise missile today. There was a time when the lack of space and carrying-capacity on such a missile seemed to preclude its being equipped with radio devices for a recall; there being no human beings on board, of course, it had none of the "inherent" advantages of recallability and redirectability still so often touted by the U.S. Air Force for the manned bomber. If technology later made such radio-recall devices small enough to fit into the warheads, the fear remained that an enemy might be able to decode the necessary signals and thus blunt any attack merely by sending out the recall signal itself. As better coding systems develop, some of this objection might also be overcome, with the result that this kind of communications gap might ultimately be closed.

There is also a problem a little further off in the future, analogous again to Hornblower out in the Pacific, that is, the prospect of a future "war in space," fought out by fully automated space platforms that might have to be fired and ordered into action well in advance of any engagement, or else preprogrammed to take action on their own initiative, much as British naval captains were occasionally authorized to do. "War in space" may never happen, but if it does, one advantage may be that it will bring about little or no death and destruction on the Earth. A disadvantage, however, is that such a war may occur some time before it is known about on Earth, and it may take some time for signals to get up from Earth to stop it.

We would rather aspire to a situation in which communications flow along at a leisurely but effective pace and where each side can afford itself the luxury of issuing orders of "when in doubt, do not fire" (rather than that most awful of alternatives: "unless you are clearly directed otherwise, fire").

The submarine-launched ballistic missiles (SLBMs) constituting each side's Strategic Reserve Force (SRF) are in many ways the model of the kind of low-urgency weapons system we would aspire to, capable of being withheld by communication from the national capital and (as long as no breakthroughs occur in antisubmarine warfare—ASW) of waiting for quite a while before coming into use. The proposal has been advanced at times in the past that the urgency of any such use be reduced further by keeping such submarines on both sides deployed out of firing range of their targets, such that days would have to pass before any trigger could ever meaningfully be pulled, forcing each side to ponder still further the course it wished to take in a crisis or in a limited war that had still not escalated to all-out war.

Our ideal, to be precise, would thus be to slow weapons down while keeping communications speedy and clear. "Real-time" surveillance of the battlefield, where the weapons subjected to this surveillance are moving *slowly,* is not a problem for mankind. The problems with speedy communications arise when weapons impact is also rapid and when communications play an instrumental role in making such uses of weapons effective. "Strike while you have the chance" thus translates too soon into "strike while you have him on your scope," and rapid communications then become an amplifier of urgency rather than a dampener of it.

We have already outlined a prescription for the desirable form of weaponry. Broadly, amid some important difficulties of definition, we must favor weapons that could be classed as defensive and avoid those that would more merit the offensive title. We must seek weapons that impose the higher casualties on whoever strikes, and the lower casualties on whoever has been struck, whether the exchange rates involved be missile warheads versus missile warheads, or ships versus ships, or tanks versus tanks.

Straightforward military professionals may regard this approach as a possible distraction from the pursuit of victory. Should anyone sacrifice an increment of battlefield effectiveness, merely because of calculations about exchange rates on offense and defense, merely because of what arms controllers would label as "crisis stability"? Traditional military analysts would welcome a reinforcement for the defensive if, and only if, it worked as a reinforcement for the combat effectiveness of their own forces; they would similarly welcome any reinforcement for the offensive, whenever this strengthened their forces.

Yet the national interest applies not only to winning wars, but to avoiding them in the first place. When a limited war is underway, the national interest includes winning it, but also avoiding the escalations that amount to a disaster for winner as well as loser.

To serve these more complicated purposes, strategists need to guard their leisure in war, and even to guard the other side's leisure. A harried opposing command structure may fight less effectively, but it may also lash out in rash moves that hurt everyone.

Notes

1. The final, unnecessary Battle of New Orleans is described in Francis F. Beirne, *The War of 1812* (New York: E.P. Dutton, 1949), 353–73.

2. C.S. Forester, *Captain Horatio Hornblower* (Boston: Little, Brown, 1939).

3. On the sea battle, see Oliver Warner, *Trafalgar* (New York: Macmillan, 1959). On the land battle, see John Naylor, *Waterloo* (New York: Macmillan, 1960).

4. One of the most readable accounts of the preemptive tensions governing the initiation of World War I is still Barbara Tuchman's *The Guns of August* (New York: Macmillan, 1962).

5. For an earlier discussion of some of these techniques, see Stephen J. Andriole and Gerald W. Hopple, "They're Only Human: Decision-Makers in Command and Control," *Signal* 36, no. 7 (March 1982):45–49.

12

Substituting Conventional for Nuclear Weapons: Some Problems and Some Possibilities

Using conventional warheads instead of nuclear warheads is surely one of the most tested and reliable ways of limiting a war. Ever since the introduction of atomic weapons at the very end of World War II, strategists and laymen have been impressed by how limits could be imposed on war,[1] as some targets are hit and not others, as some weapons are used and not others. The end result of these limitations has been that the worst of all wars, an all-out thermonuclear exchange, is never fought.

It is always debatable whether such limited war is good news or bad news. For the person who in 1945 thought that all future wars would be avoided, because of the damage that was possible when such wars went to the absolute, limited wars are bad news, and the Korean, Vietnam, and other wars have come as an unpleasant surprise. For another person who expected that wars would still occur, but feared that the next such outbreak of fighting would mean the end of mankind, limited war has been good news, since armed conflicts do not have to mean the termination of all communication and cooperation with one's adversary.

In the abstract, this is how the limited war phenomenon might have pleased or disappointed two different Americans in 1945. The same question can be posed as a retrospective exercise for an American student today. Should we lament the existence of nuclear weapons, or should we be glad of these weapons' existence? And should we then lament, or be glad of, the possibility of limited war? Compared with

George H. Quester, "Substituting Conventional for Nuclear Weapons," *Ethics* 95, no. 3 (Spring 1985):619–40. Reprinted with permission of the University of Chicago Press.

what was considered a normal volume of warfare during earlier decades of the international system, the years since 1945 have probably seen less of such warfare, since the ominous possibilities of a thermonuclear war have worked to deter some wars that otherwise might have occurred, for example, along the NATO Central Front. Compared with the possibility that *all* war would be deterred, however, the limited wars fought elsewhere around the globe have been a disappointment.

The conventional/nuclear choice is much more real and immediate, of course, for West Germans and West Europeans. Would they not have been exposed to a replay of World War II by now if thermonuclear weapons had not existed? Would not a "limited war" in Europe, if it could be kept from escalating (perhaps through the adoption of some "no-first-use" policy and the withdrawal of nuclear weapons from the potential battlefield area), not basically amount to such a replay of World War II? A replay of World War II would surely be preferable, even for these Europeans, to a first run of World War III. But peace is surely preferable to any such "limited war" replay.

Limits have been based on territorial boundaries, as in Korea where fighting was kept inside the two halves of that country, and not escalated out to sea or north into Manchuria. Limits have been maintained by the use only of surrogates; neither the Soviet Union nor the United States has forces fighting in Angola, for example. Above all, limits have been maintained by observation of a major qualitative distinction, that between conventional and nuclear explosives. While engineers in a nuclear weapons laboratory may take pride in designing nuclear warheads of ever lower yields and perhaps of very low radioactive impact, the distinction between a dynamite explosion and a nuclear explosion has remained something that anyone can notice and that everyone trusts everyone else to notice.

Why Limits?

Whether we regard limited war as good news or bad news, therefore, we might conclude that the conventional/nuclear distinction is of priceless value for the maintenance of limits. Anyone hoping that the use of nuclear weapons could be limited, since some other firebreak would be observed once this one had been crossed, is burdened by having absolutely no practical experience on his side. Since much of the continuation of limits in warfare is based on carrying forward experience (the experience accumulated in the wars that gave a nation some practice), the conventional/nuclear firebreak thus looks all the more formidable.

Yet, before we enshrine this distinction so completely, we ought first to consider what the core logics of limited warfare might be. If the greatest advantage of the conventional/nuclear distinction stems from its simple salience and recognizability, this salient visibility may not be as important for one logic of limitation as for another.

Broadly one can think of at least six distinct arguments for why the sides to a war might avoid hitting certain targets, thus imposing a limited amount of damage on their adversaries even while a war is underway. Four of these arguments originate from the time before the invention of nuclear weapons, thus supporting the traditionalist military strategist who scoffs about whether "limited war" is such a new idea. But two very central arguments are indeed quite new.

The first traditional argument for limits is simply that of morality. The laws of war discourage and forbid the deliberate or unnecessary destruction of civilian targets. Realists about international politics will disparage the strength of this argument, in light of the depradations of World War II. Yet those who believe in an afterlife will feel some trepidation about unnecessary escalations of violence, as will those who fear the reactions of the neutral bystanders here on earth. It was such reactions, of course, that brought the United States in on the side of the British and French in World War I, sealing the defeat of Imperial Germany. If one's submarines sink merchant ships, the Americans become angry. If one's troops shell a cathedral, other neutrals become angry. If one destroys a cathedral, moreover, God may become angry.

A second traditional reason for avoiding hitting cathedrals, for example, and aiming instead at military targets was that the hitting of cathedrals would be a waste of ammunition. If the central aim of one side in a war is to be to disarm the enemy as quickly and effectively as possible (this will not always be the aim, of course), then the application of accuracy might indeed involve sparing some culturally valuable targets on the other side. The purest form of counterforce *can* involve an avoidance of countervalue.

A third traditional argument simply reflected the fact that wars were being fought over territorial spoils, so that it would be folly to destroy the prize in the process of winning it. A military leader might thus spare a cathedral simply because he looked forward to being crowned emperor in it or because he intended to add the cathedral and the province in which it was located to his territory. Frederick the Great's Prussian army, in being sent to seize Silesia from the Austrian Empire and from Maria Theresa, was surely instructed to be careful not to inflict unnecessary damage on what would become an important new portion of the Prussian kingdom.

Related to this matter is a fourth traditional argument for care in aiming one's fire. This argument stemmed from the fact that many of the people around a battlefield might be friendly to one's own side. Perhaps a nation was simply in the process of recovering territories that had been temporarily occupied by a foreign invader. Perhaps that nation had the support of some dissident minorities within the territories of its enemy, or even the support of a majority of the population in the enemy's country. For example, it would have been foolish for U.S. bombers to kill too many Frenchmen or Czechs in the process of air attacks on German military forces in World War II, for doing so would have meant disabling the people Americans love, the soldiers the United States was about to recruit.[2]

All of these arguments are sufficient to support the traditionalist who questions whether limited war is a totally new concept or phenomenon. Yet these arguments are now outweighed by some new considerations, as a result of the tremendous destruction that can be inflicted by the biggest of nuclear weapons and of the vertically dimensional means of delivery that can carry such destruction back to the enemy's targets, even when he has been winning on the immediate battlefield. Two distinctly new arguments for limiting one's attack, for aiming carefully, emerge from this combination of nuclear warheads with bombers and missiles and submarines.

First and foremost, one will avoid destroying an enemy's cathedrals and his cities now because he can always so totally devastate one's own. His cities must remain intact as the hostage by which one persuades him to leave one's own intact, and vice versa. If any thermonuclear attack should befall one's own cities, it is not obvious what would keep his from being attacked, and vice versa. This is a mutual bargaining exchange, by which each side deliberately and consciously foregoes a fair amount of countervalue destruction, even destruction that would not have been ruled out by any of the four traditional reasons for restraint, simply because the other side is practicing similar restraint. Even if the destruction of a city or a cathedral would have made sense in terms of defeating the enemy (perhaps not being anticipated as some prize to be acquired), it may well now be spared. These limits depend very much on being seen as an exchange by both sides. Each side must know that it is getting something in the exchange, that there is a firebreak or a line behind which the other side is staying.

Second, as a crucial ingredient to this kind of limitation process, it is important for each side that the other retain command and control over its forces. To keep one's own cities secure, one must not only keep the other government *desirous* of maintaining restraints, but one must also keep it *able* to maintain restraints. An attack that cripples the ability of the opposing ruler to communicate with his missile commanders might thus be very counterproductive to this goal of limitation.

Advantages of a Conventional Strategy

Since nuclear weapons are ordinarily greater in destructive impact than conventional explosives, we might offhandedly conclude that avoiding their use serves each of the six discrete arguments for limited war that we have listed. Yet there will be instances, as the labors of Los Alamos or Livermore bear fruit, in which a nuclear warhead would be just as free of collateral damage, perhaps even freer.

If the importance of the distinction is to stem from its qualitative salience, its visibility to both the parties to an exchange, then this aspect of the conventional/nuclear firebreak may be most relevant to the fifth argument on the list.

With regard to not wasting ammunition (the second argument) or avoiding the destruction of valuable prizes and the destruction of cherished friends and allies (the third and fourth), or preserving the enemy's command and control (the sixth), what one actually does is considerably more important than the appearance of what one does. If someone could make the case that a nuclear attack would stand a better chance of avoiding collateral damage, then it would be largely counterproductive, for these parts of the war-limitation process, to use conventional warheads instead.

Even with regard to morality (the first argument), what one actually does should be more important than what one is seen to be doing. God and history will discover the truth in any event whether innocent civilians were exposed needlessly to suffering. The neutral gallery of Swedes and Indians and Zambians may be more affected by the appearance of what is happening, of course, so that the substitution of nuclear warheads for conventional, even if it had genuinely saved lives in some elegant and esoteric approach to military targeting, would probably draw their condemnation, perhaps even directing their moral and material support to the adversaries.

We thus see the interaction of two distinct considerations about restraint on weapons used or targets aimed at. One is the assessment of greater versus lesser damage; the other is simply finding some visible line of distinction.

The two considerations may at the moment blend together well for the conventional/nuclear distinction. Yet technology marches along. Later we will consider cases in which the delivery systems originally intended only for nuclear warheads might now have become accurate enough to make attacks (against an intended target) with conventional warheads effective (thus sparing the unintended targets). But the same technology may also offer up some very small nuclear warheads, which perhaps would offer an even more decisive attack on intended targets, again with markedly less unwanted collateral damage. If this option were to become a larger part of the picture in coming decades, our two considerations backing a respect for the conventional/nuclear firebreak would no longer be so strongly reinforcing to each other.

One already can note an incongruity among many of the other lines of restraint that have been observed in the limited wars fought since 1945. For example, bombing was kept south of the Yalu River in the Korean War. This was important to Beijing, Moscow, and Washington as an observable distinction of restraint, but would the total destructiveness in the war really have been greater if the U.S. Air Force had been allowed to use its conventional bombs on both sides of the Yalu? Most of the weapons banned for war may be more destructive and horrible than the ones allowed, but this is hardly an ironclad rule.

Tear gas is forbidden for use in armed combat, while napalm is not. Surely a reversal of the line of distinction here would seem more humane.[3] Vietnamese and Cambodians are allowed to fight against each other with backing from the United States and the Soviet Union, just as these two superpowers use leftists and rightists in El Salvador. Would the local population suffer more or suffer less if these local wars were fought instead by Soviet and U.S. paratroops flown in for the purpose, with the Asians and Central Americans being held in reserve as "weapons imposing too much collateral damage." Most of the wars fought since World War II have been fought on, or over, dry land, with very little warfare (the 1982 South Atlantic War for the Falkland-Malvina Islands being the great exception) being fought on, or over, the high seas. Yet the damage to civilian life in such wars might have been less if exactly the reverse had been the rule (a war fought "all at sea," for instance, might reduce civilian losses even if nuclear weapons were used).

Any limit is better than no limit, where the object is to see that the final escalation to all-out thermonuclear war does not occur.[4] Yet the "any limits" that we use are often only those that we have stumbled into in the past, and then retained and reused as a matter of recognizable custom. We sometimes thus forbid categories of weapons or draw boundaries around battlefields in ways that do not seem to relate very well to calculations of immediate civilian suffering, and this action stems from the larger considerations of grasping for any stopping point whatsoever.

As has been noted, this tension among the considerations underpinning a limitation process has been the least on the conventional/nuclear distinction. Yet, extrapolating from the logic of the other firebreaks observed in war (and then crossed from time to time, as in the sinking of ships in the Falklands war, or the Iraqi use of poison gas against Iran), we must bear the possibilities of such a tension in mind for the nuclear firebreak as well, lest a technology that offers interesting new options suddenly spring some nasty surprises on us. Despite this caveat, it is still likely that the conventional/nuclear distinction will retain its appeal and value as a firebreak for limiting war.

As one surveys the arms control proposals that have captured popular support over the years, one can note an interesting pattern to the proposals for regional limitations. In general, the world's common sense is always that "less is better" in the use of weapons. Where particular regions are demarcated, however, we have seen proposals for nuclear-free zones, whereby nuclear weapons would not be deployed or used within a particular area. And we have seen proposals for disengagement, whereby the conventional forces of the United States and the Soviet Union would not be deployed within a certain area, perhaps amounting to the creation of a buffer zone between the two superpowers.

Clearly, there is more to arms control than simply "less is better." For the sake of symmetry, one could present a parallel proposal for a zone in which *only* nuclear weapons would be deployed, and no conventional weapons. Or one could propose a zone in which only the superpowers had troops, with no local troops deployed. The latter proposal might indeed have some redeeming advantages, on the theory that Moscow and Washington would feel less hot-blooded than local governments and local forces about the future of Lebanon, West Berlin, or the Koreas. Yet it has not ever drawn the world approval that is sometimes accorded to disengagement. And no one has ever proposed a nonconventional weapons zone.

The asymmetry here thus reflects intuitions, intuitions that may accord well with reality, that some kinds of weapons and deployments are qualitatively worse than others. There is thus m⸍ re to a preference for conventional weapons over nuclear than simply the usual sticking to any limitation that could once be gotten into practice. Perhaps the world is simply expressing a simplistic moral reaction in preferring that local forces occupy a territory rather than alien superpower forces, or in preferring conventional weapons deployments and conventional arms races to the nuclear equivalent. But the latter preference still has a great deal of reinforcement in realistic considerations of the damage in any nuclear exchange.

Losses in a Conventional Strategy

If it makes sense to forego using nuclear weapons, as long as the adversary power does so as well, even if both sides are fighting an active war with conventional weapons, we thus have what is also often described as a "no-first-use" policy.[5] Whether or not such a policy has been declared, it has been accepted in practice for all the wars fought since Nagasaki. One central topic of the discussion here is whether such a policy should also cover all the wars that could conceivably be fought. If the United States accepted no first use for Vietnam and is accepting it for Central America, should the nation accept it as well for any wars in Europe, staying below the nuclear/conventional firebreak if fighting were to erupt there just as the United States would in other corners of the world?

Anyone proposing an explicit no-first-use policy for the United States is usually addressing himself specifically to the areas of South Korea, the Persian Gulf, and the NATO Central Front. Other parts of the globe already are governed by a de facto U.S. inclination to avoid the use of nuclear weapons, even if the United States were threatened with a military defeat in the conventional exchange.

What about the territorial integrity of the United States itself? Would Robert McNamara and his associates favor the non-use of nuclear warheads, even if the home areas of the United States were being invaded by Communist ground forces? It is easy for an advocate of no first use to scoff at the question as a pointless academic abstraction. As things stand, the National Guard of each of the states could indeed probably repulse any invasion by the Soviet marine corps, so that "deterrence by denial," the preservation of peace by traditional approaches to military operations, would take care of itself.

But the question is not quite as abstract and unworldly as this. Much can happen in the next two decades, as conventional military balances will remain unpredictable. It is not completely guaranteed that what is happening in Central America will not happen in Mexico as well. People like Robert McNamara could thus answer the hypothetical question in either of two ways, each of which is troublesome. Very simply, in terms of the logic, such people could declare (1) that the United States would never use nuclear weapons first under any circumstances, a morally consistent position, (2) or that the United States should never use nuclear weapons first outside its own borders, a position more consistent with what has normally been imputed to states pursuing their selfish national interests.

Perhaps the United States would never use nuclear weapons first, even if it were about to be totally defeated and occupied by any enemy, with all its cities falling under enemy control. But this answer runs counter to all of what analysts have presumed about the role of nuclear weapons in international politics since 1945, and it has thus far been proffered by only one of the world's nuclear powers, by the Chinese.

Beijing's official policy on the use of the nuclear weapons acquired after 1964 took a new and interesting form in a categorical and explicit endorsement of no first use.[6] Again and again, the Chinese have stated over these two decades that China will never use nuclear weapons unless another country uses them first, even if the contingency posed was a U.S. invasion, or later a Soviet invasion.

But other possessors of nuclear weapons have not exactly followed suit. Moscow recently issued an endorsement of no first use, but it is hardly as categorically or repeatedly put forward as the Chinese statement. France, in the clearest contrast, is very explicit that French nuclear weapons would certainly come into use, even if no one else had used such weapons, if ever any conventional invasion penetrated the boundaries of France itself. If forced to answer the hypothetical question, McNamara and his coauthors might well have to admit that, yes, they would use nuclear weapons if the United States itself was about to be overrun.

This hypothetical ultimate policy of the United States and the less hypothetical policy of France thus pose serious problems for convincing countries like West Germany to accept a shift to a totally conventional defense of Western Europe. Unless McNamara and like-minded people are prepared to go as far as the Chinese, categorically rejecting a use of nuclear weapons even in the direct defense of the United States itself, they will not substantially alter the feelings of those West Europeans who regard a conventional occupation by the Soviets as comparable to a nuclear war. And, unless the French opt to withhold the use of their own nuclear arsenal, as long as the Soviets have not yet used theirs, any U.S. policy of no first use would be undercut by the independent nuclear decisions of one of its allies.

So, there are numerous objections that can be raised to any shift toward conventional warheads and preparations for an exclusively conventional war. Relatively few of such objections will apply to how a war would be fought once it had broken out, for here the ability to limit escalation will almost always be enhanced by having avoided the use or presence of nuclear weapons. More germane are arguments that such weapons' presence in a potential battlefield area, and their potential for use, will work to keep wars from breaking out in the first place. If the Soviets know that an attempt to seize Hamburg by a conventional aggression will lead to the use of nuclear weapons, and probably to uncontrollable escalation, they will not attempt such a seizure.[7]

What we are discussing here might thus amount to a substantial undermining of the logic of extended nuclear deterrence. Investing in substantial efforts to provide for a conventional defense may be a very humane move, but it also telegraphs the message to the other side that the United States is more afraid of nuclear war now, more reluctant to use the prospect of a global disaster to head off aggressions against its allies.

All is well and good if a reliable conventional defense is developed in the process, or if U.S. strategists find sufficient means of punishing aggressions by conventional attack.[8] A surefire tank killer may make it impossible for Soviet tank forces to gain any part of West Germany. Knocking down every bridge in Poland may make it equally impossible for Soviet tank columns to advance. Hitting valued civilian targets inside the USSR might make the Soviets reluctant to continue a conventional advance.

But the patterns of effectiveness in conventional warfare since 1945 have seemed considerably less predictable and stable than the patterns of what would be all-out nuclear war. Thermonuclear weapons look "new" and "revolutionary," but they are now reliably blunt and destructive, as assured destruction continues to be assured. By contrast, the outcomes of tank versus tank battles, or contests pitting precision-guided munitions (PGMs) against tanks, or PGMs against any important military or civilian targets, are highly unpredictable, with each new round of warfare in the Middle East seemingly disproving the conclusions obtained from the previous round.[9]

What if U.S. strategists therefore develop an airtight defense for the NATO Central Front for 1990, allowing the United States once and for all to rely on "deterrence by denial" rather than "deterrence by punishment," allowing it to move all the nuclear warheads out of the prospective combat area, thus markedly reducing the likelihood of escalation if war breaks out? Would the United States not then face the prospect that such defenses would be capable of being circumvented again by 1995, as new technology was brought to bear to favor the Warsaw Pact once more over NATO, or to favor the offense over the defense? What if U.S. strategists uncover very elegant ways to use conventional warheads against targets inside the USSR, and the Soviets then augment their defenses enough to blunt any attack depending on such warheads?

Soviet Responses to a Conventional Limit

One objection to a shift toward conventional weaponry, as part of a no-first-use and nuclear-free-zone arrangement, might be less powerful than many people believe. This objection has to do with an issue of verification. If the United States withdraws its nuclear weapons from South Korea or from the NATO area, how can it be certain, in the absence of extensive on-site inspection, that the Communist adversary has done the same?

The answer can never be air-tight; there might be some occasions (as we shall discuss later) on which the Soviets would wish to escalate to the use of nuclear weapons, perhaps if they were doing very badly in the conventional war.

Yet it is all too plausible that the Soviets would not want to conquer a radioactive Western Europe, but would be interested in capturing this prize because of its future value to their economy (that is, they would feel about Western Europe the same way as Frederick the Great felt about Silesia). If we are correct in drawing this analogy to Silesia, the Soviets would welcome the U.S. decision to shift from nuclear to conventional weapons on the battlefield and would also (without any verification or inspection policy to assure this) find it very much in their own interest to follow suit.[10] The logic of escalation is that the presence of *either* side's nuclear weapons in the battlefield area amounts to a tripwire, making it likely that the conventional/nuclear threshold will be crossed simply in the heat and confusion of battle. Having seen NATO pull its own nuclear weapons back to rear areas to avoid the risks of escalation to all-out war, the Soviets would be very foolhardy to replace NATO tripwire nuclear warheads with their own.

The more serious fear involved in conventional/nuclear decision has all along been that a denuclearized NATO Central Front would be too inviting to a Soviet conventional aggression, offering the prospect of an invasion whereby the Soviets would seize a valuable prize. If conventional weaponry does not offer some new approaches to effective defense, to a "deterrence by denial," in Glenn Snyder's phrase, rather than a "deterrence by punishment," then this fear will remain a serious one. But the prospect of Soviet cheating, in failing to match the Western performance in some shift to a nuclear-free-zone arrangement, does not play much of a role here at all.

Under what circumstances would the Soviets nonetheless want to escalate to the use of nuclear weapons, if the war had so far been fought only conventionally? Under what circumstances would the Soviets wish to pose the *prospect* of such escalation? As with U.S. decisions, these are two distinct questions; though they are easily blurred and confused with each other, they require very separate answers.

To begin with the first question, the Soviets are sometimes conjectured to have devised some very elegant uses of nuclear weapons that would speed their advance to the English channel and preempt the use of whatever nuclear weapons are based in the NATO area, while still avoiding most of the collateral damage that would make Western Europe worthless as a prize, and presumably also avoiding the risks of escalation to all-out nuclear war that would make every prize worthless.[11] If U.S. nuclear weapons had been withdrawn from the NATO area, this preemption mission would presumably be vitiated, but some of the other applications might still apply.

All of this reasoning is very much subject to doubt, however, precisely because of the extreme difficulties all parties have encountered in trying to predict and encompass the damage that nuclear warheads would inflict, and because the first use of nuclear warheads by anyone, anywhere, has such unpredictable consequences in terms of the human communication and calculation of the war limitation process. If the Soviets have any good chance of scoring a victory in Western Europe by the use only of conventional weapons, they would surely be foolish to poison the winds and risk much greater escalation by introducing nuclear weapons merely to speed up this victory.

But what if the Soviets were unable to break through NATO's defenses, having been given a bloody nose in the first rounds of conventional warfare? Having failed to break through, the Soviet forces might find themselves in a stalemated situation, or might be facing the prospect of being pushed back into Eastern Europe, as NATO suddenly became intent on liberating some territories from Communist rule.

Here the two questions become interestingly separated. If merely denied the conquest of Hamburg or Frankfurt, would the Soviets feel driven to escalate to nuclear warfare, with all its possible consequences, rather than suffer a defeat? Probably not, by all we know and have seen of Soviet behavior. Might the USSR wish the West to believe it plausible that such Soviet nuclear escalation could occur, perhaps in the hope of intimidating the West into not mounting an effective conventional resistence? Perhaps yes, although the price of this kind of "extended nuclear deterrence" would be great if it stampeded the NATO command into bringing its nuclear forces back into the theater, or committing them to use.

If denied more than victory, facing the loss of East Germany, Hungary, or Poland, would the Soviets want to escalate to nuclear warfare? More likely the answer is yes, yet all the same doubts have to be voiced here that have been expressed so often about the credibility of a U.S. nuclear escalation, if only Western Europe were being lost. Would the Soviets want the West to sense the *prospect* of such nuclear escalation in such an event? Almost surely they would.

The central hope being explored in this chapter is that new Western applications of conventional warheads might amount to an effective military instrument, substituting for the threat of nuclear escalation, literally substituting for nuclear warheads on the front of some delivery systems. No one can deny the importance of the counterquestion as to whether the Soviets would sit still for this, would match this shift from nuclear to conventional preparations. Yet the question hardly hinges on verification or on commitments to the sanctity of treaties. Rather, the willingness of the Soviets to sit still for a conventional war will be a matter of particular scenarios and will also be a matter of reality versus bluff, or actual practices versus the prospect of practice.

We have been considering at least four kinds of situations or possibilities here, capable of being outlined by the matrix in figure 12–1. Will the United States and NATO keep nuclear weapons in the potential combat zone, yes or no? Will the Soviets use nuclear warheads in any aggression against West Germany, yes or no?

It is often assumed that the Soviets would have to use nuclear weapons in any war if U.S. and other NATO nuclear weapons remain deployed near the combat zone, on the presumption that such nuclear weapons would come into use willy-nilly in any event (this is outcome A in figure 12–1). And the hope of those who favor a withdrawal of NATO nuclear weapons, as part of a shift to conventional options, is that the Soviets would find it to their own interest to follow suit, on the arguments just stated (outcome D).

Skeptics about the advantages of NATO's denuclearizing the battlefield contend that the Soviets might use nuclear weapons (outcome B) even if all U.S. and NATO warheads had been put out to sea or held back in Britain, Spain, and the continental United States. This is where the issue of verification is raised so often.

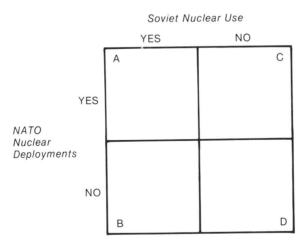

Figure 12–1. **NATO Deployments and Soviet Nuclear Use**

The counterargument is that this possibility is indeed unlikely unless NATO had defended itself so well against the first round of a Soviet conventional attack that the defenders were suddenly advancing into the Ukraine (a very unlikely working out of this contingency, perhaps, but never impossible, given the wide ranges of unpredictability in the outcomes of land warfare and the unpredictable loyalties of all the Eastern European armies allied with the USSR).[12]

Considerably more likely, ahead of this insertion of Soviet nuclear warheads into conventional war, might be a Soviet all-conventional attack even when U.S. nuclear warheads remained in place in West Germany (outcome C), an attempt by Moscow to disarm and disable U.S. nuclear weaponry without using any of its own such weapons, that is, an attempt to win without crossing the nuclear threshold.

We shall now address some special possibilities of substituting conventional warheads for nuclear, in a variety of missions the United States might have to undertake in a variety of wars. But it never should be forgotten that what the United States can do, the Soviets can do as well. This is particularly bad news when the Soviet countermove undoes the benefits of a U.S. move, or when the combination of moves somehow compounds crisis instability, leaving both sides worse off then before.

Such a Soviet matching response is somewhat less bad news when it works to restrain escalation, or reduce crisis instability. That the Soviets might be contemplating a conventional commando-type attack on the nuclear weapons depots of the NATO forces is bad news if it signals a Soviet intention to invade West Germany, or sets up some kind of unstable confrontation in which each side feels better off striking first. But compared to the same Soviet preemptive moves executed by means of nuclear warheads, such planning could still be very good news for a reduced likelihood of destruction in Europe in any future war and a reduced risk of escalation to an all-out World War III.

The Ultimate Substitution

We are certainly not unaccustomed to balancing conventional weapons more generally as alternatives to strategic nuclear weapons. Additional antitank weapons might make additional intercontinental ballistic missiles (ICBMs) unnecessary. A very reliable conventional defense of NATO would eliminate the need for threats of nuclear escalation.

The remainder of this chapter will use this logic in examining the possibilities of a matter discussed less often, the *direct* substitution of conventional warheads for nuclear, a substitution on the very same delivery systems, missile or bomber, perhaps aimed at geographically very much the same targets.

We will begin by digging into the early 1980s debate about new options for strategic nuclear war, often portrayed as "limited nuclear war," and into the technological developments thought to be nourishing the excitement about these options. We will then have a try at translating them into conventional options.

The many possible uses of strategic nuclear weapons have indeed become a lively topic again,[13] in ways that disturb those who regard any liveliness here as a threat to peace, and in ways that may also amuse closer students of the history of strategic planning for such weapons, as some old wheels get reinvented, again and again.

What are the various technological changes that might explain such a rekindling of interest now? One important development is the substitution of multiple warheads for single warheads on ballistic missiles (a technologically elegant way of rendering ineffective any antiballistic missile defenses, but a development basically quite threatening to the stability of missile confrontations).

Another interesting development, also reinforcing the U.S. ability to bypass possible defenses, comes with the cruise missile's ability to fly in at very low altitudes.

Developments of nuclear warheads also continue, but not with quite as spectacular results. Bombs are surely capable of being large enough in the yield, even if the test ban has circumscribed the signatory states from showing them off in public. Nuclear weapons have also been made much smaller in yield (becoming the so-called mininukes), but they would still produce large and very destructive explosions.

Much excitement has been generated about the neutron bomb, also labelled the enhanced-radiation weapon, allegedly a warhead that would kill much more by a flow of deadly neutrons and correspondingly less by blast and heat (although the amount of blast and heat is still hardly negligible). This author would contend, however, that the technological achievement of the neutron bomb is exaggerated by friend and foe alike. If it were as much different from ordinary weapons as it is described as being, a major strategic revolution might indeed have occurred; but it is not that much different.

The impact of all these developments on strategic planning, it is argued here, is considerably less important than the last major change that we must discuss, the technological change that has been the most significant of all: the dramatic increase in possible accuracies.

More than the addition of multiple warheads, more than the introduction of penetration means to bypass the defenses contemplated on either side, more than any new development of nuclear warheads, the achievement of extreme accuracies for ballistic and cruise missiles has gotten the nuclear strategic targeting discussion going again. This accuracy has led a James Schlesinger or a Colin Gray or a Leon Sloss[14] to argue that nuclear weapons can be used to do more than deter by mass destruction, so that other options on the use of the U.S. nuclear arsenal need to be considered, so that targeting debate needs to be reopened. The possibility for surgical strikes and for very effective strikes against difficult-to-hit targets is enlivened much more by the diminution of CEPs (Circular Error Probables) than by any increase or decrease of likely yields on nuclear warheads.

Enhanced accuracies are thus now widely viewed as lifting the nuclear taboo, a taboo that made U.S. strategists plan only for the use of conventional weapons in limited wars, holding nuclears in reserve as a deterrent. Yet there is an interesting paradox about this discussion that will grip us for the remainder of this chapter. If such accuracies are now great enough that they can offer attractive targets for finely tuned nuclear escalation, they may also offer very attractive options for attacking such targets instead with conventional warheads, rendering the possibility of nuclear escalation (with all its pitfalls, risks, and costs) unnecessary again.

The creative targeter may have been frustrated until now by the inaccuracy of missiles, an inaccuracy that would have made any nuclear strike a very destructive and massive countervalue exercise. Yet, if freed to apply his creative ingenuity to the application of mininukes delivered by high-accuracy missiles, he might find even more of an outlet for creativity in planning strikes with conventional warheads.

If the accuracies of ballistic and cruise missiles are now as great as advertised, strategists must surely assign some more thought and speculation to possible uses of such delivery systems with conventional warheads. The advantages of maintaining the nuclear/nonnuclear firebreak remain very great indeed. If the United States were capable of destroying a key power generator in the USSR by using an ordinary dynamite warhead hitting directly on target, would this option not be far more valuable to cultivate for dealing with some of the scenarios of Soviet aggression than the option of using nuclear warheads (which after all are still always held in reserve to be brought to bear later)?

Just as on the battleline itself, where high-quality conventional antitank munitions would substitute for so-called tactical nuclear weapons, such a conventional-for-nuclear substitution might be workable for various kinds of counterforce strikes at Soviet military capability. And the substitution could work also for countervalue strikes, for various kinds of carefully graduated retaliation. Limiting a war has not meant sparing the other side *all* punishment. Rather, it has meant imposing some punishment to put the enemy in the mood to terminate the war, while maintaining a robust list of intact hostages to keep him in the mood to forego all-out escalation.[15]

The general trend in the analysis of deterrence problems since 1977 has been to argue that a U.S. response that is not "rational," that does not serve some purpose other than mere spiteful retaliation, will be too incredible to shield Western Europe. This author thinks that this kind of reasoning is premature and too pessimistic from the standpoint of U.S. interests.

The consequence of this kind of premise has nonetheless been a search for practical war-fighting adaptations for nuclear weapons that rely in part on the miniaturization of nuclear warheads and in larger part on enhanced accuracies for missile-delivery systems. All of this, of course, is quite rightly described as a move to erode the conventional/ nuclear distinction.

Some of the logic of this premise has to be accepted on its face; at least it cannot be brushed aside when so many analysts outside and inside the United States government insist on endorsing it, stating that the United States would be better off if it had options, in the event of a Soviet aggression against Western Europe, that were not simply suicidal escalation. Yet the same technologies that have enlivened thinking about applications of nuclear weapons can be used to stand the problem on its head, to create more interesting applications of conventional warheads, and that approach is what is being explored here.

New Options to Explore

We might begin by contemplating some possible applications of cruise missiles or ballistic missiles, fitted with conventional warheads instead of nuclear, to be used to frustrate Soviet military capabilities, rather than greatly punishing the Russian people.

If the accuracies of the newer cruise missiles are as good as anticipated, they might provide a substantial augmentation of NATO defenses, in a manner not nearly so likely to escalate into World War III. If Soviet armored forces rolled forward, the array of Western cruise missiles would be fired to attack the railway and highway bridges, airports, and fuel dumps, and other logistical targets upon which the Soviet advance depended. The mathematics would be very different from those of an attack on the strategic missile silos back in the USSR. If some large fraction of such tactical targets could be destroyed, it would not help the Soviets very much to know that 30 percent of such targets had survived. A Western attack that destroyed 70 percent of the tactically relevant targets in Poland would be a great success, forcing the Soviets themselves to escalate into the nuclear war that might lead to World War III, or forcing them instead to retreat. Bridges are not so easily rebuilt once they have been destroyed, nor are tunnels. The gauge-change points between the Soviet and East European railways have always looked like inviting targets, and they might indeed be vulnerable to conventional attack as well, if only the CEP can be brought down enough.[16]

There is absolutely no denying that conventional warheads would be somewhat less effective in this situation than nuclear. A conventional warhead might destroy a railroad bridge, but only a nuclear warhead could destroy an entire railway marshalling yard in a single shot. A tunnel on the Trans-Siberian Railway might with good luck be blocked by a conventional warhead, but it would more surely be blocked using the nuclear. Yet there is equally no denying that a reliance on conventional warheads would be far less likely to cause escalation; such a reliance would mean avoiding crossing the most important firebreak of limited war, avoiding the opening of calculations of radioactive fallout, and so forth.

Given the likely increase in the cost of cruise missiles and the likely erection of defensive barriers against them, it might strike many analysts as wildly unrealistic that they should be squandered in the delivery of conventional warheads. When discussing the war scenarios of the European theater, analysts often make reference to a published Soviet military doctrine that seems to assume that nuclear weapons are sure to be used from the very outset of such combat.

Before all this is written off as an idle speculative exercise of professors inclined to abstraction, however, we might simply remember the use of the B-52s in the Vietnam War. Who would ever have predicted in 1961 that this splendid vehicle for delivering the H-bomb to the Soviet Union over ranges of ten-thousand miles would become assigned instead to delivering "iron bombs" of TNT over the short range from Thailand to North and South Vietnam?

Such a use of the B-52 indeed made sense as part of an effort to avoid escalation to more general war and as part of an unsuccessful effort to cripple the Communist advances in the south by attacking the logistical lines from the north that supported them. (Incidentally, such a use made a mockery of the program budgeting Secretary McNamara had introduced in 1961, by which budgetary items were labelled not by the type of weapon purchased, but by the end purpose they were to serve. The B-52 was clearly in the strategic warfare package in any 1961 budget, but its use "in anger" in the end was to come instead in tactical war.)

Like the B-52, the cruise missile in the future might be used at shorter range and with conventional warheads. Also like the B-52, however, it would be impossible to offer an adversary any assurance that such weapons could *only* be used in these modes. Any cruise missile can be stretched in range by readjusting the balance of warhead weight and fuel weight (as well as by adding some auxiliary fuel tanks). One way to reduce warhead weight is of course to go to nuclear warheads, with their tremendous increase in explosive power, and their tremendous strain on the limits to any war. The straightforward arms controller would thus worry about what can verify the inclination to limited use here and what can assure the other side of a less escalating targeting approach.

The reassurance here is not impossible to find. Each side in any limited war must rely not just on predetermined limits to its adversary's weapons and military capacity, but also somewhat on the adversary's good sense. Limited war does not entail being disarmed, so much as holding back the use of the various weapons one indeed has ready. Such mutual recognitions of the opponents' good sense are of course reinforced by what Thomas Schelling identified as the core of tacit communication, the ongoing day-by-day pattern of restraint that implicitly signals an intention to continue restraint.[17] If the first cruise missiles fired in a European war steer for railway bridges in Poland, and strike with conventional rather than nuclear detonations, the Soviet leadership will get a signal that the West has for the moment chosen to try to keep the war nonnuclear. (This of course assumes that the Soviet attackers have also elected to hold back their nuclear weapons, which would be a signal to the West that the Communists as well preferred to remain at the conventional level.) The pattern of where the cruise missiles landed would similarly be a Western signal of what the geographical limits to the exchange were slated to be.

In selling the Soviets, during the SALT II negotiations, on the counting rule for the MIRVing of strategic missiles (the rule by which any missile tested with multiple warheads is assumed to have such warheads), U.S. negotiators may have generated a major logical problem for future strategic situations in which the direction of the imperative is reversed. The Soviets, with a great deal of justice, can contend that every U.S. cruise missile capable of carrying a nuclear warhead must be assumed to be so armed, since the United States, in the absence of verification to the contrary, might obviously find it to its advantage to sneak into the more potent nuclear weaponry. But what if a nation in the future could achieve greater strategic leverage of equipping a dual-capable weapon with a conventional warhead? How does the counting rule function then? Can we even imagine clandestine removals of nuclear warheads from U.S. missiles, as they are given TNT warheads instead?[18]

Using an intercontinental strategic missile, or a long-range cruise missile, with a conventional warhead might still often be labelled an enormous waste of money, at least until some design work is done to ensure that the United States has effective nonnuclear warheads for such vehicles. Breakthroughs in conventional warhead design are never likely to be as spectacular as those on the nuclear side. Nevertheless, some important possibilities are within reach in this area as well. Ordinary conventional explosives have been developed with a higher yield-to-weight ratio, perhaps doubling the explosive power per ton of weight. New modes of driving the warhead into concrete or into other forms of protective armament prior to detonation of the explosive similarly offer greater "kill probabilities," whether the target is an airfield runway, or a bridge, or a railway marshalling yard.

Conventional Targets inside the Soviet Union

Much of the current excitement about new and different uses of *nuclear* warheads is spurred by alleged Soviet inclinations toward war-fighting attitudes, toward the seeking of victory and political power in any future war, and by alleged Soviet preparations for the civil-defense sheltering of Communist party leadership and key workers, or even the evacuation of Soviet cities.[19]

Many of the proposals for Western nuclear responses to such Soviet options founder on the fact that nuclear destruction would be much more difficult to contain and channel than the needs of any careful "surgical strike" would require.[20] The argument is that all this U.S. thinking about careful and effective responses to Soviet civil defense and war-fighting techniques might have a much greater a payoff if it were shifted to the application of *conventional* warheads.

Two very unrelated developments are now likely to expand the U.S. ability to differentiate among kinds of destruction: the improvement in U.S. missile accuracies, and the Soviet investment in additional civil-defense preparations.

The general point about civil defense is thus two-edged. A Soviet capacity for evacuating cities is clearly worrisome, in that it might one day embolden the Politburo to undertake an aggression, thinking that less of its population and work force would suffer as a consequence. Yet such an evacuation capability also offers U.S. strategists a much longer list of alternative targets and opportunities for leverage in trying to dissuade the Soviets from beginning or from continuing such an aggression. It simultaneously makes the U.S. strategic problem more difficult and more interesting. Hanoi's civil-defense system, in a paradoxical way, cooperated in 1972 with the U.S. Air Force in holding down the number of casualties from the B-52 air strikes, thereby making such strikes more possible; similarly, the USSR's investment in civil-defense preparations does not only make Soviet toughness more worrisome, it also allows the United States to undertake forms of attack that it might otherwise consider too likely to lead to escalation.

If the United States were thus to limit itself to conventional explosives, as part of a policy of keeping a cap on escalation, would it also for the same reasons still have to confine its attacks to targets outside the Soviet Union? Perhaps. Perhaps not. Of the two thresholds to be crossed, the conventional/nuclear line may be considerably more sensitive than the line of the formal boundaries of the USSR.

Firing anything whatsoever into Soviet airspace would of course be the crossing of an important threshold, one that has not really been violated before (the U-2 does not count). If not handled properly, it might still stampede the Russians into an unwanted response. Yet we might be talking here about the firing of a single missile, or just a few, so that the risk of the incoming salvo being mistaken for a full nuclear strike would be substantially reduced. Public declarations could also be made in advance that the United States in some situations reserves the right to strike at the USSR itself with conventional arms delivered by missile.

If one felt very much obligated to assist the People's Republic of China in a military engagement with the USSR, for example, an engagement that had not yet gone nuclear, would there not thus be great payoffs in a conventional-warhead missile strike against the tunnels of the Trans-Siberian Railway? If the United States could destroy a bridge or a dam or a Soviet government building by conventional means, it would have shown substantial punch without yet crossing the nuclear firebreak, without throwing away the most important lid there is on escalation.

The day will probably never come when a nonnuclear warhead will be powerful enough, whatever its accuracy, to destroy an ICBM missile silo or a hardened command post. The more that U.S. strategists get in the habit of assigning conventional warheads to any strikes inside the Soviet Union, the more the United States will reassure the Soviets that it will be limiting itself to what could be called "good counterforce," to attacks on their ground force strength, their ability to project power into other territories and out to sea, that is, their conventional forces; and the less the United States will cause any apprehensions about "bad counterforce," including attacks on Soviet missile silos, or Soviet command-and-control, or the shelters of the Soviet leadership. The latter are the kinds of targets the United States should try to avoid for fear of putting the Soviet leadership into a position of "use them or lose them" with regard to their own nuclear missiles.

Under all circumstances, the appropriate U.S. response to the various Soviet strategic ploys is never so clear and obvious. The United States always wishes to retain *most* of its leverage, while applying *some* of it—to turn back Soviet aggression, while at the same time maintaining the deterrence of the worst Soviet attacks on the United States, the attacks that have not yet occurred.

For example, if Soviet cities were evacuated, under what circumstances should the United States try to inflict substantial casualties on the population that has been moved out into the countryside? Similarly, what damage should be inflicted on evacuated cities? Rather than destroying an empty city outright, are there things that the United States could do short of this that would be more effective for its purposes? Could the United States somehow destroy only parts of a city, perhaps the parts most central to the maintenance of future political control by the Soviet authorities?

If only conventional warheads were to be used, residential areas might be spared while government buildings and communications and data storage centers (that is, the equivalent of City Hall) were destroyed. Alternatively, bridges and railroad connections through the city might be attacked, or whatever major industrial facilities were contained in it.

All of these are targeting options that have captured attention inside the U.S. government since the third year of the Carter administration, with Presidential Directive 59 demonstrating some of this interest,[21] and with the options being part of the sales pitch for cruise missiles and the MX. And arguments for all of these options have been easy to debunk when they claimed that a nuclear warhead would be required.

Yet without the tremendous and often unpredictable collateral damage of a nuclear warhead, some of these scenarios would be less easy to debunk. The problem of keeping the Soviets out of the mood for aggression against Western Europe remains real, moreover, and is not just the product of febrile imaginations in the Reagan or Carter administrations.

Even with conventional warheads, U.S. strategists will certainly have to be on guard against becoming excessively enthusiastic about the possibilities of fine-tuning attacks on an enemy, as they so ambitiously sort out whom to hit and whom to spare. Historically, the United States has often been disappointed with the "precision bombings" that have been attempted. Yet the clear upshot of the improvement in CEP is that some kinds of sorting are becoming more possible, such that certain kinds of surgical strikes that would have been impossible in the past will not be so in the 1990s or beyond. With the application of conventional warheads, it should at least be possible to spare most of what the United States wishes to spare in any such surgical strikes, while new accuracies increase the likelihood that the nation will destroy what it wishes to destroy.

Service in Deterrence versus Use in Combat

If a deterrent force works well, it is demonstrated in use. We are hardly arguing here that the United States should look forward to directing conventional-warhead cruise or ballistic missiles at targets in Eastern Europe or within the Soviet Union itself. The suggestion instead is that it might be healthier and wiser to regard such conventional responses, rather than nuclear responses, as the bounty offered by missile accuracy, responding to the argument, now so often heard in Washington, that the best deterrent is a military response that the United States could actually bring itself to undertake without committing suicide.

One should stress other reinforcements for NATO defenses, moving away in this area from a reliance on nuclear escalation, including extensive deployments of new PGM (precision-guided munitions) anti-tank weapons, the "smaller brothers" of the accurate cruise missiles and ballistic missiles we have been discussing here. The prospect of many Soviet tanks being destroyed as they advance by antitank guided missiles (ATGM), while their reinforcements are having difficulty getting through Poland because too many bridges have been destroyed by cruise missiles, may be sufficient to deter Moscow from ever launching an aggression into West Germany in the first place.

Will we ever see cruise or ballistic missiles striking at bridges in Poland or at tunnels of the Trans-Siberian Railway, or in a demonstration shot at some shelters for the Soviet leadership? One hopes that it will never have to come to this.

As an aside, will we indeed see cruise missiles ever come into use with conventional warheads anywhere, once and for all showing what they can do? The possibilities here, somewhat more removed from U.S.–Soviet military actions, are perhaps a little more real, just as the B-52s never came into use inside the USSR, but saw previously unimaginable service in Vietnam.

One can imagine such a truly "surgical" (no radioactive fallout, little collateral damage) use of conventional-warhead missiles in at least one important and serious situation. Turning to the nuclear proliferation front, suppose that the United States had strong evidence that a regime like Colonel Qaddafi's in Libya was embarking on a diversion of fissionable materials to nuclear warheads. The world consensus might indeed be supportive of a move to head this action off, as long as it was not too messy and as long as it did not itself entail the use of nuclear weapons in battle. The destruction of the reactor or plutonium-separation plant in question, by a direct hit with one or two conventional-warhead missiles, might be exactly what the world would applaud.

In summary, we must stress that any substitution of conventional threats for nuclear threats will have to remain debatable for all the reasons cited at the outset. Such a substitution makes wars easier to limit, almost beyond a doubt. Yet making wars easier to limit can make them more likely to happen.

The primary task of U.S. strategic procurements remains to see to it that the United States will always be able to retaliate if the Soviets use nuclear weapons. As a consequence, the United States will also always be able to escalate to the use of nuclear weapons, even if the other side has not used them in battle, but is merely advancing by the use of conventional weaponry.

Cultivating additional conventional options does not change what is possible in this regard, but it may change what the Soviets expect the United States to do. If the United States shows too much interest in conventional weapons options, does it betray an unwillingness to use nuclear weapons first?

This author is not yet convinced that the United States should reassure the Soviets that it will never use nuclear weapons if Western Europe is invaded. Nevertheless, the promising applications in such a situation of conventional weaponry should indeed be explored. If analysts within the U.S. government itself continue to insist, moreover, that the United States cannot be counted upon to escalate merely because of its pledged word and treaty commitment, but would do so only if it acquired new nuclear war-fighting options, then the choices will thereby have been changed. For the nuclear war-fighting options have too many collateral effects to give the United States any of this "rational" deterrent that is allegedly so needed; and something like conventional options may then have to be substituted, whether we like it or not.

Notes

1. For a very clear analysis of the limited war phenomenon, see Morton H. Halperin, *Limited War in the Nuclear Age* (New York: John Wiley, 1963).

2. For the analogous argument within the context of nucler war, see Bernard S. Albert, "Constructive Counterpower," *Orbis* 19, no. 2 (Summer 1976):343–66.

3. On the relative damage potential of different kinds of chemical weapons, see Carnegie Endowment for International Peace, *The Control of Chemical and Biological Weapons* (New York: Carnegie Endowment, 1971).

4. This idea was outlined early and well in Thomas C. Schelling, *The Strategy of Conflict* (Cambridge: Harvard University Press, 1960), 53–80.

5. On the arguments for a no-first-use policy, see Richard Ullman, "No First Use of Nuclear Weapons," *Foreign Affairs* 50, no. 4 (July 1972):669–83.

6. A good discussion of Chinese declaratory and actual policy on nuclear weapons can be found in Jonathan D. Pollack, "China as a Nuclear Power," in *Asia's Nuclear Future,* ed. William H. Overholdt (Boulder, Colo.: Westview, 1977), 35–66.

7. This is the argument that Henry A. Kissinger came to in his third book, *The Troubled Partnership* (New York: McGraw-Hill, 1965). See also Bernard Brodie, *Escalation and the Nuclear Option* (Princeton: Princeton University Press, 1966).

8. The possibilities of a conventional defense at the tactical level are discussed in John L. Mearsheimer, *Conventional Deterrence* (Ithaca, N.Y.: Cornell University Press, 1983), and Johan J. Holst and Uwe Nerlich, eds. *Beyond Nuclear Deterrence* (New York: Crane Russak, 1977).

9. Paul F. Walker, "Precision-guided Weapons," *Scientific American* no. 245 (August 1981):37–45.

10. For an interesting argument that the Soviets are *not* planning earlier use of nuclear weapons in a European War, see Philip A. Petersen and John G. Hines, "The Conventional Offensive in Soviet Theater Strategy," *Orbis* 27, no. 3 (Fall 1983):695–739.

11. An example of the argument that the Soviets have standardized on planning for early nuclear escalation can be found in Joseph D. Douglass, Jr., "The Theater Nuclear Threat," *Defense Science 2001+* (December 1983):23–37.

12. Samuel Huntington, in his own chapters of the book he edited, *The Strategic Imperative* (Cambridge, Mass.: Ballinger, 1982), presents an argument that the United States should welcome a capability for plunging into Eastern Europe if the Soviets have attacked Western Europe.

13. For a much quoted illustration of this kind of thinking, see Colin Gray, "Nuclear Strategy: The Case for a Theory of Victory," *International Security* 4, no. 1 (Summer 1979):54–87.

14. Leon Sloss and Marc Dean Millot, "U.S. Nuclear Strategy in Evolution," *Strategic Review* 12, no. 1 (Winter 1984):19–28.

15. For some early speculation about such scenarios, see Klaus Knorr and Thornton Read, eds., *Limited Strategic War* (New York: Praeger, 1962).

16. See Edward J. Ohlert, "Strategic Deterrence and the Cruise Missile," *Naval War College Review* 21, no. 3 (Winter 1978):21–32.

17. Schelling, *The Strategy of Conflict.*

18. For a discussion of some of the verification problems with cruise missiles, see Thomas K. Longstreth, "Cruise Missiles: The Arms Control Challenge," *Arms Control Today* 13, no. 4 (May 1983):1, 7–10.

19. An example that attracted a great deal of attention can be found in Richard Pipes, "Why the Soviet Union Thinks It Could Fight and Win a Nuclear War," *Commentary* 64, no. 1 (July 1977):21–34.

20. For some very well-researched skepticism about U.S. capabilities for

limiting damage in a war that has become nuclear, see Desmond Ball, *Can Nuclear War Be Controlled?* (London: International Institute for Strategic Studies, Adelphi Paper no. 169, 1981).

21. A discussion of PD-59 can be found in Louis René Beres, "Presidential Directive 59: A Critical Assessment," *Parameters* 11, no. 1 (March 1981):19–27; and in Colin S. Gray, "Presidential Directive 59: Flawed but Useful," *Parameters* 11, no. 1 (March 1981):30–37.

13
Avoiding Offensive Weapons and Strengthening the Defense

The case to be presented here is on behalf of an old distinction, between offense and defense in military weapons, a distinction not given enough attention in contemporary analyses of international security matters. This distinction has surely been much abused in recent decades, with every country claiming that its own policies are entirely defensive and accusing its rivals of being prepared for offensive aggressions; this explains part of the reason that the distinction is no longer used as much for serious analysis. Yet, as will be argued here, the distinction is still real, and it is important.

An Unfortunate Bias against Defense

While the world's civilian political leaders all pretend to be interested only in defense (hence the United States now has a Department of Defense and no longer a War Department), the professional military officer often pretends to see no real distinctions between defense and offense. But in actuality, these professional officers have a great, if unadmitted, bias against the defense and in favor of the offense.

There are several reasons why such officers have become prejudiced against the defensive side of weaponry and military tactics. Defenses are often seen as oriented toward a complaisant status quo, too much encouraging stagnation in military thinking and military preparedness. The weapons of the defense tend to be immobile weapons, tied down into permanent fortifications, and thus are perhaps more difficult to upgrade and improve. Military officers who become

This chapter was presented as a paper at a May 1982 conference in Buenos Aires on "Arms Control Issues," sponsored by C.A.R.I., the Argentine Council for International Relations.

enthusiastic about defensively oriented fixed fortifications in the U.S. armed forces are accused of having a "Maginot mentality," a commitment to permanent preparations for a fixed view of war, allegedly the approach that led to the French defeat by the Germans in 1940 (this myth of the uselessness of the Maginot Line ignores the fact that the Germans did not go through the Line, but around it).[1]

One hears that military officers of the U.S. Army have no hope of reaching the rank of general by being experts on minefields. Similarly, officers did not expect to rise to the highest ranks in an earlier day by being specialists in coast artillery, a branch of the army that could never attack a foreign enemy unless he was first attacking U.S. shores. The roots of a bias against defense might thus be traced to the substance of the issues, as interpreted in light of recent military history, but another part of the bias must be traced instead to the self-interests of those committed to a military career.

To admit or stress the potency of defense is generally to admit lesser needs for military appropriations, for such a defensive military technology serves to leave each side less threatened by the other, more able to hold its own if attacked. If the emphasis on defense was predominant, for example, when two nations of mountaineers confronted each other, each knowing the ambush positions in its own hills very well, then it is possible that neither side could profitably attack the other. Consider a "confrontation" between Austria and Switzerland, in which the Austrians would easily beat off a Swiss attack, and the Swiss could easily beat off an Austrian attack. Here it becomes much more difficult for military establishments to increase their own appropriations and career prospects by describing their potential enemies as "ten feet tall," since nature cuts all aggressors down to size when they cross into another country.

By contrast, when the emphasis on the offensive looks more predominant, it might become impossible for the two sides to a confrontation ever to be simultaneously secure, or for their two armed forces ever to be told that they had enough in the way of resources.

It is all too possible that emphasis on the offensive will predominate from time to time, causing wars or causing arms races. But it is all too tempting for military officers to act as if the offensive was more important *all* the time, for doing so serves the military's career interests, and this accusation might be directed today at the military professionals in many areas of the globe.

One result of this bias toward offense is that military officers tend to avoid confronting the distinction between defense and offense. Some typical military clichés: "Any weapon can be used offensively or defensively"; "The best defense is a good offense"; "Offense or defense is a matter of the enemy's intentions, rather than of his capabilities."[2]

What we have here is a seeming reluctance to face the possibilities of choice. It can be illustrated by a conversation with an Israeli general, who was asked whether it might not be better for peace if Israel were to maintain a larger standing army, even if this had the price of lowering mobilization potentials somewhat, that is, of lowering the maximum wartime size of the Israeli armed forces. The argument for reducing the reserves and maintaining a larger standing army is that reserve structures too much tend to reward whoever moves first and fastest during any Arab–Israeli crisis, precisely what we shall come to define as the offensive. In short, such reserve structures give Israel a greater capability in the event of war, but they also make war more likely. The general admitted that the tradeoff existed, but within a sentence or two was again questioning whether there was ever a real distinction between arrangements favoring the defense and favoring the offense.

Military professionals have, of course, not always pretended to be so blind to the offense-defense distinction through history. France, under the influence of Maginot, with the bitter memory of the trenches and machine guns of World War I, took the defense very seriously and wedded its military thinking to the defense. Prior to World War I, France had by contrast been committed to a very explicit theory of the offense, based on the writings of Ardant du Picq, a theory that an army always fought better on its enemy's territory than on its own, a theory that, when matched against the German Schlieffen Plan, contributed to the outbreak of World War I.[3]

Perhaps the French, being an unusually logical people in the tradition of Descartes, are more prone to seeing clear differences between a commitment to the defense or the offense. Perhaps it was rather that the times and trends of military technology moved more slowly in earlier decades, giving analysts more time to reach one conclusion or the other. Yet one does not have to be French, or unusually logical, to identify some important differences here. And even if the times are moving rapidly, one can sort out differences that will matter a great deal.

Factors Favoring Offense or Defense

What kinds of factors favor the offense, and what kinds the defense? As has been noted, systems that stress mobilizations of reserves favor the offense, precisely because each side would be racing to build up its forces first and then would be tempted to strike before the other side had completed its own mobilizations. As reservists put on their uniforms and get on their trains, there is a race to get to the frontier and to win "the battle of the frontiers," since whoever gets there first can push into the enemy's territory to disrupt his mobilization. Much of the outbreak of World War I has to be blamed on this kind of offensive advantage derived from mobilization systems, and it has been a serious problem as well in the confrontations between the Arab states and Israel, given the heavy Israeli dependence on mobilization of reserves.

When one's reservists have been mobilized, one knows that they cannot be held in the military indefinitely, because the civilian economy will suffer too much. One is thus tempted to "strike while the iron is hot." Nothing could be worse than to demobilize and then be attacked by an enemy that had belatedly gotten his forces up to full strength. Weapons systems and weapons arrangements that offer only a temporary battle potential inherently bias generals and admirals toward attacking, toward favoring the offensive.

Another factor favoring the offensive is mobility. When an advancing army can bring its fighting power along with it, without too much of a loss of such power, it has less reason to sit still. When forces can be quickly grouped and regrouped, the enemy can be suddenly outnumbered at one particular sector of the battle line, facilitating a breakthrough. Tanks thus have normally favored the offensive,[4] as have all forms of artillery mounted on mobile platforms. Troop-carrier aircraft similarly favor the offensive, allowing the Soviets to fly Cuban troops quickly into Africa, or allowing the U.S. Air Force similarly to fly in the French Foreign Legion.

Related to mobility, an extended range of weapons systems, especially of ships and airplanes, favors the offense. An airplane that is more limited in range is sometimes labelled an "interceptor," much more useful in its own airspace than in the airspace of the enemy. By contrast, a modern U.S. fighter-bomber is capable of carrying substantial weapons payloads considerable distances into the enemy's airspace.

Airplanes in general tend to favor the offensive whenever they can get into and over the enemy's territory. Like reserve forces, their ability to fight is limited in time, as they will soon have to land to refuel. Hence, they become weapons to be used earlier rather than later. Having one's own airplane over an enemy's airbases is surely preferable to having an enemy's airplane over one's own airbases.

The same is all the more true for aircraft carriers, where whoever has gotten his planes into the air over the enemy fleet has a tremendous advantage. Equipped with aircraft carriers, the fleets of Japan and the United States had become tilted toward a taking of the offensive by 1941, with the Japanese surprise attack at Pearl Harbor simply being the realization of this situation. If the two fleets had been equipped with battleships instead, such a surprise attack would have been far less tempting.

So, what kinds of weapons favor the defense? As was suggested earlier, any weapons that are very much tied to particular terrain have this effect. One's fixed fortifications are useful if the enemy has taken the initiative to launch an attack, but they serve no purpose for attacking him. Minefields similarly require that the enemy set foot on one's own soil, whereupon he may have his foot blown off.

Some of what is done in the name of defense may simply amount to a substantial investment in the pouring of concrete, with the French Maginot Line and German Siegfried Line of World War II serving as not such ludicrous models. To repeat, the Germans exploited the gap in the Maginot Line along the French–Belgian border by simply going around it. They would not have had such an easy time penetrating directly through the Line. When the Germans had to retreat to their own Siegfried Line in 1944, they made good use of these prepared fortifications, halting the advancing British and U.S. tank columns, prolonging the war into 1945.

Other terrain-specific military skills similarly strengthen the defensive. When mountaineers know their own mountains, but would be lost in the mountains of their neighbor, the defense is reinforced. When some troops are specialists in fighting in jungles, and others in deserts, and others in built-up urban areas, the result is that each is stronger in their own special kind of territory and is less capable of attacking the other in his kind of territory, again a discouragement for the taking of the military initiative and a reinforcement for the defense. In the 1948 Arab–Israeli war, the Jordanian Arab Legion was better at fighting out in the open desert, but the Israeli Haganah was better at fighting in the built-up areas of Jerusalem.[5] The ultimate cease-fire line reflected this distribution of skills.

Hilly ground in general favors the defense, an intuitive observation based on the difficulty of moving upwards against people who do not have to move. By contrast, flat desert country has tended to look like tank country, allowing for rapid movement and free-flowing battle, and thus favoring the offense.

As has just been suggested, urbanization may favor the defense, in that it obstructs free movement. What used to be called the "North German plain" may have changed drastically in the years since World War II, as the prosperity of West Germany has filled this area with buildings, especially along and close to the paths of the major Autobahns. Someone jokingly referred to this German urbanization as "the most extensive man-made fortification since the Maginot Line,"[6] and it may well have this kind of defensive effect, since Soviet tanks would surely be unable to move through at a clip appropriate to any blitzkrieg. What was once the North German plain thus has become the "West German traffic jam," offering NATO infantry many points from behind which it might fire antitank weapons at advancing Soviet armor.

Another factor favoring a defense is a system of militia reservists tied to local terrain. Whether or not a nation can establish this kind of system is, to a large extent, a matter of national heritage. The Swiss Army has a tradition of training its males between the ages of eighteen and fifty for defending positions in their home areas, learning all the good positions for an ambush, preparing to destroy the bridges and tunnels, training for the same positional warfare that their fathers and grandfathers did. Some analysts have advocated the establishment of such a territorially based militia system in West Germany,[7] but the German tradition is different. Unfortunately for the likelihood of peace, the German reservist in the past was drilled for getting on a train to fight a war in France, rather than for fighting in prepared positions near his own village. This system of reserve mobilization was quite different from systems that have deep roots in Switzerland or Sweden; it was a system more inclined to be offensive, rather than defensive.

Since tanks favor the offense, it should generally follow that antitank weapons favor the defense, by cancelling out some of the power of the tank and by making it harder for an aggressor to roll forward with so much mobile firepower.

It would be foolish to argue that such offensive or defensive inclinations in weaponry, or in general military and political situations, are always easy to sort out. Any critic of the central distinction can note how complicated some interactions can be. Antiaircraft guided missiles might seem defensive, for example, but suppose that such missiles are mounted on the backs of tanks, shielding the advancing tanks against air attack, or that they are otherwise mounted on mobile platforms. Clearly, the "bottom line" in a final analysis of impact may not be so easy to settle.

Yet to cite difficulty in sorting out the answer to a question is never the same as saying that there was no important question in the first place, or that there was no real distinction to be assayed. At the end of any change in military technology, or change in military deployments, or change in overarching political confrontation, there will be an end-product change on one important question, the question that determines all of what we have been labelling offense or defense: Did the changes in the end increase the military advantage of attacking, of moving to take the initiative in a crisis, as opposed to sitting still and waiting for an enemy's attack perhaps to come? If it did, the net change was in the direction that should be labelled the *offensive*. Did the changes instead in the end decrease the assumed advantage of attacking and rather counsel that one should sit still during a crisis, waiting for the other side to lose battles and make a fool of itself by attacking? If it did, the net change should be considered a reinforcement for the *defensive*.

There is thus a final answer here, such that serious analysis cannot ignore or brush past the question. What is at stake is the likelihood of war or peace. Offensive weapons tend to make wars more likely, because they cause crisis to become wars.

A crisis might be defined a perceived increase in the likelihood of war; the crucial question then is whether the military arrangements push each side to respond such a *perceived* increase by *actual* moves toward war, toward forward motion and the attack. When rumors of war are thus self-confirming, the world is in more trouble. Defensive weapons are the kind that tend to reduce the risk of such self-confirming predictions.

Some Complications

A few important qualifications need to be noted before we conclude that defensive weapons are thus always preferable to offensive ones.

What if one side has defensive weapons and the other does not? The side possessing fixed fortifications might have nothing to fear, but its neighbor might be wide open to attack, with the superior power then electing to become the aggressor whenever it was so inclined.

What if one side very much outnumbers the other in totals of forces? Would a predominance of defensive inclined weapons ensure the peace in such a case? Very possibly not, for the superior force might elect to aggress anyway, accepting whatever tax was imposed by trenches and machine guns and mountain barriers, intent nonetheless on a final victory. A tilt toward defensive weapons does not guarantee peace; what it does contribute is a wider margin of stable and non-threatening force-ratios, a greater elbow room in comparisons of forces. Without tanks on either side, it is probably much easier for a smaller army to stand off a larger. When tanks are present everywhere, by contrast, it might be menacingly possible for either side to strike and win, if it only struck first.

Another most important caveat is that we are discussing only the *military defensive* here, systems that reward the side sitting still in terms of the comparative losses of troops, aircraft, or warships. We would be entering a very different discussion of defense if we began thinking of shielding civilian populations against wartime destruction, as with the antibomber or antimissile weapons that are intended to ward off nuclear attacks on cities. For reasons of the complicated logic of nuclear deterrence, this kind of *population defense* could be very threatening to peace, panicking the side that was about to lose its ability to inflict massive retaliation, panicking it perhaps so much that it might launch a nuclear war while it was still able to do so.

The humane philosopher might think it much more important to concentrate on shielding civilians rather than soldiers. But for purposes of reducing the likelihood of war, it is much more urgent to shield soldiers, to shield them against the initiatives and surprise attacks of their adversaries so that such adversaries do not see any incentive to begin a war in the first place.

One sees this counterintuitive logic very clearly in some U.S. analytical discussions of antiballistic missile (ABM) defenses. An ABM system merely shielding the land-based intercontinental ballistic missiles (ICBMs) of the United States against attack by Soviet ICBMs would be desirable, for it would reduce either side's incentive to fire such missiles (that is, it loads the situation toward the defense instead of the offense, in terms of missile exchanges). Such ABMs protecting instead the people of the United States against attack could be very destabilizing and therefore undesirable, making more likely a war nobody wanted.[8] Missiles that protect missiles are good, missiles that protect people are bad. This message is still difficult for Americans and others to accept.

Another problem in any world move toward a defensive orientation in weaponry would be well illustrated by Argentine attitudes on the Malvinas, that is, the situations in which the status quo or distribution of territorial control is regarded as unjust. If the British had deployed extensive antiship and antiaircraft defensive systems to the Falklands before the Argentine attempt to take back the islands, Argentina might perhaps never have felt able to make the attempt. The world might have welcomed the barrier to recourse to force, but Argentines might rather have seen it as a military reinforcement for an apparent British intransigence about negotiations.

There are some other irredentas around the world still in dispute, just like the Falklands-Malvinas. The side possessing such territories rarely thinks of itself as unjust. But the side lacking such territories instead feels that it is the height of injustice for its claims to go unrecognized. Happily, however, they are not many such territories around the world, that so much serve as an irritant. On a much broader scale, liberals think it the height of injustice that Poland is governed by a Marxist regime, while Marxists think it equally unjust that El Salvador is governed by a non-Marxist regime. But would we welcome a world in which all such senses of injustice were relieved by military action? This is exactly the kind of warlike world we are very eager to avoid.

In cases like that of the Falklands-Malvinas, therefore, the outside world is still not likely to lament an introduction of defensive systems, even while that world might be willing to sponsor genuine negotiations on the issues. As was the consensus in the days of the League of Nations, war and military offensives are something everyone probably will wish to avoid under virtually *all* circumstances, even while realizing that there must therefore be alternative peaceful ways of addressing and redressing grievances.

A very different interpretation, however, of problems with defenses is illustrated by the Argentine occupation of the Malvinas, and similarly by the Turkish seizure of a portion of Cyprus, and by a number of Israeli ventures in the Middle East. What if one side suddenly makes a quick move, by surprise, to capture a small and finite piece of territory and thus confronts the losing party and the world with a fait accompli? This possibility, sometimes labelled "smash and grab," would exploit the inherent difficulties all countries have in keeping their defenses manned and ready at all times. Something gets seized early on Sunday morning, and—by the time the aggrieved party is ready to counter on Monday—the now defensive impact of ground, air, and sea weapons can be counted upon to settle in, reinforcing the new status quo so suddenly established.[9]

In part this is what Argentina was seeking to accomplish in the islands, and the impact of new weapons like Exocet almost confirmed the value of this model, as it proved more difficult for the British to recover their Falklands than London had anticipated. What if the Soviets suddenly seized Hamburg and then announced that they favor peace? As Clausewitz noted, the aggressor is always the first to cry "peace"; it is the side trying to undo the departure from the status quo that rounds out the two-sided military effort prerequisite for there to be a "war."[10]

Yet in most corners of the world, the amount of territory that could be seized in such a sudden "smash and grab" operation is not significant enough to be a cause for worry. Rather than suddenly seizing Hamburg, the Soviets and East Germans could long ago have instead seized West Berlin. What deters them is not any layer of military defenses, but rather the elementary economic deterrence of ongoing East–West trade relationships, the same kind of factor that deters Communist China from seizing Hong Kong.

Just as the world will have to devote some attention to nonmilitary ways of handling the territorial disputes that are the object of deep and genuine irredentist sentiments, so it will have to be particularly clever at devising deterrent projections for areas vulnerable to smash-and-grab operations. Economic and political relationships of interdependence may suffice to accomplish this deterrence in many of those instances about which one would otherwise have worried militarily.

It should be noted that the Argentine occupation of the islands in the South Atlantic was very finely tuned, with very little "smash" in the "smash and grab." It was precisely its surprise and subtlety and sudden offering of a fait accompli, that then so much alarmed the outside world, alarmed the world more than the Argentine government had probably anticipated.

Difficulties of Implementation

One should not assume that anything like total control can be exercised over whether the military technology of the future will favor the offense or the defense. Much of this decision is made by Mother Nature, as the technology naturally in one decade favors the defense more, and in another favors the offense. The point is rather that strategists do have some choices to make, choices in the avenues of military research and development to be pursued, choices in the weapons to be procured, and in the strategies to be designed. Simply to pursue all avenues of scientific research, "wherever the opportunities lead us," is just as much of a know-nothing approach as to deny any distinction between offense and defense in the first place.

When nature is being kind and we exploit this situation to the fullest, we might establish the kinds of defensive postures that make war very unlikely and that relax all the powers that matter, even during political crises. When nature is being unkind to us, offering up new options that favor the initiative, the attack, and the offense, we still would be well-advised to do our best to compensate. To keep some strength for the defensive, for the second strike (at the strategic nuclear level as well as at the conventional theater level), is to offer all the governments that matter more time to think and to risk less of the frenzied panic that might cause a totally unwanted war.

But what if the other side is not matching the United States in a commitment to defensive, stabilizing armaments? What if the Soviets are investing in multiple-warhead missiles or continue to invest heavily in tanks? Can the United States commit itself to single-warhead missiles or to antitank guided missiles (ATGMs) if the other side is not doing its part to ease tensions?

A naive or excessively argumentative U.S. congressman might contend that the United States should not or cannot make any moves toward defensive armaments unless the Soviets also do their part. But the reality is that a nation like the United States must serve its own best interests, regardless of what its adversary might foolishly be doing on its side. If strategists urge that the United States invest in antitank weapons and in fixed fortifications looking vaguely like the Maginot Line, it is not so much as an unreciprocated gesture to appease an adversary, but rather because U.S. interests are well served by this kind of policy; U.S. chances of winning a war if it begins will be enhanced, just as will be the chances that no war will begin in the first place. The United States would dearly love the situation in which a Soviet tank attack on Western Europe, if it came, would be repulsed, repulsed without the nuclear escalation that could destroy the entire world. Even more, the United States welcomes a situation in which the Soviet tank attack never occurs in the first place.

Admittedly, by investing in defensive weapons, the United States does the Soviets a favor, since such weaponry would be of no help to the United States if it were ever to try to liberate Poland or the Ukraine. More importantly, the United States does itself a favor.

If the Soviets were to see the implications and reciprocate, the United States would of course welcome their doing so, as they chose to invest in antitank weapons themselves or fixed fortifications, but reduced the totals of their tanks. Indeed, there are kinds of weapons, basically defensive weapons, that would cause little fear of an "arms race," such that any lack of a mutual verification to assure each side that the other was restraining its military procurements would not greatly upset either side. Suppose that rumors were to emerge that the Soviets had invested in vastly larger numbers of antitank rockets than had previously been admitted and had secretly erected a belt of fortifications along the borders between the USSR and Poland or Rumania. Would not everyone in the West heave a sigh of relief at this Soviet "clandestine armament"?

Political Aspects of Defense

The abstract possibility of any extensive Soviet and Warsaw Pact investment in fixed-fortification defensive military arrangements has another drawback that must be noted, however, illustrating one more possible problem in a largely defensive weapons bias. The West German government has been reluctant to invest too heavily in minefields and fixed fortifications on its side of the line because of the costs of purchasing scarce and valuable agricultural land, and because such fortifications would symbolically mean an acceptance of the division of Germany. Soviet fortifications on the East German side of the line might be militarily stabilizing and reassuring for any crisis situations, but would similarly reinforce the impression that East Germany is never to be merged again with West.

Aside from signaling permanency of division, fixed fortifications, by being so visible, may signal permanency of hostility. It is sometimes alleged that the United States and Canada would never have become truly friendly if they had not first signed a treaty in 1817 for the demilitarization of their common boundary.

Yet the argument cuts two ways. The U.S.–Canadian boundary remained somewhat fortified for quite some time, in part because of exceptions and loopholes in the treaty, and in part because of cheating on both sides. In the meantime, the political problems solved themselves, so that the remaining fortresses of the frontier became pleasant historical museums and parks.[11]

English-speakers have an old saying, that "good fences make good neighbors." When we get good locks on our doors, we do not have to worry whether a neighbor might have stolen something every time we have inadvertently misplaced it. A stress on defensive weapons is thus analogous to giving all of us in a village good locks, without giving ourselves ways of breaking through the locks of others.

Will there ever be an occasion on which the United States might favor the offensive rather than the defensive? Some major writers on military strategy in the past, including the preeminent Clausewitz, could indeed be read as favoring the offensive.

Many of us might once have favored it, for offense produces world empire and world law and order, when carried to its ultimate extreme. If one side can conquer everyone else, as the result of having strong forces that do not lose their power as they travel great distances (that is, having offensive weapons, and not being stymied by defenses), then the world might come to accept a single ruler, and the subjects of war and international politics might fade from the scene. This is what happened when the Roman legions, with their ability to march great distances and arrive fully prepared for battle, extended the Roman Empire and the Pax Romana as far as human habitation seemed to require. Such empires perhaps fall sooner or later, but Pax Romana lasted for some four hundred years, during which time there could not really have been an academic discipline studying international relations and international anarchy and the problem of war and peace. Many of us would have been out of jobs as professors and authors, but the world was much more civilized as a result of the empire's existence, at least in some regards.

The civilizing union that the Romans achieved has had a nostalgic appeal for many continental European military strategists, not just for

Clausewitz, and also for European philosophers and political theorists. This idea may have been part of what drove Philip II of Spain to try to conquer Britain and the rest of Europe. This idea helped to keep the title "Holy Roman Empire" in use until the time of Napoleon.[12] And in part it spurred Napoleon forward to try to unify Europe under French rule, standardizing it on the metric system, introducing the peace of offensive-weapons-leading-to-conquest.

The British dominance of the seas after Trafalgar perhaps comes the closest to matching the monopoly power of the Romans, based also as it was on the offensive power of the sailing vessel, which could sail great distances from the English channel to attack ships or coastlines anywhere around the globe. Could any nation aspire to such a monopoly today, extracted from an ability to exploit the offensive? The answer is entirely negative, because of the introduction of nuclear weapons, weapons that give the Soviet Union or France or China an ultimate veto over anyone's desire to conquer the world. Whoever was about to be conquered now, to be submerged into some new kind of Roman Empire and Pax Romana, would threaten, as its last gasp of military independence, to destroy the cities of the conqueror, to devastate the new "Rome." Nuclear weapons negate the realization of battlefield victories, as retaliatory destruction against cities and civilians can be inflicted by going over the top of the battlefields, or under them by means of missile-carrying submarines.

In light of this fact, and in light of other world orientations toward pluralism and separate sovereignties, we have thus come to favor the defensive cast of military technology, rather than the offensive. Rather than new Roman legions, we need Swiss militia. Rather than forward motion, we may desire fixed fortifications.

Defenses at the extreme can produce what in English has been called "phoney war," or "sitzkrieg" (instead of "blitzkrieg"), a war that is formally declared, but then leads to no military operations or casualties on either side, as each side sits waiting, hoping that the other will be so foolish as to attack.

This was allegedly the situation between the German Siegfried Line and the French Maginot Line for the first months of World War II, a situation not so fortunate, of course, since it did not extend to the Eastern Front where German panzer columns were slicing through Poland. The possibility can just as clearly be illustrated in the contrast between the outbreak of World War I on land and on sea. On land, the bias was toward offense, toward "real war," as all the powers had to race to mobilize their troops, to get them on trains and then head toward the enemy's interior, with cries of "Nach Paris" interacting very unproductively with matching cries of "A Berlin." At sea, something very different occurred, in a pattern that could have prevented World War I altogether or converted it into a "phoney war" if only it had been seen as applying on land as well.

The competition between Britain and Germany regarding the construction of dreadnought battleships had indeed been an important political factor worsening relations between the two countries. But the military impact of this kind of warship, unlike the later aircraft carrier, was very much toward the defensive. When the kaiser asked his admirals what the German navy should do at the declaration of war, the answer was that it was best to stay on the German side of the North Sea, hoping that the British fleet would make the mistake of coming steaming across, whereupon it could be sunk. When the British government asked its admirals what they proposed to do, the answer was symmetrically the same, to wait on the British side of the North Sea, hoping that the German fleet would make the mistake of coming steaming across on the attack, whereupon the Germans could be sunk.

The facts of World War I were to prove that the defensive was predominant on land also, as the machine gun and trench were to make forward motion very disadvantageous. The tragedy of the outbreak of World War I was that the generals had not correctly perceived this defensive inclination, as the admirals had at sea, but instead assumed that the offensive was preponderant.[13] The outbreak of real war (a disastrously real war, rather than "phoney war") was the price here, a war that probably would not have occurred otherwise, since the nations plunging into it were tightly linked by culture and economics, not nearly as hostile to each other as are many neighboring countries in today's world. World War I, in its outbreak, is the model of what we might hope to avoid.

If the military professional and the military weapons designer were to succeed in making wars "phoney" and in making crises and war-possibilities boring, they would thus have done their countries some considerable service. Instead of the message of any crisis being "Shoot first and ask questions later," the message would be "Ask questions, for we can still shoot later if the need arises."

The logic of this approach was understood clearly enough, at least until the Reagan administration came into power, with regard to strategic nuclear weapons. ICBMs based underground and submarine-based ballistic missiles (SLBMs) have a great advantage over the earlier manned bomber systems, for they did not seem to reward the side initiating the attack, but rather work *militarily* to the benefit of the side riding out an adversary's attack. Bomber crews used to race for their aircraft, fearing that enemy bombers were about to appear over them, but the image with regard to Polaris submarine crews and Minuteman missile silos became one of supreme patience, since the United States would never have to "launch on warning" or "launch under attack," but rather could retaliate at leisure after taking the time to make sure that there had actually been an enemy attack and after ascertaining the facts on who had launched such an attack.

By contrast, the extremely accurate multiple-warhead missiles now coming into the inventory suggest advantages for striking early at the enemy, for striking first. The fact that nature is steering the United States in this direction is very unfortunate.[14] At least as unfortunate is the apparent failure of the Reagan administration to take this change seriously enough as a threat to peace, the change to an offensive rather than defensive leaning in the confrontations of strategic forces.

The logic of stability has thus been understood, at least for much of the time, with regard to strategic nuclear weapons; the major complaint is that it has not been applied nearly as much to conventional weapons where it also has some very serious implications for the future likelihood of war.

The Problem of Europe

What are the prospects for an application of conventional defenses to soothe international problems in the 1980s and 1990s? In particular, what is the prospect for what has long been the most serious problem for the United States, the shielding of Western Europe against Soviet attack?

To repeat, the geopolitical nature of Western Europe has been a serious obstacle to international peace and quiet ever since 1945. Western Europe is basically a peninsula attached to the rest of Eurasia, which makes it inherently vulnerable to whoever controls the center of the continent, the Soviet Union, which is itself capable of massing and moving large masses of troops into the peninsula. For the Soviets to saturate West European defenses is basically a task of movement by rail, by wheel, or by foot. For the United States to match this threat is always a task of movement by ship or by airline, an inherently more difficult task.

Western Europe is also of extraordinary value to the United States and indeed to the entire Western world. It is the place from which most Americans' ancestors came. It is the source of U.S. culture and its philosophical and political traditions. It is also a most valuable economic asset for the world, full of innovation and energy, a valuable source of high technology and human capital. For the Free World to lose Western Europe would be a fantastic defeat. Even the *prospect* of such a loss is enough to change all of our political life. A great deal of U.S. political and military planning since 1945 has thus had to be devoted to heading off the reality of such threats and even the psychological shadow of them.

Before 1945, before the introduction of nuclear weapons, there would only have been the option of conventional defenses, possibly exploiting any advantages of a defense-oriented technology as we have been discussing here, but otherwise involving a substantial investment in troops and military equipment. Such an investment might have threatened in turn the Soviet Union with an invasion of Eastern Europe, and it would in any event have been an obstacle to the remarkable economic growth that lifted Western Europe out of the shambles of World War II. The alternative solution, basically the one adopted since World War II, has been to rely instead on the threat of nuclear retaliation against the Soviet Union, a retaliation that might or might not save Western Europe from Soviet occupation, but that would be so painful for the Communist leadership in any event that Moscow would never launch the invasion in the first place.

Perhaps this structure of nuclear retaliatory threats is thus stabilizing, in making offensive moves less likely in either direction, as well as being less of a burden to the economies involved. Yet the risks in such a reliance on nuclear retaliation are not negligible. A minor war might break out someday, after riots in East Germany, say, or an act of Soviet interference in Yugoslavia, with nuclear weapons being introduced almost automatically thereafter.

This is not to argue for total reliance on conventional defenses or for a withdrawal of U.S. tactical nuclear warheads from the NATO theater or for any declaration of no first use. Rather, it is a plea for a quieter exploration of the conventional possibilities for strengthening NATO, slowly reinforcing (and only ultimately replacing) the underpinning for Western European security that has depended so much on nuclear threats. To make this possible at a lower material cost and in a way that does not automatically threaten and panic the Soviet leadership, it should be realized as a NATO augmentation exploiting defensive weapons and defensive techniques, "defensive" in the more rigorous, nonpropagandistic sense we have been discussing here.

Are strategists right in their implicit premise that the Soviets would have attacked Western Europe by now, if the prospect of nuclear retaliation or of a conventional warfare defeat had not been there to deter them? Unfortunately, the West will never know what Soviet intentions have truly been over the years since 1945, for their documents will never be captured for academic study and analysis in the way that Hitler's documents were as part of the unconditional surrender at the end of World War II. The introduction of nuclear weapons stands in the way of "world empire" and also in the way of "unconditional surrender."

Seemingly confirming Western worries, or at least causing a continuance of uncertainties leading to worries, has been the heavy Soviet investment in tanks for these decades, an investment that amazes U.S. military officers, who would like to have more tanks for their own armed forces, but who nonetheless see the Soviet army's table of organization as being unreasonably "tank heavy." Why has Moscow made such a provocative investment, without which much of U.S. and NATO concern might long age have receded? At least three theories can be advanced.

First, the Soviets might actually be intent on one day invading the West, on occupying Hamburg, Frankfurt, Brussels, and Paris.

Second, the Soviets might see massive tank arrays as the most visible and effective way of suppressing any East European desires for decommunization and independence. The mere presence of such forces reminds one and all of the Soviet invasion of Hungary in 1956 and of Czechoslovakia in 1968.

Third, the Soviets may recall their own experiences with Hitler in 1941 and with Napoleon in 1812, when a rolling defense was what finally drove the invader back out of Mother Russia. This amount to endorsing the cliché that the "best defense is a good offense," since the invader can be counted upon to make some mistakes, mistakes that the defender's mobile armored forces can then move in to exploit.

The difficulty with this third interpretation of Soviet tank procurements is that the tank totals in Soviet inventory far excede the totals in NATO. If the Soviets are truly afraid of an armored advance by the

U.S. Army and the Bundeswehr, resembling the attacks of the Wehr-macht in 1941, they have vastly overensured themselves against this menace, ensuring their defense with enormous numbers of particularly offensive weapons. As has been noted, the West would heave a huge sigh of relief if the Soviets were to invest heavily instead in antitank weapons, which might prove to be equally good insurance against a U.S.–West German advance, but would pose far less of a threat to the political future of Western Europe.

Just as the Soviets might have been able to justify *some* tanks as insurance against the possibility of an aggression by Western tanks, NATO commanders are then tempted to ask for more tanks on their side, as insurance against Soviet capability. "The best antitank weapon is the tank" is the way their feeling is voiced, in yet another cliché suggesting that there are no qualitative differences among types of weapons.

It is quite correct that some tanks should be included in the appropriate force designed to repulse an enemy's armored attack. The ability to exploit the temporary confusions of an enemy advance by one's own counterattacks may be an essential part of any overall defensive posture. Yet the West would surely miss an opportunity if it elected to match the adversary entirely with the same kind of vehicle. It might be far more effective and/or far more stabilizing to concentrate mainly on other kinds of counters to Soviet tanks, for example, new antitank guided missiles (ATGM), a part of a most interesting range of new weapons called precision-guided munitions (PGM).[15]

PGMs have been defined as weapons that offer a very high kill-potential, once the intended target has been identified. When the target is a metal object against a nonmetallic background, such as a naval vessel on the water, an airplane in the sky, or a tank rolling across the battlefield, the skill required of an ordinary soldier for destroying such a target may now be minimal, perhaps comparable to operating a home-movie camera, or playing a video game in the kinds of game parlors now so widespread around the United States.

We earlier defined offensive weapons as weapons that can move, and defensive weapons as those that punish movement. In future wars, it may well be that for a tank to move will be to give away its location, and giving away its location will greatly increase its chances of being destroyed by these new PGMs. The new precision-guided antitank guide missiles will, therefore, very plausibly have a defensive effect.

Similar conventional war battlefield effects may be achieved by the many breakthroughs now being made in communications and in command-and-control systems, allowing the national force commanders to have a view of the battlefield that is almost "real time" in the currency of its data. Rather than the "fog of war," in which commanders must continuously guess about the location of enemy forces and even about the location of their own forces, the battlefield will be much more open and visible, as satellites orbiting over the Earth give a continuous picture of tank and ship concentrations.

Surprise attack and mobility have always been an asset for the offensive, since the aggressors could group their forces to engage only on a particular sector of the frontier, breaking through because the defender had no way of knowing where the attack was coming and thus was forced to spread his troops too evenly. Even if a three-to-one advantage in troops was normally needed to overcome the defense, forces on the offensive might be able to break through by arranging to surprise the defender in piling up a seven-to-one advantage in a particular zone.

With real-time surveillance and modern data-processing techniques, it may now become much more difficult for attackers to inflict such a surprise, since the defense can quickly shift its own reserves to negate any advantage for the mobile attacker. Once again, a hope emerges that new technology, if analyzed and exploited properly, can be harnessed to reinforce the defense rather than the offense, reducing more of whatever tension arises during a political crisis.

Some Conclusions

The discussion presented here will not be instantly welcome to the outright advocate of disarmament, for whom all weapons are bad. The argument here has been that some weapons are bad, but that others (those that discourage the launching of attacks) are good (while some may make little difference one way or the other in terms of stabilizing or destabilizing international confrontations, but simply waste the resources expended on them).

The term *defense* is used a great deal in international propaganda, for everyone wants to have a defense department, and no one politically wishes to admit even considering taking the offense. Japan thus has Self-Defense Forces, rather than an army, navy, or air force. President Kennedy, in warning the Soviets about deploying missiles to

Cuba in 1962, objected to "offensive" weapons, while not objecting to "defensive" ones.

Such uses of the "defense" label, as noted throughout this chapter, amount to a polemical abuse of what is still a valid and helpful analytical distinction. In the reality of this distinction, the concept of defensive policy is not overused, but indeed gets too little attention, since the internal psychology of the professional military is too much inclined toward the offensive, for all the historical and bureaucratic reasons noted.

The maintenance of peace in the world will require a great deal of effort, indeed a great variety of kinds of effort. Greater political and social communication across the boundaries can work to reduce the hatreds or tensions causing wars. Slowing the spread of the very deadliest of weapons, nuclear weapons, will reduce the chance that a madman could plunge the world into a holocaust simply by firing a few missiles. Reducing the temptations of a first strike, the temptations of the offensive, can finally play an important role in peace keeping and avoiding any repeat of the outbreak of World War I, a war without too much hatred or too many madmen, but "a war nobody wanted."

Notes

1. For details on the Maginot Line, see Vivian Rowe, *The Great Wall of France* (London: Putnam, 1959).

2. An example of such a disparagement of the offense-defense distinction can be found in Richard Burt, *New Weapons Technologies: Debate and Directions,* Adelphi Papers No. 126 (London: International Institute for Strategic Studies, 1976).

3. Ardant du Picq, *Battle Studies* (Harrisburg, Penn.: Military Service Publishing Co., 1947).

4. On the offensive inclination of tanks, see John Mearsheimer, "Maneuver, Mobile Defense, and the NATO Central Front," *International Security* 6, no. 3 (Winter 1981–82):104–22.

5. See Larry Collins and Dominque Lapierre, *O Jerusalem* (New York: Simon and Schuster, 1972).

6. Paul Bracken, "Urban Sprawl and NATO Defense," *Survival* 18, no. 6 (November–December 1976):254–60.

7. For an earlier example of such a territorial-militia proposal for West Germany, see the discussion of the von Bonin Plan in Klaus Knorr, ed.,

NATO and American Security (Princeton: Princeton University Press, 1959), 251–53.

8. Such an analysis of ABM is endorsed in Jan M. Lodal, "Deterrence and Nuclear Strategy," *Daedalus* 109, no. 4 (Fall 1980):155–75.

9. See Steven Canby, "NATO: Reassessing the Conventional Wisdoms," *Survival* 19, no. 4 (July–August 1977):164–68, for some discussion of possible Soviet "smash and grab" threats to Western Europe.

10. Carl von Clausewitz, *On War,* trans. Michael Howard and Peter Paret (Princeton: Princeton University Press, 1976), 370.

11. On the demilitarization of the U.S.–Canadian border, see Edgar W. McInnis, *The Unguarded Frontier* (Garden City, N.Y.: Doubleday and Doran, 1941).

12. Nostalgia for this Roman unity is discussed in F.H. Hinsley, "The Development of the European State System since the Eighteenth Century," *Transactions of the Royal Historical Society* 11 (1961):69–80.

13. On the military decisions on the outbreak of World War I, see Ludwig Reiners, *The Lamps Went Out in Europe* (New York: Pantheon, 1955).

14. The centrality of the stability issue on strategic weapons is discussed in Albert Carnesale and Charles Glaser, "ICBM Vulnerability: The Cures Are Worse than the Disease," *International Security* 7, no. 1 (Summer 1982): 70–85.

15. On precision-guided munitions, see James F. Digby, *Precision-guided Weapons,* Adelphi Paper No. 118 (London: International Institute for Strategic Studies, 1975.)

14
The Future of the
U.S. NATO Commitment

W estern Europe has been special for the United States, special enough to produce the defensive commitments central to the structure of the North Atlantic Treaty Organization (NATO). Yet will it remain so? This is the question about which we will worry throughout this chapter. To attempt to answer whether U.S. commitments to Western Europe can persist, we will first have to ask ourselves what made Western Europe, indeed all of Europe, ever become so special for the goals and commitments of U.S. foreign policy.

It is possible to identify and outline at least three major interpretations of U.S. foreign policy in general, interpretations in contention with each other now, as Americans try to understand themselves and their role in the world. We will outline these interpretations and then attempt to relate them to our interest in Western Europe.

A first interpretation to be considered, the most critical of U.S. foreign policy, is what could be called a "radical" or Marxist perspective. This is the view that the United States is worse than most countries in terms of being a threat to peace and the other good things of life, precisely because it is the most capitalist country in the world, thus the most burdened by the alleged internal failings and contradictions of capitalism. The domestic failings of the capitalist system, including an unequal distribution of resources and the unemployment of large numbers of workers, lead to imperialist adventures abroad in a fierce

This chapter was delivered as a paper in November 1983 at the Tenth National Security Affairs Conference, National Defense University, Fort Lesley J. McNair, Washington, D.C., and was published in the conference proceedings, William Buckingham, ed., *Defense Planning for the 1990s* (Washington, D.C.: National Defense University Press, 1984).

competition for markets in which to dump surpluses of production, and this leads to arms races and wars.

A second interpretation could be labelled the "power-politics" approach; it assumes that all countries in the world are guided to the same extent in their foreign policies by a pursuit of power. This is the view that the United States is the same as all other countries, "an ordinary country," in the title of a book by Richard Rosecrance,[1] with statesmen like Wilson, Acheson, or Kissinger behaving no differently from a Bismarck, a Clemenceau, or a Churchill.

The third interpretation is what most Americans would have endorsed until quite recently as best describing their own country; it is what might be labelled the "American liberal" perspective. This is a view that the United States is and has been better than other countries; having an unusually successful and appropriate model to offer the world, Americans have ventured out into the world mainly to help other peoples achieve the same happiness through freely elected regimes and by the economic successes that flow as a consequence of such political democracy.

This liberal view would have impressed almost all Americans as the most apt interpretation of U.S. foreign policy during all the years before World War II and most of the time since. The power-politics view was introduced and somewhat popularized in the years immediately after World War II, with the writings of Hans Morgenthau playing a central role here.[2] Such advocates of "realpolitik" argued that they were offering previously naive Americans an antidote to shock and disappointment about the behavior of others and an antidote to hypocrisy about themselves.

The "radical" view, whether it be of a Marxist or non-Marxist stripe, only began to attract a wider following during the Vietnam War, as many Americans (on campus and off) began to convince themselves that their country was imposing unnecessary troubles on the third world, resisting the forces of "socialism" because the demands of American profit margins somehow required such resistance. These Americans concluded that political democracy was inappropriate for places like Vietnam, Cuba, or Angola, as "economic democracy"—a more equal sharing of wealth—would be far more important than political democracy, than free elections or freedom of the press, with the latter "bourgeois" institutions having to be sacrificed if they got in the way of "socialism."

Testing Theories of U.S. Foreign Policy

How do these interpretations of U.S. foreign policy affect the nature and the durability of U.S. commitments to Western Europe? The radical interpretation does not normally so much relish being tested against Europe, since its favorite cases involve places like China, El Salvador, or Guinea. Can one prove American capitalist selfishness and greed by the Marshall Plan? If Lenin's interpretation of international conflict among advanced societies (a conflict allegedly explaining world wars and arms races) is to be believed, it surely was a short-sighted and foolish move for U.S. industry to build up such a powerful trade rival as West Germany. One remembers the hopeless task of the lone Communist member of the Württemberg Parliament in 1948 opposing the granting of the requisite approval for the delivery of Marshall Plan aid. "The Americans will dump their surpluses on you, their surplus grain, their surplus butter, their surplus manufactures . . . ," he warned, to which all the rest of the Parliament responded by chanting, "Great news; hurry it up; the sooner, the better."

So, Marxists and radicals feel on more comfortable ground when snatching up case studies of U.S. foreign policy for Central America or for anywhere else in the third world. This dichotomy, on which kinds of cases suit the radical or the liberal, will itself play an important role in the future development of U.S. commitments, a point to which we shall return a little later.

The second interpretation, that of power-politics, might find Western Europe's value for the United States relatively straightforward to explain. The primary issue is whether such a "realistic" set of categories really captures the entirety and the essence of American sentiments here. The NATO countries are valuable for the resources they offer, their raw materials (one constantly encounters arguments now that the Middle East and southern Africa are even more valuable in this regard), but especially their industrial capacity for converting such raw materials. If the industrial potential and human energies of the West Europeans were to fall under Soviet control, Moscow's option for developing military weapons systems would be strengthened (once all of such resources had been digested, or in part wasted—the standard Communist pattern), as would its option for enhancing the civilian living standards of the USSR (either or both of these options being regarded by realpolitik theorists as standard goals for ordinary countries).

Another kind of power-politics consideration would point simply to the geographical space of Western Europe rather than to its resources or industry. One is better off defending his own home in someone else's backyard—an old adage of national self-interest in a world of uncertain power distributions. Yet, persuasive as this might sound, it would clearly seem still more relevant to Central America than to Western Europe.

A last kind of power consideration is a little more psychological and less economic or geographical. If the United States has once stated its willingness to defend an area, and then backs out of such a commitment, its commitments everywhere else will come under more scrutiny and challenge. The initial commitment to the defense of an area might be quite haphazard and accidental, but the continuation of such a commitment thereafter becomes very important. The U.S. investment in the maintenance of the status quo in West Berlin illustrates this point extremely well. The very existence of a Western enclave in Berlin looks like in retrospect a sleep-walking exercise, based on premises about continuing Allied cooperation after the defeat of Hitler's Germany, and generating an unnecessary irritant for U.S.–Soviet relations when this cooperation did not continue.

West Berlin is not an economic asset; rather, it is a drain on and a liability to the economy of West Germany. West Berlin is not a buffer contributing to the defense of Western Europe or the United States. (When the commitment to Berlin was established, the United States was not particularly fond of the Berliners or of Germans in general; in 1948 they still looked like "Nazis," but the experience of the Soviet blockade and the U.S. airlift changed this image substantially.) Instead the U.S. commitment to West Berlin arose, was continued, and has been continued to this date, because to surrender it might weaken U.S. power (image being an ingredient of power) all around the globe.

Perhaps the U.S. commitment to all of Western Europe and not just to West Berlin may be derived in part from the psychological considerations of precedent stemming from past commitments. But this factor probably plays a larger role in the U.S. commitment to South Korea, and in the retention of the enclave base at Guantanamo in Cuba, and even perhaps in the maintenance of the ban on Soviet nuclear deployments in Cuba, won in President Kennedy's "finest hour" in the 1962 Cuban missile crisis.

All of these power considerations—economic resources, geographical position, or the dangers of setting precedents of surrender—may thus not be unique enough to Western Europe to explain the depth of U.S. commitments to NATO. They suggest that the United States is seriously interested in Western Europe, but that its attentions normally would be placed elsewhere.

It is when we apply our third perspective, by which Americans generously and altruistically identify with the happiness and well-being of others, that the depth of the attachment to Europe begins to make more sense. Americans care about more than markets for their capitalist entrepreneurs and about more than power. Europe is the mother continent for most Americans, in terms of ethnic heritage, and it is the source of language for all Americans, English- or Spanish-speaking. More important, Europe is the place from which the United States has drawn its culture and philosophy, its ideas about political freedom and democratic elections.

Americans may feel sympathetic toward all human beings abroad, and eager to share with them the institutions and arrangements that have produced happiness within the United States. Yet it is perfectly normal psychologically to identify the most, vicariously, with people who resemble oneself, "people like us." Except for Canada, Australia, and New Zealand (countries that would also be shielded by the same U.S. military commitments and "nuclear umbrellas"—if they ever needed to be shielded) there are no places in the world that quite so much resemble the United States. Beyond the simpler psychological feelings of identification, the Western (and Eastern) European countries remain places where Americans assume that political democracy can work (even while the applicability of free institutions has been cast into some doubt in places like Vietnam or El Salvador).

In some eighteen to twenty-five countries in the world free election systems still function, and the majority of these are in Europe. A few very radical Americans might question the appropriateness of such free elections—of political democracy—even in nations like Britain or Denmark, even in the United States, but this attitude reflects a skepticism about liberal values that has gripped only the tiniest minority of Americans.[3] Far more Americans might now have their doubts about the workability or applicability of political democracy in the underdeveloped world, a conclusion that this author regards as very premature and unfortunate, but which all the more serves then to explain why Europe is special and why it may well remain special.

The three broad interpretations of U.S. foreign policy would each thus have to be measured against the U.S. pattern to date of committing itself to NATO's defense, as we extrapolate into the future the interpretation that best seems to explain the past. As has been noted, the radical interpretation is full of inconsistencies where Western Europe is concerned. The material power-politics explanation is plausible, but it has some ins and outs, as Europe alternates between being a power asset and a power liability. Does having Western Europe on the U.S. side enhance its strength or tie it down?

The liberal interpretation, that the United States is bound to Europe by philosophical values and by ties of culture and heritage, is the most persuasive, for it readily acknowledges that Europe has been a "liability," an "entangling commitment," a commitment that the United States wanted to make for its own sake, rather than as a means to ends anywhere else on the globe. Some Americans still have aunts living in Europe, while others could not begin to trace their ancestry back to the crossing of the North Atlantic, but most Americans are far from forgetting the links across the ocean for which NATO is named.

Western Europe is thus special in its value to Americans, but additionally it is vulnerable; and it may be unique in combining such value and vulnerability. The forces capable of being mobilized by the Soviet Union can ride or walk to Paris, while the U.S. forces needed to redress the balance would have to arrive by sea or by air, logistically always a more demanding process.

As was noted earlier, the United States is committed to another peninsula reaching out from Eurasia, that being South Korea. This commitment raises many of the same problems over the years on continuity of commitment, feasibility of conventional reinforcement options, and credibility of threats of nuclear escalation. Yet the U.S. interest in Korea is much more explained by power-politics considerations of precedent than by liberal identifications with the people and life-style of the Republic of Korea. Having once shed the blood of American young men in defending South Korea, the United States would fear the consequences of the world's seeing the nation back away from such a defense now, throwing away whatever was won in 1950. By comparison, the politics of South Korea hardly merit the label of political democracy. The energies of the Korean people obviously win some admiration among Americans, and the growing community of Korean-Americans may produce new links in the future, but one wonders whether the United States could be persuaded to pledge a defense of Korea if it had not already carried out such a defense once before.

Australia and New Zealand are other places that are just as valuable to the United States by liberal perspectives, and so is Japan, after the remarkable transformation in image and reality that occurred after 1945. But these places are not as geopolitically vulnerable as Korea or continental Europe, for they do not sit in the path of a possible advance of Soviet tanks. Britain and Ireland are similarly valuable, but less vulnerable.

In the near future, the Persian Gulf area might gradually gain similar high status coupled with great vulnerability, such that all the tense lessons of uncertain commitments and hypothetical threats of escalation that the United States learned from NATO and from Korea would have to be applied there as well. In this case the tie would not stem from any liberal identification, as with Europe or Australia, or from considerations of the power of precedent as in Korea and the original commitment to West Berlin, but rather would stem from the more material power-factor of the enormous oil reserves in the region. The U.S. commitment to Israel in the Middle East may thus be exceptional, in that it stems from the same altruistic motives of identification as apply in NATO. Israel is a "liability," rather than an asset, despite its unhappiness when any U.S. government official ever phrases the situation this way. It is a nation that the United States wishes to shield against attack, merely because Americans love the people and admire the political style they set, rather than because of their contributions in oil or industry, or their sturdiness as some kind of strategic buffer. (Lest the radical explanation be forgotten, does anyone wish to argue that the United States defends Israel because it is seen as a market in which to dump surplus manufactures, or because U.S. investment capital wishes to purchase and operate plantations there?)

We can also label nations in this "valuable-vulnerable" category as "the fifty-first states." Reassuring as this phrase may sound to worried allies, one should probe it a little more deeply for meaning. It suggests that the United States would go as far in defense of such areas as it would go for California or Massachusetts, thus probably meaning that the United States would escalate to nuclear war in response to an attack on these areas. Conversely, one cannot imagine such a label being applied to, or such a likelihood of nuclear escalation on behalf of, say, Thailand or Zaire.

"Fifty-first states" become such because they are extraordinarily valuable to the United States. They also tend to become such because they are vulnerable, because the question of their survival is posed when hostile neighbors present threats of armored assault.

Considerations of precedent impose demands of continuity; the country that is threatened is reassured, and then continues to be reassured into the future. Our linkage becomes a little circular. "Fifty-first states" get nuclear umbrellas extended over them. But the extension of the nuclear umbrella solidifies and continues the special "fifty-first" status.

Dynamics of American Self-Image

What would we then predict about the trends over time in such a U.S. commitment to NATO? The Vietnam War worked to destroy what previously had been a predominant (and therefore often unarticulated) American ideological consensus behind the liberal position. Almost every American, asked in 1948 whether the far corners of the world would be happier if they were governed in the same manner as Minnesota, would have responded affirmatively, whether the corner be Bavaria or Bulgaria, Angola or Cambodia; and most of such Americans would have viewed their country's foreign policy as intended to facilitate such an ultimate spread of the free-election system, of what one should call, to be precise, "political democracy."

Given the costs, frustrations, and tactical deceits of the Vietnam War, however, a fair number of these Americans shifted to accepting the radical interpretation (discounting the value of the U.S. model and thus distrusting all U.S. foreign policy) or to the power-politics interpretation (by which U.S. policy is no longer anything but selfish, that is, it does not even try to be high-mindedly meritorious of trust).[4]

As the United States moves ahead in its foreign policy, in accordance with one or another of these theories about what this policy is all about, it will be enmeshed, moreover, in a dynamic process of seemingly confirming one or the other of such theories, compounding some of the new disagreements and confusions. Much of our discussion here will pertain to the possibility that the United States will settle once again into some kind of stable and persistent view of its commitments abroad. The United States has certainly gone through a change since the 1960s, but the nature and full dimensions of this change remain difficult to discern. If this chapter were about the future of the U.S. commitment to SEATO (South East Asia Treaty Organization), rather than NATO, it might amount to a depressing account of a steady erosion of U.S. commitments. But the topic here is NATO, not SEATO; and the argument here is that any despair over an erosion or termination of the U.S. NATO commitment could be very premature.

Equally premature would be conclusions that only power-political considerations will stimulate Americans from here on, or that the demands of capitalism have somehow been decisively proven as the source of all U.S. foreign-policy decisions. Although Americans have remained at odds among themselves as to which of these interpretations best fits the nation's foreign policy, the liberal commitment to contributing to the happiness of others retains a great deal of strength.

We shall try now to list the kinds of foreign-policy advice offered by the three perspectives outlined on the United States' role in the world. If the advice of the liberal perspective were followed, would the number of Americans accepting this perspective increase? If we begin with Europe, it will be argued here, this increase would occur. But what if we follow the advice of the power-politics school instead? Doing so might paradoxically pull the national consensus still further apart by seemingly confirming the logic of the radical interpretation.

The radical advice for the United States is relatively simple for the moment, captured in a way by George McGovern's campaign slogal of 1972, "Come home, America." This advice would be for the United States to withdraw from Central America as well as Southeast Asia and to withdraw from Europe as well. This does not amount to simple and straightforward isolationism; if the United States could ever be turned into a noncapitalist society itself, then it would be sending out the Marines to support revolutions of the Left elsewhere, deposing the white regime in South Africa, deposing the military regime in Chile, and so forth. Until then, however, since the United States (by this interpretation) always does wrong in the world, it should for the moment strive to do nothing in the world.

As was shown in Richard Nixon's smashing defeat of McGovern even in 1972, and by election trends ever since, the radical view has hardly come close to winning a consensus position in the United States. It rather merely influences enough of people and enough of analysis to confuse and prevent the establishment of any other view as a consensus.

The power-politics advice would be to forget everything except resources and position (and probably precedent), concentrating U.S. efforts where they most relate to its "vital interests" (somewhat narrowly or tautologically defined), therefore probably concentrating on "our own backyard," in particular on Central America and Mexico. The power-politics interpretation perhaps captures more Americans these days than does the radical position. Since the United States failed to win any gratitude in the world for its sacrifices in Vietnam and has been accused by many of being just "an ordinary country," many Americans will conclude that they may as well conform to the accusation that they are "taking care of [them]selves first." Yet the question is whether such a narrow outlook, in applications of U.S. influence in the world, can ever be consistent with the instincts of a majority of Americans. A selfish pursuit of only "national interests" or "vital interests" as an "ordinary country" might simply go against the national character. It might also paradoxically make the United States look *not* like an ordinary country, but like the radical caricature of it as an "unusually bad country."

If policymakers follow the advice of the power-politics advocates of realpolitik, for example, and concentrate the national energies and attentions on Central America (thereby also concentrating much of the world's attention on Central America), the United States might preclude the establishment of some Soviet bomber bases in Nicaragua and El Salvador (with whatever strategic difference this makes—or does not make—in a world of intercontinental-range missiles and oceans concealing missile-launching submarines). At the same time the United States seems to be supporting some of the worst examples of selfish ancien régime landlords, thus seemingly confirming the radical charges that the United States always supports economic inequality. Central America, it is contended here, would thus be a loser for anyone trying to recapture that consensus and self-confidence that used to be such important underpinnings of U.S. foreign policy. It pulls the United States into supporting former henchmen of the Somozas; it is a case made-to-order for the Marxist claiming that capitalistic vested interests explain all of U.S. foreign policy. Trying to head off the establishment of leftist dictatorships, the United States will have great difficulty in finding and supporting any true supporters of free elections, a free press, and liberal institutions. The United States will instead, out of power considerations, wind up opposing economic justice without accomplishing anything in the way of political liberty, opposing "economic democracy" without doing anything to support "political democracy." Only a single country in the region, Costa Rica, has to date shown inclinations toward the kind of liberal and free society that the United States cares about. Nicaragua, El Salvador, Honduras, and Guatemala have been something very different.

For purposes of getting Americans to feel good about their foreign policy again, a region full of Costa Ricas would be needed. And there is one, of course, in the very NATO area we are discussing in this chapter. For liberal purposes, a focus on Western Europe (*and* on Eastern Europe) is thus just the opposite of a concentration on Central America. It is an "easy case" for the liberal perspective, and a loser for the Marxists, just as Central America is a "tough case" for the liberals, and a winner for the Marxists.

If the United States pursues the liberal instincts of its people, beginning once again with the area where they are least open to challenge, it renews the American people's trust in these instincts and their self-confidence in the appropriateness of being active anywhere at all outside U.S. borders.

For Central America, as for Southeast Asia, and earlier for China, many Americans have now concluded that "they will lose their freedom under the Communists, but at least they won't be starving anymore; and besides they wouldn't have any freedom under our allies either." In the European case, illustrated so very nicely by Poland, the juxtaposition is just the opposite: "They lost their freedom under the Communists, and they are worse off economically than ever; and they are people like us, perfectly capable of living well under a system of free elections."

With regard to Europe, however, the Europe of NATO and also the Europe of the Warsaw Pact, Americans can feel as they felt after World War II, with nothing to apologize for. The evidence is clear that Western Europe shares U.S. satisfaction with the liberal political system and with the economic consequences of this political system. The evidence is similarly clear that Eastern Europe yearns for this kind of political system and for its economic concomitants.[5]

The events of 1968 in Czechoslovakia demonstrate this point. Those of 1981 in Poland show the same. The election in 1978 of a Polish pope amounted only to a more spectacular reminder of the sense that East Europeans were "people like us" in their wants and inclinations, people greatly dissatisfied when these wants were frustrated by Soviet foreign policy, people hoping that U.S. foreign policy will do as much as it can to counterbalance Soviet power.

One should not exaggerate how bad life is in Eastern Europe. To this author, it seems far better than life in South Vietnam since the Communist takeover, since the European Communist regimes have been forced (or have even wanted) to temper Marxism's worst intrusions into their citizens' private lives. Yet there is still much fault to find in the political and economic life-style of every one of these regimes, certainly when compared with their opposite numbers on the NATO side of the line. Life is not too poor in East Germany (with a per capita living standard considerably higher than that of the Soviet Union). Yet compare this standard with that of West Germany. And compare the relative political freedoms. We know how the comparison would strike most Germans if the Berlin Wall were to be torn down. Life is not too drab or too politically constricted in Hungary. Yet compare what is tolerated in Hungary with what has been accomplished in Belgium or Denmark.

NATO may simply amount to the Western commitment to keeping Denmark from becoming like Hungary. This is equivalent to arguing that Americans will remain tied by liberal sentiments to the outside world and that they will remain particularly tied to Europe, because Europe is the case that best exemplifies the relevance of such sentiments. When the transplanting of the U.S. model of political democracy did not seem to "take," when it seemed doomed to be perverted or frustrated, as in Vietnam or Nicaragua, Americans lost some of their self-confidence and enthusiasm for an active foreign policy. But Americans certainly still have something to offer for "people like us."

This author personally thinks it tragic that Americans have come to doubt the relevance of their institutions for the other corners of the world, because this attitude can verge on a kind of racism by which only Europeans (and the Japanese, as new "Europeans") are somehow "people like us," people "cut out" for the democratic process. Yet the fact remains that situations like those in Indochina and Central America have worked to blur the relevance of free press and free elections for underdeveloped areas (although India might show how such free institutions can indeed be of value even in surroundings of economic poverty). The day may come when Americans are again confident that free elections are as important for India and Singapore and Cambodia and Nicaragua as they are for Belgium and Denmark and the United States; that day is now some distance off. But (happily) very few Americans would as yet entertain doubts about Belgium and Denmark.[6]

Remaining Problems

Before taking the U.S. commitment to NATO too much for granted, however, we ought to work through a list of possible sources of trouble.

First, there are no new waves of immigration from the NATO countries to renew the ties of kinship that may have started such fundamental identifications in the first place. The economic boom that came along as a most welcome by-product of the liberal political system in the NATO area terminated the earlier pattern of Western European migrations across the Atlantic, while the border guards of the Iron Curtain stemmed any similar flows from Eastern Europe. Some observers thus conclude that this will end all the "special relationship" feelings within another generation or two, as the flow of family mail ends, as more and more Americans conclude that Europe is a distant and foreign place.

It should be stressed, however, that most Americans already have lost track of their cousins in Europe; it is not clear that the U.S. commitment to political freedom for a place like Norway depends on the Norwegian-American vote in Minnesota. The U.S. cultural and philosophical commitment is probably deeper than all this and thus less vulnerable to the most recent patterns of immigration.

Second, it is entirely possible that West Europeans will not identify with Eastern Europe as much as Americans do, with results that are confusing and perhaps quite upsetting for the links we are discussing here. This point has already been illustrated in the differing responses to the suppression of the Solidarity labor movement in Poland; the average American was more upset than the average West German or Frenchman. In many ways, of course, this makes perfect sense, for a typical American city is an amalgam of nationalities, while a typical European city is not. Americans may thus be more truly "European" than the Europeans, since they see the cultural whole, while those living on the continent of Europe see only the parts. Germans see themselves as very different from Poles, while Frenchmen see themselves as very different from Hungarians. Standing at a distance, at the remove of an ocean, one realizes that the Europeans actually have a great deal in common (as compared with the civilizations of other continents perhaps), and this is a great deal that is also held in common with the United States.

Americans might be upset by parochial attitudes among the Europeans, just as they have been upset in the past when such parochial attitudes produced World War I and World War II. Yet one good feature of the Cold War has been that such intra-European ethnic differences and rivalries have been substantially deemphasized. Ideological considerations of freedom versus Communism, of political democracy versus economic democracy, have been trumpeted on both sides, pitting East German against West German, discouraging French–German rivalries and German–Polish rivalries. Americans may at times feel themselves *leading* a general European concern for the liberty of all Europeans, West and East, rather than following such a concern, but this kind of leadership role has not totally perplexed them in the past and should not kill their interest in Europe for the future.

Third, it is inevitable that the economic interests of Western Europe will not be identical to those of the United States. Trade rivalries will persist, since everyone likes to find steady customers and worries if someone else is beating him to them. The governments in all the democracies have moreover had to abandon any "hands off" attitudes toward their economies, being now expected to produce full employment and low inflation if they wish to be reelected. Given the complexities of the economic interrelationships, it may be difficult to maintain any kind of real trust among such democratic governments whereby all of them resist (and are trusted to resist) the temptations of thrusting inflation and/or unemployment onto someone else, of playing "beggar thy neighbor." When such economic disagreements are then compounded with arguments about the economic costs of maintaining NATO's military defense, amid suspicions in the United States that the West European countries are relaxing too much and relying too much on U.S. military strength and not doing their fair share, the irritation that has always seemed to threaten NATO commitments will persist.

The prosperity of Western Europe is a strong piece of testimony for the general advantages of the liberal political system, especially when compared with the failures of the Marxist regimes in Eastern Europe. Such prosperity has perhaps made Western Europe a troublesome trade rival for the United States, but very few Americans would resent or regret the West German economic miracle or the rest of the European boom. Yet some Americans will see this now as a sign that Western Europe should take on more of the burden of its defense, perhaps all the burden. The European NATO members are geopolitically vulnerable to attack from the East, but they are economically capable of fielding some powerful military forces. Poland's economy is a mess, that of Belgium is not; and economic prowess still converts indirectly into military prowess. But this is a very familiar issue by now, having emerged virtually with the completion of Europe's economic recovery after the Marshall Plan. It is still an argument among friends.

Lenin and his disciples would predict that arguments about who gets to sell automobiles will pit nations against each other, in crises like the one that caused World War I; but anyone more committed to liberal thinking would regard the competition between German and U.S. automobile manufacturers as a necessary and healthy part of the entire economic process. Americans like to be able to sell. But, for ideological reasons, they do not like to feel that they are able to sell only because some artificial restriction kept buyers from having any other choice. Competition is the proof that one deserved to sell, and Americans are really not sorry that they generated competitors by their generosity in the years after World War II.

Fourth, this "old issue" of NATO burden sharing is matched by another "old issue" on the links of West European defense to threats of U.S. nuclear escalation. Rather than mounting a large and expensive conventional force to repulse any Soviet advance into Western Europe (what could be labelled a policy of "defense," or "deterrence by denial"), the United States has ever since the 1940s come to depend on threats of nuclear attacks on Soviet forces and on the Soviet Union itself (what is more often labelled a policy of simple "deterrence," or "deterrence by punishment"). This has raised troublesome issues (for three decades now, ever since the Soviets acquired nuclear weapons of their own) about the rationality and credibility of such responses by the United States and about the wisdom of a Western European dependence on such threats. Reliance on threats of nuclear escalation has surely allowed the West Europeans to escape with lower military expenditures and lower commitments of man-years to military service, thus importantly making possible the economic growth and prosperity that characterized the 1950s, 1960s and 1970s. Yet this reliance has always included the prospect and possibility of nuclear war, and the tension and foreboding that are a part of living with such possibilities.

In effect, the United States has been defending the West Germans by threatening to blow them up, along with their Soviet attackers, *if* the Soviets ever attacked. The United States has also been threatening to blow itself up in such a case. West Germans and other Western

Europeans and Americans have reacted periodically by questioning and denouncing the apparent irrationality of this policy; at other times they have settled back to be content with it, on the "rationality of irrationality" assumption that such threats are fine as long as they never have to be executed, that the Soviets will never attack a Western Europe they know will be destroyed as they conquer it (with the Soviet Union and the United States and much of the rest of the world being destroyed in the same process).

The West is presently encountering another wave of such doubt and criticism about the rationality, morality, or wisdom of a reliance on nuclear deterrence, amid demonstrations against the deployment of cruise missiles and the Pershing II in West Germany, and parallel anti-nuclear demonstrations in the United States. Consistent with what has just been said, it is possible (even likely) that this is merely part of an ebb and flow that saw similar expressions of opinion after the Carte Blanche exercises in West Germany in the late 1950s. It is also possible, of course, that something deeper and more permanent will emerge, as the U.S. NATO commitment that has been so heavily a nuclear commitment could be threatened and overturned, not because of any change now in American sentiments about Europe, but because of new American and European aversions to the basic threat of nuclear war.

A fifth problem for a continuation of the U.S. commitment to NATO will appear for those Americans with a historical memory that "entangling alliances" and overseas commitments have never been a normal part of U.S. foreign policy, so that it is somehow "unnatural" for several hundred thousand American young men to be stationed in Germany and this unnatural situation will have to end sooner or later. While very few people would endorse an "isolation" policy anymore, quite a few might still put forward such an intuitive impression of what is "normal," regarding the U.S. defense of Western Europe therefore as temporary and abnormal. These people would regard as unconstitutional any foreign country's being the "fifty-first state."

Such a view is a little difficult to categorize in terms of the trichotomy of liberal, radical, and power politics. It borrows from the liberals a recollection that most of the overseas entanglements of the past would have involved participation in some foreign imperial regime's selfish quests for more power, with the United States being able to nurture and enjoy its own democracy only by staying clear of such intrigues. Side by side with the liberal identification with democracy abroad has thus been a traditional aversion to overseas military operations and commitments, a sentiment of "back to normalcy" and "come home, America," for years enshrined in the annual debate about the Mansfield Amendment for a U.S. troop withdrawal, showing up now in other forms of discussion.

This view in turn borrows from the power-politics perspective the idea that it is natural for states to take care of themselves rather than altruistically to make sacrifices on behalf of others, with the logical corollary that the European NATO states should now be carrying most or all of their own defense burden and not relying on U.S. soldiers. The presence of U.S. troops on the continent of Europe would thus be viewed as a temporary and abnormal arrangement, as perhaps a transitory adjustment to the temporary weaknesses of the United States' allies after World War II, but surely not as something that can be continued endlessly into the future.[7]

This American memory of an absence of "entangling alliances" is so strong that one can only with difficulty argue against it. Yet there is much counterevidence to suggest that whenever it was *possible* for the United States to intervene with beneficent effect, throughout its history, that it has indeed intervened.

The sweeping generalization is that the United States has somehow been intent on isolation in all sectors, but a narrower generalization has sometimes been substituted, that the United States was perhaps more interventionist in Asia for most of the nineteenth and twentieth centuries, and isolationist with regard to Europe. If this was so, however, it was not because of lack of interest in events in Europe, but rather because of a great differential in how much impact Americans felt they could have in the two areas. In Asia and in the Pacific, the United States could play a balancing role. On the continent of Europe, however strong the vicarious involvement, the United States was too much outweighed by the forces of the established powers.

But rather than being uninterested in the welfare of others, the United States has been a model for revolution ever since the success of its own revolution, by its very example destabilizing and threatening the ancien régime back in Europe and elsewhere, offering sanctuary and safe haven for those revolutionaries who had to flee when their uprisings were suppressed. The United States endorsed the French Revolution of 1789 when all the powers of Europe disapproved of it. It endorsed the Greek revolution against Turkey in 1831. It endorsed the revolutions in Germany in 1848. Any bias the United States had toward the Far East in past allocations of energies thus results not from what Americans cared about (Americans cared about the whole world, convinced that any part of it could benefit from the form of government they had tested on themselves), but rather from what seemed possible. Any bias Americans might have today toward Europe is (as noted) derived very differently, from a conclusion arising quite recently that perhaps only Europe and the transplants of Europe will be suited to this democratic form of government.

The United States intervened seriously in Europe, of course, as part of an effort to end World War I, and then again in World War II, and then ever since. This period is rather prolonged to merit any label of "abnormal." That the United States retreated into self-conscious isolationism after 1919 was at least in part a fluke, the result of personality clashes between Woodrow Wilson and the Republican leadership of the U.S. Senate. Public-opinion polling had not yet been begun in the early 1920s, but more informal opinion sampling suggests that a majority of Americans indeed favored joining the League of Nations.[8]

The United States' failure to accept the Versailles Treaty came partly in response, of course, to a disillusionment with its World War I allies, who in negotiating the treaty showed themselves more interested in petty territorial gains than in Wilson's idea of "making the world safe for democracy." If European conflicts were ever again to become as nationalistic as they appeared in 1919, Americans might once again become disillusioned, vowing to withhold support for either side. Squabbles about secret treaties, promising away places as obsure as Fiume, could never be as important as the institution of free elections and freedom of the press.

Yet one of the unique features of the Cold War years is that such ethnic and nationalistic disputes have been substantially deemphasized. Considerations of ideology threaten Europe with war or conquest, rather than considerations of language and ethnicity. The Communist leadership (to its credit) has largely eliminated the kinds of ethnic feuds that used to pit Hungarians against Rumanians, or Poles against Germans, much as the European Community experience and the prosperity of the NATO area have deemphasized such historical feuds. The vicious experience of Fascism and Nazism probably contributed the most, of course, to Europe's putting such considerations of ethnic nationalism away.

What pits two armed camps against each other today is not

whether Germans or non-Germans will get to be top dog, an old-fashioned conflict of selfishness, but rather an issue of comparative judgment on what is best for all people, for all Europeans. It would thus probably be a mistake to rate the altruism of the Soviet leadership as being any lower than the altruism of American liberals. Rather than merely living up to the power-politics interpretation of Soviet national interests, the leaders of the Politburo most probably sincerely (alas, quite erroneously) believe that Poles and Germans and Frenchmen would be happier if they were governed in the style of Byelorussia. The United States' problem in defending NATO, or in bringing liberalization to Poland, would be simplified if the Soviets were not governed by such high-minded, but erroneous, beliefs.

Americans, quite rightly, believe that Poland would be happier if it were governed like Minnesota or like Denmark. Soviet leaders, quite wrongly, believe that Poland and Denmark will be happiest if governed along Marxist principles. Therefrom springs much of the risk of war in Europe ever since 1945. Therefrom also springs a deeper commitment by the United States, for it is defending its NATO partners on very important issues, issues just as significant as those that engaged the United States in 1917 and in 1941, issues far more important than what emerged in 1919 as the narrow concerns of Lloyd George, Clemenceau, and Orlando.

The situation would thus be very different if one were suddenly to hear West German or Belgian statesmen and men on the street stressing how anti-Russian or anti-Polish they felt, rather than how anti-Communist. As long as the issue is one of ideology, rather than nationality, however, Americans are less likely to become disillusioned again with their European partners or with the cause of NATO, and there is no "normalcy" of withdrawal here to retreat to.

In summary, during it entire history, the United States' "normal" pattern has been to be quite engaged in any issues as important as the difference between political democracy and hereditary autocracy, between political democracy and Fascism, or between political democracy and Marxist dictatorship. The United States has never been an "ordinary country" in this regard, because it was unique, after winning its independence, in its form of society and of government and in its role as a model for the world. Despite some more cynical commentators in other societies who would insist that the United States is an ordinary self-interested state, and despite the injunctions of some U.S.

power-politics-oriented theorists of international politics—that the United States *ought* to be exclusively self-interested and "ordinary"—this is not in the U.S. character.

Sixth, and finally, as a worrisome problem of U.S. commitments to NATO, we must return once more to the uncertainties about average Americans' self-image in terms of how they view the U.S. role in the world, and to our three-way debate on whether the liberal, the radical, or the power-politics perspective best explains the successes and failures of U.S. foreign policy since 1945, or since 1890, or for all of the nation's history. In the days when Americans were almost monolithically inclined to accept the liberal interpretation, there was no occasion to discuss it; most Americans accepted it silently and almost subliminally. The debate with other interpretations has brought the issues into the open, which is intellectually very desirable, but it has also meant that the United States now lacks consensus and is unpredictable as to where it is headed. If the United States engrosses itself more in Central America, trying to be "like all other powers" in looking mainly to national power, then the credibility and persuasiveness of the radical image of U.S. foreign policy may be enhanced, leading Americans to see themselves as "worse than most," with unforeseeable consequences also for the depth and persistence of U.S. commitments to Europe. If nothing else, U.S. commitments to NATO might become strained because the West Europeans themselves could more often accuse the United States of being "like all the rest" or "worse than most," questioning U.S. judgment, and causing Americans then to resent the apparent European lack of gratitude or solidarity. Those Americans who in the 1960s came to endorse U.S. foreign-policy interpretations that stressed the alleged needs and drives of capitalism or the inherent goals of power-politics were matched by a number of West European scholars and ordinary people who also endorsed such perspectives, less complimentary interpretations no longer suggesting that the United States was an unusually good country. Some of this attitude was simply a reflection of radical chic on European campuses or of a desire among older Europeans to uncover the same greedy self-service on the part of the United States that had so often been demonstrated by the European powers. Yet much of it reflected the impact of the horrors and the frustrations of the Vietnam War. Far fewer Europeans would have had to twist logic to see the 1944 liberation of France or the Marshall Plan as "power-politics" or as the workings of an exploitative and mercenary capitalism.

Conversely, the more the United States commits itself to Europe, to both Western and Eastern Europe, the more it will remind everyone of the kinds of conflicts with the Soviet Union that reflect well on the United States and that help to recapture the confidence and admiration of West Europeans. This is hardly because Europeans are so self-centered that they care only about their own futures. As was pointed out earlier, West Europeans may not even care so strongly, on any selfish basis, about what happens in Poland or Czechoslovakia. Rather, it would be because the facts in Poland or Czechoslovakia so clearly support the American vision of the world, while any such proof of the American vision is less easily discerned in the current situation in El Salvador.

The logic of post–World War II U.S. foreign policy, and indeed of U.S. policies during World War II and World War I, and perhaps for all of U.S. history, is exemplified by American feelings about Europe. While it is reasonable to ask about the durability of U.S. commitments to NATO, it is misleading to presume that such commitments are somehow "abnormal." The NATO commitment is much more truly in the "fifty-first state" category.

Some Conclusions

Let us try here to put the problems of the NATO security alliance in perspective. Disputes and problems do exist, but they are too easily exaggerated by those who forget the overarching identity of interest pulling the United States into its West European commitments in the first place.

Americans who study the fractions of gross national product allocated to defense by the different NATO countries typically begin to feel exploited, with this feeling growing as the European partners have prospered. Why should the largest alliance partner make the greatest contribution when it is no longer so much the richest partner? (While Belgian, Dutch, and Danish expenditures on defense continue to lag, the problems are not entirely ended by West German efforts to increase defense spending; a defense effort that ceases to be primarily American, but instead relies primarily on the growth of the Bundeswehr, may cause new anxieties based on older historical memories.)

Yet it is all too easy to exaggerate these issues, since the Mansfield

Amendment probably never spoke for as many Americans as some might have feared. The United States was for long the most prosperous member of the alliance and still is so by some yardsticks of measurement. Quite apart from who is best off in terms of per capita GNP, or in terms of balance of payments, it is also historically normal for the largest member of a military alliance (even an alliance in the old sense) to expend more effort than the smaller members. Moscow does "more than its share" within the Warsaw Pact.

Beyond these considerations, moreover, the United States may be "exploited" precisely because of the visibility of the feelings of identification discussed earlier, just as some children may feel exploited by the aging parents they love ("exploited" at least by the exchange standards that would apply between strangers—but the United States and Europe are not "strangers"). Hoping each year that the NATO countries would deploy a few more troops of their own, the United States nonetheless has been continuously prepared to deploy its young men to Western Europe, to have them fight and die there if an invasion were to come from the East, and to have them serve as proof that far more awesome military counters to aggression were likely to follow.

This subject leads us soon enough into the alleged European–U.S. "debates" about military strategy. Could it be that Americans look forward to fighting a war only in Europe, avoiding all destruction back in the United States? Can it be that West Europeans instead look forward to a defense in which all the nuclear rounds are fired over their heads, in a duel of intercontinental missiles devastating only North America and the Soviet Union? All of such abstractions are hopelessly misleading for what the defense debates have really been about since the 1950s.

Americans and Europeans agree almost totally in hoping that a Soviet attack will never come and in welcoming preparations that discourage such attack. If an attack were to come, Europeans and Americans would agree also in lamenting nuclear damage on either side of the Atlantic, just as they lament the damage inflicted in a war limited only to the use of conventional weapons, just as all members of NATO would also lament the fall of any segments of territory to Communist conquest.

This is a very demanding list of the kinds of damage everyone seeks to avoid. Americans then disagree among themselves, as West Europeans in general disagree among themselves, as to how to balance the items on this list against each other. Some Americans and some

Europeans ever since the 1950s have wished to place primary stress on deterring and preventing the Soviet attack in the first place, relying heavily on the threat of nuclear escalation posed by having U.S. troops and tactical nuclear weapons already in place. Relatively smaller deployments of U.S. troops, and of German and other European troops, are required by this nuclear approach, thus sparing all the alliance members some monetary and human costs in peacetime (another important consideration is that these costs are shared by all concerned).

Other Americans and other Europeans have shared a worry ever since the 1950s about the nuclear damage that would ensue if deterrence were to fail, thus wishing instead to augment the conventional defenses of NATO so that the response to a Soviet attack would not so quickly have to become a thermonuclear war. The cost of such an approach might be that it would make it easier for Soviet leaders to contemplate an aggression; also, more young men from both sides of the Atlantic would be tied up in military service.

Compared to the disagreement *within* each country on these choices, the disagreement *between* countries is minor. It is a mistake to see such disputes as pitting national interests against each other, as Mansfield and Gallois and many others have done, for the most serious disputes are instead spread across the alliance, between the different schools of thought on how best to serve the community interest. It is similarly a mistake, a mistake the press is terribly inclined to make, to view Europe as more détente-minded than the United States, or as less détente-minded; leaders like Reagan, Schmidt, Kohl, or Mitterand may face more telling opposition within their own countries than they face from their alliance partners.

Notes

1. Richard Rosecrance, ed., *America as an Ordinary Country* (Ithaca, N.Y.: Cornell University Press, 1976).

2. Hans Morgenthau, *Politics among Nations,* 5th ed. (New York: Knopf, 1978).

3. For an illustration of the questioning of liberal democratic values even for the United States itself, see Michael Parenti, *The Anti-Communist Impulse* (New York: Random House, 1969).

4. The loss of American self-confidence in the value model of political

democracy is outlined in Ole R. Holsti, "The Three-headed Eagle: The United States and System Change," *International Studies Quarterly* 23, no. 3 (September 1979):339–59.

5. For a discussion of some of the issues, see Klaus Bloemer, "Freedom for Europe, East and West," *Foreign Policy* no. 50 (Spring 1983):23–38.

6. For this author's more extended discussion of a "double standard" by which Europe and the more developed world is seen as appropriate for a system of free elections, but the non-European underdeveloped world is not, see George H. Quester, "Consensus Lost," *Foreign Policy* no. 40 (Fall 1980):18–32.

7. For a European view anticipating such an exhaustion of the U.S. commitment, see Hedley Bull, "European Self-Reliance and the Reform of NATO," *Foreign Affairs* 61, no. 4 (Spring 1983):874–92.

8. On the disillusionment of Versailles, see Thomas A. Bailey, *Woodrow Wilson and the Lost Peace* (New York: Macmillan, 1944).

15
Assessing Soviet Power Away from Europe

T he intention of this chapter is to survey the reality of the Soviet power position for the sweep of Asia from the Middle East to Korea and Japan. It surely will not conclude that the West has no causes for concern with regard to such Soviet power. Serious problems remain, even as these problems continually change form. Yet prudence sometimes produces a "worst-case scenario" caution that misses possibilities that can be exploited, and that can also miss the respects in which the adversary himself feels insecure. As the Soviets watch the Persian Gulf or South Asia, or Southeast Asia or Northeast Asia, they may see as many burdens as opportunities, burdens that postpone or even solve U.S. problems in some cases, burdens that may generate new or worse problems for the United States in others. Not every force that is hostile to the United States on the Asian continent is a natural ally for Moscow.

In looking at the other side of the Soviet strategic situation, some of the analyses might thus come across as wishful thinking, as U.S. analysts again and again uncover complications for the Soviets, complications that give Moscow a difficult hand to play, rather than an easy hand overloaded with trump cards. Precisely because of the complications of the world, however, these difficulties for Moscow will not always be such welcome news for the United States either. Not every force that is hostile to Moscow is such a comfortable ally for the United States.

When threats of nuclear proliferation are involved, the United States may still have a common interest with the USSR in heading it off.[1] Even when threats to petroleum energy sources are the issue, the two superpowers, and the two alliances over which they preside, may have more than one might think in common and less reason for conflict.

This chapter was presented as a paper at a National Defense University conference on the Pacific Basin in March 1984, at Fort Lesley J. McNair, Washington, D.C.

Some Confusing Links between Inputs and Outputs

One can always try to assay the strength of a major power in some region by returning to the objective raw data of military inputs. How many troops and how may tanks do the Soviets have in Asia and where are they deployed? How many aircraft does Moscow command, with what ranges and carrying capacities, and what bases from which to fly them? How many missiles, with how many nuclear warheads, are now available for targeting cities or military targets around Asia?

There is little doubt that the Soviet Union has made impressive gains by all of these yardsticks.[2] Airbases in Afghanistan are now at their disposal; they may also have bases in South Yemen and Ethiopia. The naval base at Cam Ranh Bay seems now to be entirely Soviet in its operation. New fighters, fighter-bombers, and bombers have been deployed, with greater capabilities than the aircraft they replace (facing new aircraft on the adversary side that are also, of course, better than the ones they replace). The total of Soviet ground forces along the Chinese border remains quite impressive, having risen dramatically at the end of the 1960s without diminishing troop or tank totals in Eastern Europe, and then remaining at this high level through the 1970s even when forces in Eastern Europe were growing in fighting power.

The replacement of older SS-4 and SS-5 medium-range nuclear missiles with the SS-20 has complicated any kind of accommodation for Asia and for Europe, because the newer missiles, in addition to being more accurate and equipped with multiple warheads, are quite mobile. This mobility may offer some stabilizing advantage for crisis situations, in that they will be more difficult for the West to locate and target. But the same mobility makes for easy moves back and forth from Europe to Asia, so that countries at neither end might ever feel really assured that they had been relieved of this missile threat.[3]

Yet military inputs do not result in an output of military power or political influence in any automatic one-to-one pattern. Some of the growth in Soviet military capability has been matched by growths in non-Communist military capability, as the development of better and better military technologies leaves all sides more capable. Some of the enhancement in Soviet capability may also be redundant. Since the Soviets already have many ways of destroying Tokyo or of sinking tankers coming out of the Straits of Hormuz, it is not always so obvious what Moscow gains by investing in yet another means of inflicting these kinds of punishment.

Finally, some of the enhanced Soviet deployments of military tools may even be counterproductive, creating problems for Moscow rather than solving them, or at least reflecting some deeper problems that the Communist system was already going to encounter all along. If the Soviet leadership now seems to keep on reaching for aces, it is not beginning with such a pat hand.[4]

The Persian Gulf

It may seem entirely plausible that Moscow would like to control some or all of the Persian Gulf region. The entry of Soviet forces into Afghanistan has thus struck many as consistent with a master plan in this direction, as have all the Soviet intrigues in Syria and Libya, and in the other Arab states in the Middle East. Yet not a few unanswered questions remain on the Soviet prospects here. Can the Soviets so easily establish control over the oil-producing states? Has the intervention in Afghanistan really been so much spurred or designed with this object in mind? And, if the Soviets did win control over some of the oil regions, would Moscow elect to withhold oil from the West? Or might Moscow paradoxically make considerably more of such oil available than has been the pattern with OPEC (Oil and Petroleum Exporting Countries)?

From the perspective of U.S., West European, and Japanese energy needs, a Soviet takeover of a state like Kuwait, Abu Dhabi, or Iran, is surely not the worst that the West has to look forward to.[5] Far more of a problem might arise in a takeover of these oil fields by any new domestic regimes that, for ideological or religious reasons, decided that the flow of dollar earnings was undesirable and that oil production should thus be cut back. If Saudi Arabia were taken over by a new Islamic fundamentalist government, would it not be more likely to reduce oil production, convinced that the import of consumption goods from the West was evil per se, convinced that the oil should best be kept in the ground until its exploitation can be handled in a morally appropriate fashion? Conversely, if Iran were taken over by the USSR (itself an unlikely prospect), would the Soviets not actually increase the oil production of the new "Iranian SSR" to the maximum, being as intent as ever on earning hard currency by sales to the free world?

No one in the West is going to root for the Soviets to win military and political control over Kuwait or Qatar or Saudi Arabia. Given the great risks of destruction and escalation and the greater ease of onward movement across the Gulf, no one will even root for a Soviet takeover of Iran. Yet the important point is that the West will also not be able to see a Soviet takeover as the very worst that could happen. The current status quo is surely preferable to an extension of Soviet power. But will fortune permit "the current status quo" as an available and attainable option (the option that was denied the United States in Iran)? Compared to some other possibilities, for example, to a totally antimodernity approach in some locally grounded revolutionary movement, the West would have to consider Communist domination preferable.

Can one really imagine the Communist world and the West endorsing a shared interest in the production and export of oil from a troubled region, perhaps with Soviet naval vessels sharing the convoy duties of the U.S. Fleet in the Straits of Hormuz, or with Soviet troops guarding oil wells pumping oil to Japan? Lest this sound too wildly imaginative, we might simply note that one such situation already exists, as Cuban troops in the Angolan enclave of Kabinda guard oil wells pumping oil to the American Gulf Oil Company, while the oil wells are occasionally attacked by the anti-Communist rebels supported by the CIA. One could perhaps wait in vain for Gulf Oil to adopt Andrew Young's description of the Cuban presence as "stabilizing," and it would be unwise to attribute Cuban behavior here to any lingering commitment to détente. Rather, we see a convergence of the real material interests of the two sides. Quite simply, the Marxist regimes very much need hard currency, and the democracies normally very much need oil.

More than worrying about the Soviets' seizing the oil fields, the West might have to worry about their devastating these fields in the process of trying to seize them, as "scorched earth" tactics took their toll, as no one would then for a time have access to the energy flow normal to this region. The Western world would worry about the sheer fragility of such a valuable resource. Yet what is valuable for the West is valuable for others as well, and this prospect of devastated oil fields can also be counted upon to work to deter Soviet advances into the region, for a worldwide increase in the cost of energy would impose additional stringencies not just on Italy and Japan, but also on Hungary and Poland. Again, we have a situation that is full of problems and worries for all sides, rather than simply a handful of trumps for

Moscow. And, we have an indirect trump for the West, in that some of these risks and problems amount to an additional deterrent to any Soviet military aggressions. If Afghanistan were rich in oil, it might have been gobbled up by the USSR much earlier. *Or,* it might never have been attacked by the Soviets at all.

What is best for the United States and its friends, with regard to the Middle East and especially the Persian Gulf, is hardly what is best for the Soviet Union and its allies. But what is the worst for one is hardly the best for the other side either. One form of "worst" here would be widespread nuclear weapons proliferation, followed by the use of nuclear weapons in combat, perhaps all too quickly lapping up into the Soviet Union itself because of the short geographical distances involved, then soon drawing in the United States as well.

Another form of "worst" would be the prolongation and extension of conventional wars, like that between Iraq and Iran, with both the superpowers failing to benefit from the war, with both the superpowers really being unable to decide what side they wish to be on. Such wars can drag down civilization in the area even if they do not become intertwined with nuclear weapons proliferation. They do great damage even if they do not interfere with the exporting of petroleum products.[6]

Still another form of "worst" that is not good for adversaries pertains particularly to the amount of energy extraction from the Persian Gulf region. For selfish reasons of national interest, the Soviet Union cannot be looking forward eagerly to denying the West the energy resources of the Middle East. A Soviet advance into the region that produced devastation in the process would be to the good of no one. A Soviet move otherwise to hold back petroleum would also not be to the real interests of the Soviet leadership.

Afghanistan

Returning to the Soviet motives for invading Afghanistan, one might wish to go slowly about crediting the Soviets with worries about an Islamic fundamentalism lapping over into the Soviet Asian republics from Iran. Decades of Communist rule and of secret-police control have cultivated a greater legitimacy for atheistic outlooks, such that an ayatollah would seem to have less latent power.

Yet downgrading Soviet concerns here does not mean that one can erase them entirely.[7] The "revival" of Islamic fundamentalist political movements has indeed come as a surprise to many observers, with the possibility of a string of dominoes falling from Iran to Afghanistan to the Uzbek SSR not being so much less plausible than the possibility of similar dominoes toppling from Iran to Kuwait to Lebanon. What the Soviets certainly faced in Afghanistan in 1978 and 1979 (and what they still face) was the first possibility of an already established Marxist regime being overthrown by a guerrilla insurgency, the kind of guerrilla insurgency for which the Soviets and the Chinese and others had for so long claimed a special Marxist significance.

Guerrilla war may indeed be a "way of life" for the tribal and hill peoples of Afghanistan, closely linked to their very traditional Islamic outlook on all matters of life.[8] It is indeed difficult for a liberal American to know with whom he is to identify, if one major issue between the Afghan freedom fighters and the Marxists centers on whether women should be allowed to learn to read. As tenth-century Islam battles against a Marxist vision of what the twenty-first century should be like, the United States might rather be content to let the conflict drag on inconclusively. And drag on is very much what it is likely to do, reducing (as is illustrated in the annual votes of the United Nations General Assembly) the standing of the Soviet Union in Asia and elsewhere.

South Asia

The deployment of troops into Afghanistan brings the Soviets somewhat closer to the Straits of Hormuz and to the Persian Gulf (even if the roads from Afghanistan across Iran might be less appropriate than those already open from Soviet Azerbaijan straight south). Yet the deployment also brings Soviet forces closer to Pakistan and, across Pakistan, closer to India. Was this the intention of the Soviet advance, or was it more an inadvertent by-product? Does it offer the Soviets advantages in intimidating Pakistan, or in offering assistance of a political and military kind to India, or in intimidating India? Or are there enough reversals in this linkage to amount to an actual power drawback to the Soviets, as the Pakistanis are driven more into an alliance with the United States, and the Indians are forced to fear the momentum and extent of the Soviet geographical advance? However much the typical Indian policymaker or opinion-leader may dislike having Pakistan as a neighbor, he might even more dislike having a Marxist regime on the western frontier, a regime controlled and pacified by the processes demonstrated in Afghanistan.

Nothing is black and white here. It would be foolishly counterintuitive to label the Soviet advance into Afghanistan as a victory for the democratic world and as a defeat for the Soviets. Yet it is not a victory for Moscow either (at least not yet). With many people in India as well as in Pakistan openly rooting for the Afghan guerrillas and pointedly drawing analogies to Vietnam, and with the Afghan guerrillas imposing substantial costs on the Soviet forces, Moscow may well have reason to regret having destroyed an earlier Afghan neutrality, even as Washington and New Delhi continue to regret this as well.

India is a very important country. One of the largest countries in population, it is also the principal example of a functioning political democracy outside the economically advanced countries, a demonstration that free elections and freedom of the press do not have to be sacrificed simply because economic development has lagged. This by itself would be reason enough for the United States to be concerned that South Asia not be intimidated or overwhelmed by Soviet military power. It is also an important reason why the Indians themselves, being concerned about protecting and maintaining their own independence, will be wary of extensions of Soviet military power.

Americans typically do not think very deeply about their reasons for caring about South Asia. Having seen so many other less developed countries give up on political democracy, they may find it too easy to forget how strong and viable such institutions are in India. Seeing most of the third world much less willing to criticize the Soviet Union than the United States, Americans forget how superficial such distinctions can be, so much a response to the perceived sensitivities of brutal Soviet character, and so unrevealing about basic Indian attitudes. How many Indians would ever wish to send their children to study in the Soviet Union if they could send them to study in the West instead? How many would choose to read *Pravda* if they could read the *New York Times?*

Despairing of hopes for rapid economic progress in India, Americans sometimes become angry at what we see as Hindu culture, forgetting the ways in which that culture has been good for setting the stage for pluralism and liberal democracy. An occasional glib commentator has even sometimes offhandedly suggested that he would welcome

Communist rule in India, because only such a total dictatorship would dare to kill off quickly the cows that consume so much grain even while they play so important a religious and cultural role in the Indian tradition. When reminded that democracy is important, the same cynic then settles for a sudden Communist coup, with the Marxist dictatorship then being terminated in another sudden coup some six weeks or so later, with democracy restored, but with this alleged bovine barrier to economic progress having been eliminated in the meantime.

All of such commentary reflects too casual and uninformed an attitude on the part of many Americans toward India and toward the rest of Asia. Too often Americans shift to other considerations of power politics as the supposed explanation for their interest, tuning out any human identifications and acting instead as if they cared about India more as a possible military base than as a functioning democracy.

In truth, India is not so necessary or valuable as military base, nor is it endowed, like the Persian Gulf or southernmost Africa, with strategically vital resources. Instead, it is important for what it represents as a model of the liberal rather than the Marxist approach. If the Soviets were really intent on extending their power into South Asia, it might just as well be for similar reasoning, with Moscow being intent on somehow proving the wisdom of Lenin superior to the wisdom of Locke, Burke, or Jefferson, or Gandhi or Nehru. If the Soviets are ideologically driven, South Asia is an acid test for the relevance of competing ideologies. If the Soviets are driven into this corner of Asia, however, they will encounter resistance from India itself, in addition to what ideological resistance the United States would be inclined to offer.

At times, therefore, the United States falls into the trap of understating its own interests in the South Asian area, or misstating them. It also often overstates the degree of Soviet influence already in place, even sometimes acting as if India were somehow already an ally or satellite of the USSR, equating diplomatic abstentions in votes at the U.N. General Assembly (usually a misleading indicator of much of anything) with deep Soviet influence, equating port calls by the Soviet Navy with the establishment of serious naval bases for the USSR, and so forth.

It is surely true, and it is surely also irritating, that India and many of the other LDCs tend to apply a double standard in their public-statements about the two superpowers, condemning the United States and its allies whenever they use military force, muting their criticisms of similar actions by the Soviet Union or its allies. One hears less vehement criticism therefore of Soviet-sponsored military actions in Afghanistan or Cambodia (although one indeed hears some) than one heard of U.S. operations in Vietnam, or of its associates' actions in Central America. As Soviet warships in the Indian Ocean are matched by U.S. warships in the same ocean, one hears more frequent protests about the latter than about the former.

Some of this criticism simply reflects the deeper links between Indian and Western society, however, indicating a double standard that actually works to the benefit of the West. Criticism of the West is criticism "within the family." The Soviets, on the other hand, are a much more alien force for Indians, and for many Asians; to them, the Soviets are like someone with whom one must deal more cautiously, someone one does not criticize as readily, someone to whom one never as fully conveys one's true feelings.

Naval Bases

Another part of the double standard just illustrated comes from special aspects of naval force deployments, producing somewhat different attitudes on "balance of power," attitudes that are not always so readily understood from a distance. In the classic balance of power on land, any state threatened by a foreign military power would welcome the presence nearby of yet another military power, as these two possible attackers might check and balance each other, perhaps fighting wars to drain off each other's military strength, more often merely deterring aggressions by the prospect that they would intervene. To keep the rest of the world divided against itself has made sense for the national security of Great Britain, and for many other countries.[9]

Why then would India not welcome a U.S. fleet in the Indian Ocean as a check to the potential of the Soviet fleet, and vice versa? The difference may well be that the seas, however important they are, do not deter life on land nearly as much as would armies back on land itself. To have several neighbors' armies checking each other may make perfect sense. To have several fleets checking each other on the high seas may only cause those seas to become more hazardous, as naval wars are threatened or are fought, or as the sea powers begin demanding onshore bases in a contest of augmenting their potential.

The United States once quietly preferred to have only the British Navy in the Atlantic and the Caribbean, rather than having German and French and other navies as well. The Japanese similarly were happier with the British monopoly than with the pluralization of naval power that showed up at the end of the nineteenth century, when China became pockmarked with German, French, British, and Russian naval bases. A monopoly fleet may not be able to apply all that much pressure on shore. When not threatened by another fleet, it may not feel so driven to demand bases on shore.[10]

This is to argue that the nations around the Indian Ocean, including India itself, may have a reason to prefer that the ocean be dominated by a single fleet, rather than being contested by two fleets. New Delhi may prefer that the Soviets keep out if a U.S. fleet is already bound to be there, or that the U.S. fleet keep out if a Soviet fleet is bound to be there; Indians could put either of such regional monopolies of naval force ahead of a duopoly, because this means less threat of a naval war and disruption of commerce on the high seas, and less pressure for naval bases along the shore. Such bases in the past were often enough established with a view to possible conflicts on the oceans, only then to become beachheads for extensive political or military domination of the hinterland.

The Indian first choice, of course, might be to have no foreign navies at all in the Indian Ocean, just as the first choice of the United States or Japan would once have been to have no European navies at all off their coasts. The issue is rather what is to be the second choice. Transplanting balance-of-power theory from continental military confrontations suggests that the next favorite choice would be to have two or three foreign navies in the ocean in competition with each other. But this analogy may be misleading, with the next favorite choice instead being, as has been suggested, a clear dominance of the seas by one major fleet.

Skeptics might still question whether the Indians have been quite as willing to object to a Soviet presence as they are inclined to object to a U.S. presence. There is, as always, some asymmetry and double standard here, but it does not really upset the general conclusion. On the presumption that the Soviet Union is indeed the more militaristic of the two superpowers (an assumption that many Indians have indeed probably internalized, even if they do not typically voice it at international gatherings) New Delhi would have concluded that the Soviets were the least budgeable from a commitment to Indian Ocean deployments. On the matching assumption that American public opinion was much more reachable and relevant, the Indian government would thus (in a manner that might simultaneously be realistic and unfair) have resigned itself to the Soviet presence, choosing to campaign against the U.S. presence.

If the naval confrontation in the Indian Ocean continues, and Soviet pressures persist, we may nonetheless see some Soviet "naval bases" appearing around the shores of Asia. Cam Ranh Bay in Vietnam surely now has this status, as do some harbors on the coasts of South Yemen; some charge that similar bases will exist on the coasts of Ethiopia, or of India itself. At least two kinds of questions need to be addressed here on the possibility of such bases. First, we will have to be careful (propaganda aside) to sort out the categories of what we think we mean by a "naval base." And second (on our major topic of surveying the Asian power advantages and handicaps of the Soviet Union), we will have to contemplate whether such bases are always an advantage, or whether they can indeed become an embarrassment and liability.[11]

First, what do we mean by having a "base"? Having access to any form of onshore assistance at all might seem to qualify, ranging from fresh fruit to shipyard services to firm ground for shore leave, except that these are services that can now normally be contracted for at many ports of the world. As long as the services could be withdrawn at any moment, the situation is hardly what the United States has at Guantanamo or the Germans once had at Tsingtao.

A firmer foothold on shore is thus closer to what we are thinking of here, with Soviet naval and army personnel garrisoning the port area, perhaps able to keep out nationals of the host country. The crucial transition point might arise on whether such a base would be usable by the Soviets without the permission of or against the wishes of the host country. Britain can use the bases it has on Cyprus and at Gibraltar without legally or practically getting permission from Cyprus or Spain. Will we ever see such Soviet capabilities embedded on the coast of India?

In addition to this degree of naval-power independence, the base might also be used to influence political and military events in the hinterland, perhaps to support subversion, perhaps to inflict a continuing and pervasive form of gunboat diplomacy.

It is precisely fears of this last kind of "basing" that make such operations sensitive around the world, so sensitive that Moscow always denies having any bases abroad, or any intention of acquiring bases. Moscow surely has been careful since 1955 not to acquire nominal sovereignty over any such enclaves, in that year surrendering the special prerogatives it had won at the close of World War II for Port Arthur on the coast of Manchuria, and for Porkkala on the coast of Finland. It is fascinating to contemplate the increased level of friction that would have developed between China and the Soviet Union if the USSR had retained its explicit base at Port Arthur in the 1960s and 1970s, having to get supplies into the enclave by boat, facing hostile demonstrations along the perimeters of the territory, and so forth.

Even at the lesser degree of significance for basing, by which the USSR might simply be able to use a base without the host nation's approval, one might anticipate substantial resentment in the 1980s and 1990s, as any such independent superpower prerogatives look like a throwback to the days of imperialism and gunboat diplomacy. Cuba wins a great deal of sympathy in the third world by the continuing existence of the U.S. base at Guantanamo, and the base surely also intensifies anti–United States irritations for many Cubans who would otherwise find little to support in the policies of Fidel Castro.

As in all the calculations offered here, it would be foolish to turn night into day, to conclude that bases on the coasts of Asia will only be a liability for the Soviets. The military and political leadership in Moscow is not blind or unaware of history, and it would never seek to establish a base at Cam Ranh Bay or facilities approximating bases elsewhere unless it saw some net advantage in having secure access to such facilities.

The point is rather that such an advantage may be much smaller in the net than U.S. strategists might previously have concluded. The Asian nations are just as sensitive to the historical precedents of such base establishment as are countries everywhere else. And what is a friendly relationship in one year can soon enough change. Given the local volatility of what happens on shore (do we have to go back very far to remember the time we were crediting the Soviet Navy with having bases in Egypt and in Somalia, before Moscow aligned with Ethiopia?), the presence of a de jure or de facto naval base could become an amplifier of irritations. Communist Vietnam may be too dependent on Moscow and too much in fear of China ever to have a falling-out with the Soviet Union. Yet any extensive Soviet naval use of port facilities on its coast might soon enough resemble the prior use made of the same port facilities by French, Japanese, or U.S. naval vessels and would certainly by portrayed that way in the Chinese or the third world press.

Again, the Soviets do not have such an easy and perfect hand to play. Intent for whatever reason on deploying naval power around the edges of Asia,[12] they pay a price in the reactions and sentiments of countries located on these edges.

East Asia

References to China and Vietnam draw the discussion to East Asia and the last round of complications for Soviet power projection. The Chinese do not trust the Soviets.[13] The Chinese, moreover, have serious quarrels with the Vietnamese, stemming from unsettled boundary disputes and historical conflicts, more recently including the harassment of the Chinese minority within Vietnam. The Chinese continue to support forces inside Cambodia opposed to the Vietnamese. The Soviets thus cannot easily exploit their relationship with Hanoi and at the same time advance their relationship with Beijing; what for a time is an opportunity soon enough turns into a dilemma, not unlike the United States' dilemma in the Middle East of trying to balance its relations with Israel against possibilities of better relations with Saudi Arabia or Jordan or Egypt.

Similar complications ensnare and divert the Soviets with regard to North Korea, where they must bid against Beijing's efforts to win favor with Kim Il Sung, while facing the fact that Kim has behaved irresponsibly on more than one occasion, posing a threat of war in the Korean peninsula that all the major powers might find difficult to control. Given the economic and general strength of the non-Communist regime in South Korea (illustrated, for example, in the scheduling of the 1988 Olympics in Seoul), both Moscow and Beijing are also somewhat tempted toward one form or another of normalization with the Republic of Korea, amid fears of serious North Korean resentment and retaliation.

Moscow thus has power assets to play in East Asia, but it is beset with a serious Communist adversary in the Chinese and with allies that for a variety of reasons are less easy to control than those in Eastern Europe. What is a nuisance for Moscow here is hardly a blessing for the West, as it might have to dread the independent decisions of Pyongyang or Hanoi more than the decisions that would have been hammered out in Moscow. Yet Moscow has to dread some of these independent moves as well and is at least somewhat distracted by the limits to alliance solidarity here.

The SS-20 and Japan

Soviet deployments of SS-20 medium-range ballistic missiles (MRBMs) illustrate very well some more of the complications being addressed here. It could very reasonably be argued that such missiles are largely redundant in their ability to hit the cities that lie within their range, since this kind of countervalue attack could always have been executed by an intercontinental range ballistic missile (ICBM) fired on a shorter trajectory. (The SS-20 indeed is the leftover of a failed ICBM, being the two stages that performed well in tests, decoupled from a third stage that was not a successful design.)

Where the SS-20 could more plausibly make some difference is as a counterforce accessory to existing Soviet conventional ground force potential. Where U.S. and NATO theater nuclear weapons were seen as a counter to Soviet tank forces, the accuracies of the multiple warheads of the SS-20 could conceivably be applied to blunt any application of such NATO battlefield nuclear forces, perhaps thus facilitating a Soviet ground advance that would otherwise have been impossible. The SS-20 hence could be argued to be militarily and strategically redundant for the vulnerability or safety of offshore places like London or Dublin, but to be very significant for places like Frankfurt and Hamburg, either preempting the Western tactical nuclear forces or deterring them (perhaps even being swapped for such forces in a mutual disarmament exchange that could be strategically very unfavorable to the West).

In terms of strategic logic, there would be no reason for peoples or governments not already threatened with Soviet conventional force invasion to become excited about new Soviet medium-range missiles. Islands off the coast, off the Eurasian continent, should be shrugging off the SS-20, while countries on the continent have much more reason to be upset. And what distinguishes Ireland from West Germany, in Europe, similarly ought to sort Japan from China, with Beijing having more practical reasons to worry about redeployments of the SS-20 east of the Urals, and with Tokyo having less.

Politics sometimes seizes upon such issues, however, and gives them a new and different life, with the result that the Soviets are discovering angry West European reactions in either category of country, those for which the new missiles might be more redundant, and those for which they would not be redundant. Apparently unwilling to dismantle or abandon such missiles once they have been produced, the Soviets have tried to assuage European feelings by suggestions that the MRBMs be deployed in Siberia, out of range of targets in Europe. Yet from such locations these missiles could reach targets in China (where they might make some military difference) and targets in Japan (where little seems added to what existed—Moscow can always destroy Japan, but cannot in any plausible way invade, seize, and occupy Japan). Hostile reactions, similar to those noted in Europe, are now appearing in both these Asian countries as well.

Those in the United States imputing the most worrisome significance to the Soviet SS-20 investments have suggested that these missiles would facilitate a new kind of intimidation, a new version of "Finlandization," as the Western European democracies might begin making unreasonable concessions to Soviet preferences. On the basis of election returns and governmental decisions it is hardly proven that any such dividends are being paid in Moscow. The impact in Japan has similarly been to nurture a new anti-Soviet feeling, linked to earlier grievances about the four small disputed islands north of Hokkaido, amplified by the shock of the September 1983 downing of the Korean airliner. Such a Japanese reaction to the SS-20 deployment, to repeat, could be discounted as largely psychological and political, rather than logical and strategic, since the USSR has already had for so long a very extensive capability for nuclear attack on Japan itself. Yet in making this potential more visible and salient, the Soviets have again played a card that may be less help than bother for them. One could visualize, with fascinated anticipation, the leaking out one day of some Soviet speculation that two of the targets for the SS-20 might have to be Hiroshima or Nagasaki; well short of this great a blow to a Japanese raw nerve, the Soviets in the deployment of their "assets" of military power have touched on nerves that are raw enough.

With regard to the four islands in dispute with Japan, Soviet policy has been in the spotlight ever since the United States returned Okinawa and the Bonins to Japan. If the Soviets had the capacity for making a generous gesture, they might get themselves off the hook but the prolonged argument and litigation that has occurred tends to get backs up on both sides, such that the concession becomes all the more difficult. It is equally difficult because the Chinese have some minor, as well as major, territorial irredentist claims to address to the USSR. To satisfy the Japanese claim might only be to initiate and to whet the appetites of the Chinese.

As was mentioned earlier, the Chinese have matched the Japanese government in grumbling about any solution of the European "nuclear arms control problem" that simply relocates the Soviet medium-range missiles farther east.[14] Much of this grumbling has to be political on the Chinese side just as on the Japanese. But a difference here is that the Soviets have, for more than a decade, had large conventional ground force deployments sitting on the Chinese border, posing at least some potential for invasion, with Beijing many times stating that a thinning out of such forces would be a prerequisite for any improvement or normalization of Soviet–Chinese relations. While all applications of theater nuclear forces to conventional combat are very debatable, amid real doubts about whether further escalation could be avoided, and about whether pronouncements of strategy on either side are genuine or merely gamesmanship, it is at least possible that the SS-20 could make some real military difference here, while it would not in the situation of Japan.

For China and for Japan the question in the end thus becomes the same as that for Europe. Do the Soviets gain in political strength, and in their ability to employ and deploy military power for their national purposes, by having brought this new round of nuclear missiles onto the horizon; or have they weakened their own political influence more than enhanced it, irritating and frightening other countries without intimidating and subordinating them? Should we anticipate some kind of Finlandization of Beijing or Tokyo; or instead will we see Japanese defense spending finally begin to rise; and will we see a perpetuation of the de facto military alliance developing between the Beijing regime and Washington,[15] despite the irritations caused by the continuing existence of an independent regime on Taiwan?

Notes

1. For a useful discussion of the joint U.S.–Soviet interest in heading off nuclear proliferation in Asia and elsewhere, see Rodney W. Jones, *Nuclear Proliferation: Islam, the Bomb, and South Asia* (Beverly Hills, Calif.: Sage, 1981).

2. An overview of some recent Soviet gains, at least as measured in terms of objective inputs, can be found in Karen DeYoung, "New Arms, Troops, Expand Soviet Military Role in Southeast Asia," *Washington Post,* 21 December 1983, A1.

3. For a discussion of the characteristics and implications of the Soviet SS-20 missile, see Raymond L. Garthoff, "The Soviet SS-20 Decision," *Survival* 25, no. 3 (May–June 1983):110–19.

4. For a parallel view by which the Soviets do not have such a strong hand to play, see Serge Schmemann, "From the Kremlin, the View is Bleak on Many Fronts," *New York Times,* 27 November 1983, p. E–1. See also David Holloway, "America's National Security: The View from the Kremlin," *Wilson Quarterly* 7, no. 5 (Winter 1983):99–111.

5. Melvin A. Conant, *The Oil Factor in U.S. Foreign Policy, 1980–1990* (Lexington, Mass.: Lexington Books, 1982), provides a more general discussion of Western fears on the future supply of petroleum.

6. On the implications of and the superpower interest in the Iran . Iraq war, see Barry Rubin, "Iran, the Ayatollah, and U.S. Options," *Washington Quarterly* 6, no. 3 (Summer 1983):142.55.

7. An extended discussion of Soviet motives in Afghanistan can be found in Thomas T. Hammond, "Afghanistan and the Persian Gulf," *Survey* 26, no. 2 (Spring 1982):83–101.

8. On the progress of the Soviet intervention in Afghanistan, see Joseph Collins, "Soviet Military Performance in Afghanistan: A Preliminary Assessment," *Comparative Strategy* 4, no. 2 (Summer 1983):147–68.

9. A very valuable discussion of the workings of the classical balance of power on land is presented in Ernst B. Haas, "The Balance of Power: Prescription, Concept, or Propaganda?" *World Politics* 5, no. 4 (July 1953): 442–77.

10. On the politics and preferences of states along the coasts contending with the very different nature of balance-of-power reasoning at sea, see Michael McGwire, "The Proliferation of Maritime Weapons Systems in the Indo-Pacific Region," in *Insecurity,* ed., Robert O'Neill (Canberra: Australian National University Press, 1978), 77–107.

11. For a fuller discussion of the nature and implications of overseas bases, see Robert E. Harkavy, *Great Power Competition for Overseas Bases* (New York: Pergamon, 1982).

12. On how U.S. naval force would have to look to Soviet planners, see Anthony H. Cordesman, "The Western Naval Threat to Soviet Military Dominance," *Armed Forces Journal International* 120, no. 9 (April 1983): 44–97.

13. A discussion of the larger flow of Sino–Soviet–U.S. relations can be found in Aaron L. Friedberg, "The Collapsing Triangle: U.S. and Soviet Policies toward China 1969–1980," *Comparative Strategy* 4, no. 2 (Summer 1983):113–46.

14. An overview of the total of current Sino-Soviet relations is provided in Thomas W. Robinson, "What Policies Should the United States Adopt to Counter the Soviet Military Threat to Northeast Asia?" *Asian Perspective* 7, no. 1 (Spring–Summer 1983):73–81.

15. The possibilities and limits of U.S. military cooperation with China are discussed in Paul H. Kreisberg, "Military Ties with China," *New York Times,* 23 December 1983, A25.

16
Some Long-Run Trends in Arms Control

W hat will follow is an attempt to scan the flow of arms negotiations, that will try to get beyond the short-run ups and
downs in such processes and look instead for some longer-
term trends and developments. Does everything more or less stay the
same (as some realpolitik analysts would assume) about the international game of power politics, such that the games involving procurement of arms or use of arms (or negotiations about the procurement or
use of arms) simply get played by the same rules decade after decade?[1]
Or are there some significant changes, changes in the backgrounds of
domestic politics or of military technology, changes perhaps in what
people know about the process of negotiations and the processes of
arms control? If any of such changes over the twentieth century have
been significant, have the resultant grand trends been in the right
direction, or in the wrong?[2]

One grand trend in the picture is now as trite as it is overwhelming
in its significance. The destructive power of the world's arsenals,
thanks to the introduction of atomic and hydrogen bombs, is fantas-
tically greater than it ever was in the past. If all of such weapons were
to be used, it could well mean the end of human life on Earth, and certainly the end of civilized life as we know it. Whatever other trends we
have to discuss here, there has certainly been an upward trend in the
importance of the arms control subject. But the interesting question is
as follows: Does such an increase in the importance of the problem
make it easier to solve, or more difficult?

The following are some other grand trends with which we shall
wish to deal as we attempt to judge whether one should be optimistic
or pessimistic about the history and trends of arms control:

This chapter was delivered at a conference on "Trends in Arms Control" sponsored by
the University of Manitoba, Winnipeg, Canada, in October 1984.

1. The inclinations of societies toward secrecy or openness about their activities, together with the premium that secrecy offers, or does not offer, for prospects of significant military victories

2. The uncertainties societies feel about their own capabilities to endure contests and to make sacrifices, as compared with the capabilities of rivals

3. The experience and wisdom, or lack of it, available to the parties in major military confrontations

4. The sheer political disposition toward peace and war of such major powers

5. The relative comparison of forces between the major powers

6. The number of powers playing an active role in international political confrontations

"Prisoners' Dilemma"

Just as war can have a variety of causes, so can failures at restraints on arms.

The first kind of problem situation we shall discuss here focuses on the initial two of the factors just listed, whether secrecy and surprise offer significant advantages in military confrontations (they do sometimes, but they do not always), and whether societies have a great capacity for secrecy (they do sometimes, but they do not always).

Some wars have thus occurred because of a settling in of a "prisoners' dilemma" situation, whereby each side is better off double-crossing and attacking the other side, and whereby each side lives in great dread of the consequences of being caught by a sneak attack. The two sides would both be better off if neither attacked, but they both are nonetheless better off attacking no matter what the other side does, and a war thus results, a war that leaves them both much worse off than if they had both stayed at peace.

The game-theoretical matrix that illustrates this situation most concisely is presented in figure 16–1. Much the same matrix could describe a situation well short of war, but a situation still worse than that of good relations and restraint in arms procurements. Here, each side is not better off attacking, but it is better off acquiring arms, in violation of any disarmament agreements, whether or not its adversary has adhered to these agreements. And each side here lives in dread of

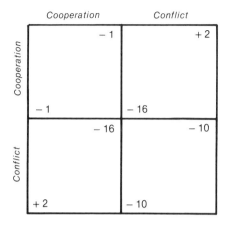

Figure 16–1. Prisoners' Dilemma

such a treaty violation by the other side. The result is again that the two sides fall into the situation of mutually counterproductive behavior, with worse results for either than if they had both kept their word.

Prisoners' dilemma does not occur all that often in real life. Yet the situation described by the matrix in figure 16–2 does occur quite often, and it resembles prisoners' dilemma closely enough to cause us a great deal of trouble. Here, for the case of war, neither side would want to double-cross the other by launching a sneak attack, but each still lives in great dread of such an attack by the other and cannot be certain of the benign feelings of the other. Applying the same matrix to an arms race, neither side might wish to cheat on a disarmament agreement, but each would very much fear the results if the other had cheated, and neither can be certain that the other would not want to cheat.

In such a case of "mutual misunderstanding," verification becomes very important, as additional arrangements for observation are introduced to reassure each side about the moves (and inferentially therefore about the intentions) of the other side. Without such verification arrangements, each side fears cheating by the other side, and each is therefore tempted to cheat a little as a hedge against this. Each side's precautionary moves are then taken by the other side as a confirmation of its worst suspicions, and a snowballing vicious cycle takes hold, in the end producing a full-blown arms race, or a full-blown war.

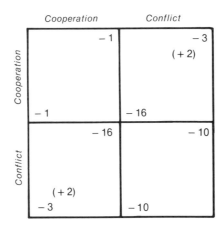

Figure 16–2. Mutual Misunderstanding

This kind of situation is a very plausible explanation of many of the arms competitions we have seen in the twentieth century. Nature changes, on making it easier or more difficult for adversaries to trust each other and to watch each other. A clever arms controller will put his ingenuity to work on steering the nature of military technology in the proper direction, finding ways to let each side feel more informed about what the other is doing.

Yet this is not the only kind of explanation for wars, or for arms races as they occur. As we survey the history of evolving patterns in arms control in the twentieth century, we shall have to face up to at least one very different explanation for arms races as they occur. This will be discussed later when we turn from prisoners' dilemma situations (or "mutual misunderstanding" situations that look like prisoners' dilemma) to something quite different, an "endurance contest."

Verification

As we attempt to sort out the ins and outs of situations favoring arms control in the twentieth century, what can we say about verification arrangements, about the openness of societies, that work to guard each side against excessive fears about an adversary's activities and intentions?

Neither side at the outbreak of World War I could know exactly whether the other was mobilizing its reserves or was deferring its mobilizations. This was an important part of the explanation of the outbreak of this war, a clear real-life illustration of the kinds of almost prisoners' dilemma situations one must dread for the future. Yet the problem was not so much in any secrecy or barriers to observation erected by the nations of Europe, but rather in the extraordinary speed and bias toward preemption that had been brought about by these mobilization plans, with their anticipated exploitation of railroads racing troops up for the battle of the frontiers.

A very important element in the problem of verification thus stems from whether one is close to or far away from prisoners' dilemma on the actual use of weapons. The mobilization schemes for the reserve armies of Europe at the outset of World War I basically caused that war to happen; that is, they basically placed an almost impossible verification burden on the two sides with regard to any restraint on the launching of these mobilizations. The risk looms that the equipment of intercontinental ballistic missiles (ICBMs) with multiple warheads, warheads of great accuracy, could similarly suggest very great advantages to striking first in some crisis. Even if such a crisis never becomes a mutually unwanted World War III, the same alleged possibilities of a counterforce attack place everyone much more on edge about whether arms restraint agreements are being adhered to.

What we all look forward to is an environment of military technology in which no one is tempted by or is afraid of a first strike. And this would also be a world in which one could shrug off fears that the other side might be cheating by 10 percent in one category or another. Since we do not have this kind of a world, much greater anxiety is expressed about the reliability of verification techniques.

Yet verification is not always so entangled in the arms control problem. An Anglo-German arms race before World War I did not occur because either side could build capital ships in secrecy; these two countries were simply too open for any such clandestine violations of an arms agreement to have been possible. Similarly, in the Washington and London naval arms agreements negotiated in 1922 and 1925, the powers involved, the United States, Britain, France, Italy, and Japan, were still open enough to make compliance with the treaty basically very likely, since any violations would probably be detected by the other parties.[3]

It was the development of what is sometimes labelled totalitarian government in the 1920s and 1930s that produced an important change in this situation, since one could not so easily have checked on the activities of shipyards or factories in the Soviet Union or Nazi Germany, or, after the 1920s, in Japan. After the defeat of the Axis powers in World War II, most of the world came under a very open liberal system again, but the Soviet Union, if anything, now approached the opposite extreme, as Stalin's regime made it very difficult for anyone's press to report on the military production or preparations of the USSR, on Soviet work on nuclear warheads, bombers, or submarines.

The issue of verification thus itself became enshrined as an East–West question from the 1940s to the 1970s, as the Soviet Union often put forward disarmament proposals that seemed quite reasonable and generous on the surface, but that were free of any arrangements for verification. When the United States and its allies rejected such proposals, they were likely to be pilloried around the world as uninterested in disarmament, as the parties to blame for a persistence of the arms race. Yet Western leaders felt that it would have been a disasterous trap to accept such Soviet proposals, since countries like the United States and Britain would have been observed by their own press and thus forced to disarm just as much as had been promised, while the unobserved Soviet Union could merrily cheat in the absence of any such witnesses to blow the whistle, hiding away a superiority in weapons that could later be cashed in for some great political return.

The United States thus kept returning to the disarmament bargaining process with matching proposals for arms reductions, each coupled, however, to extensive arrangements for inspection and verification. These the Soviets rejected, as an unjustified intrusion into their domestic sphere and as an insulting presumption that a country would not keep its word as sanctified in an international treaty. To skeptical and suspicious foreign observers, it seemed that Moscow was simply continuing to make a trap out of negotiations on arms reductions, always ready to agree to magnificent concessions on its side, never ready to submit to inspections ensuring that such concessions were actually carried out after an agreement had been signed.[4]

The exchange of propaganda and trickery, however, may not have been so totally one-sided. Skeptics about the U.S. postures of the 1950s have questioned in turn whether verification and inspection would indeed have been required for each and every proposal for restraints on arms, since some of such agreements might have been naturally fairly open to scrutiny as things stood.

Perhaps the U.S. negotiators did not really desire some certain kinds of arms restraint, but wanted to avoid the world opprobrium resulting from U.S. opposition to them; attaching extensive requirements for "on-site inspection" might thus have been a way of escaping this bind. U.S. demands for inspection might also have reflected some malicious hopes that such verification arrangements would be troublesome and destabilizing for the Soviet regime, inside the USSR and in Eastern Europe. Stalin had been careful to shut foreigners out of the USSR, and a reasonable guess was that he feared and distrusted the impact of any foreign inspectors on the attitudes and behavior of his people.

If any progress can be recorded on arms control (and there has been progress), part of it came on the diminution of the asymmetry of advantages and attitudes on verification. When only the United States stood to gain by such verification, and only the USSR stood to lose in terms of political options, the result was to deadlock the two sides in their negotiating positions, with neither inclined to retreat from its stand on this issue. Although the United States may have suffered propaganda losses in having to explain the complicated logic of verification again and again, it was not doomed always to be the loser on this propaganda front, as the argument for a need for verification was sooner or later to seem somewhat plausible to people all around the world. Some of the propaganda losses could therefore be shifted over to the Soviets. Yet the degeneration of discussions about arms restraint into a simple exchange of propaganda sallies nonetheless amounted to a loss of sorts for both sides and for all the world.

Two kinds of developments since the 1960s have worked somewhat to defuse the East–West polarization on the verification issue. Each of them amounts to a new concern for Moscow whether countries in the West could be counted upon to be so open, so self-inspected by the reporters of their own press. At first, since any closing of society can worsen the chances of arms restraints and disarmament, these two developments might seem to be bad news. Since they have driven the Soviets to cease stonewalling on the abstract issue of the need for verification, however, they may amount to some good news, with the prospect that the superpowers may ultimately be able to deal with this question without so many barrages and counterbarrages of propaganda.

The first of these developments relates to the risks of nuclear proliferation, as posed in the prospect of a spread of nuclear technology intended for peaceful purposes, and by the unfortunate inherent overlap between such technology and the kind that lends itself to bomb manufacture.[5] Since the Soviet Union was becoming worried about a clandestine manufacture of nuclear warheads in a country like West Germany, it ceased to belittle the role of the safeguards inspections of the International Atomic Energy Agency (IAEA) and instead become resolute in demanding that such IAEA safeguards be applied in all the countries that would renounce nuclear weapons while having peaceful nuclear power plants.

In a strange reversal of roles, the United States then for a time voiced some sympathies with the West German arguments, that the Federal Republic was already under the perfectly adequate safeguards and control arrangements of Euratom, the nuclear branch of the European Community, and that it was a mistake to be too suspicious about the intentions of nations signing solemn international treaties (this sounding not unlike the old Soviet argument against verification). At the same time, the Soviets pressed the worst-case arguments that German compliance with the nuclear Nonproliferation Treaty (NPT) could never be assumed unless there were safeguards in place to report any violations.

A second major development came with the disclosures after the Vietnam War and the Watergate break-in, as Richard Nixon was driven from the presidency of the United States, disclosures that the executive branch of the U.S. government had been much more able to keep secrets from its Congress, press, and public than anyone might have anticipated.[6]

Perhaps the United States could not therefore any longer be regarded as naively straightforward on the verification issue of any disarmament process, somehow setting up a country like the Soviet Union to obtain a unilateral advantage if a treaty were adopted minus provisions for verification. If the United States were comparably good at cheating about nuclear or conventional disarmament (one should remember that the democratic Weimar government of Germany in the 1920s had been quite good at bypassing many of the disarmament obligations imposed by the Versailles Treaty), then such an unverified disarmament treaty might merely be a meaningless piece of hypocrisy on each side (or worse, a contest of who could cheat the most).

If the Soviet Union has less to gain in an unverified agreement and more to lose, it can over time be brought to drop its propaganda denunciations of inspection and verification. If the United States has less to lose in an absence of verification and sometimes something more to gain, it may cease making quite as much out of this issue. To repeat, it is not always the case that verification is crucial to limiting arms or that verification is the problem.

One cannot expect any total convergence here. The USSR tolerates the presence of far more foreign tourists and newspapermen than it did in Stalin's time. Yet there are still vast areas of the Soviet Union that are completely closed to foreign visitors. The orbiting of U.S. reconnaissance satellites, after four years' use of U-2 overflights, also has freed up a great deal of information about what is going on inside the Soviet camp; yet this can never substitute for on-site inspections or the prying of the U.S. press corps.

Some of the return of the Cold War since the midpoint of the Carter administration thus has amounted to a resurgence of the verification issue. There may never be any arms control agreement presented for ratification by the U.S. Senate without someone claiming that the Soviets have clandestinely gotten away with violating the last such agreement.

Given the West's retrospective surprise at the 1970s growth in Soviet missile arsenals and in the Soviet Navy, and the addition of new Soviet weapons for ground warfare (developments that exceeded what doves as well as hawks in the U.S. political spectrum had expected), the nagging fact remains that not enough information was available to give early warning of Soviet activities and intentions in this area. Much of what is classed a "violation" may not really be so in terms of the strict wording of any international agreements. Yet the syndrome affecting the West, regardless of the precise wording of treaties, remains the same: a sense that the Soviets can deploy weapons before the West knows that they are going to do so, while the Western nations are much too open to be able to inflict such surprises very often on Moscow.[7]

The verification issue may thus abate, but it will not completely go away. Part of the reason why one might hope that it will abate has been outlined above, that the Soviets will acquire some special reasons of their own to worry about being surprised and thus come to be more accommodating in general about arrangements for warning and verification, arrangements that have sometimes been given the generic label of "confidence-building measures."

Another reason for hope in this area would come from any shifts in the background military situation, whereby double crosses, violations of disarmament treaties, and sneak attacks simply could not make as much difference. The open societies of Europe in 1914 plunged into a war because their mobilization plans had attached such a great advantage to being the first to attack. More closed societies might have been able to avoid that war, if only the offensive had not seemed so advantageous.

Verification is every bit as desirable as has been indicated here. Other things being equal, one would regret any political moves and any technological developments that ever make such verification less easy, for the price of doing so is usually to increase the amount of money each side wastes on armaments.

Yet one must also remember that avoiding such waste is not the sum total of what is valuable in the world, and reducing the inventories of arms on each side is also not the sole interest that the West has. One can imagine technical developments that may (alas) make arms races somewhat more likely, and at the same time may not make wars more likely, perhaps even making them (under certain assumptions) less likely. The development of cruise missiles, in ground-launched, air-launched, and submarine-launched varieties, may be an example of such a paradoxical development. Such missiles, which may be usable with conventional as well as nuclear warheads, will be more difficult to observe and to count, so that each side will thus have to worry somewhat more about whether the other side is cheating. Yet the same cruise missiles amount to a substantial reinforcement for the second-strike retaliatory capabilities of each side, offering both the United States and the Soviet Union ways of destroying each other's cities from additional submarines, the submarines equipped only with torpedo tubes and originally not at all designed for this strategic retaliatory role. But as long as such cruise missiles do not lend themselves to some kind of elegant attack on the other side's nuclear strategic forces, their impact on the likelihood of war may be altogether what U.S. strategists want, as always at the price of reensuring that an all-out nuclear war would indeed be very horrible. The strongest case against such cruise missiles is therefore not that they are bad, but that they are probably already redundant, since the vulnerability of other strategic delivery systems for nuclear warheads has been overstated.

Endurance Contests

We have thus far dealt almost exclusively with the kinds of arms races, or kinds of wars, that are caused by the fears and temptations of the double cross. These contests are exacerbated when each side overrates the hostility of the other side and underrates the adversary's interest in peace. These are the kinds of counterproductive conflicts that may be eased if each side has some augmented means of watching the moves of the other.

Yet some very different kinds of situations can cause wars, or arms races. As can be seen in the matrix in figure 16–3, nations may fight wars or prolong arms procurement contests because each side expects the other to quit first. Each side would be better off quitting here, rather than prolonging the contest (this is very different from the situations discussed earlier). But each side knows that the other side would also be better off quitting rather than prolonging the agony, and the gains for being *the second to quit* can thus be enormous.

In a prolonged war, such as the guerrilla contest in Vietnam, the second side to quit was the winner of political power over the entire nation.[8] In the case of an arms procurement contest, the second side to quit could be left with a definite military superiority, and could perhaps be able to cash in on it thereafter in political terms as well.

This kind of contest therefore does not continue because each side overrates the hostility and bellicosity of the other. Rather, it persists because each side overrates the other's desire to make peace or the other's desire to shift its production back to the goods of peace. Ending this kind of contest does not require verification of what people are

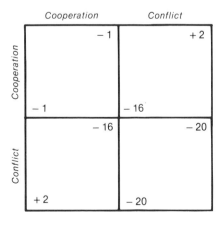

Figure 16–3. Endurance Contests

doing; rather it requires disentangling the claims and counterclaims as to how willing each side was to persist in the arms race.

Suppose that the Soviets reject a U.S. offer to forego building some missile on the grounds that the United States was not going to build that missile anyway and thus was offering a nonconcession; this is a perfect illustration of this particular kind of syndrome. A parallel example can be found in the unsuccessful Anglo-German negotiations about the limitation of capital ship construction in the years before World War I. The German negotiators rejected as unfair the British proposals for a naval holiday on the grounds that the British would get to stop in a position of being ahead and that—without any negotiated restraint—Germany would have produced more new ships in the next several years than would Britain. When the British countered that—in the absence of a negotiated restraint—Britain would have produced more ships than Germany, the talks foundered, not on any unverifiability of the proposed agreements, but on a prior inability to come to terms on what would be a fair agreement.[9]

A reader might then conclude that all that was in question here was the logical and choronological sequence of an arms control process. First one hammers out an agreement and then one sees to it that it is executed. Yet what is being offered here is less an essay in chronology and more a task of identifying key problems at all stages of the process. Under some circumstances, one can skip entirely the contest of wills where the bargaining chips are trotted out in opposing claims as to what would have happened. At other points, one is completely crippled by this fundamental uncertainty, for each side can quite genuinely not be sure whether any deal is fair, cannot be sure that it is not giving up too much and getting too little. (Under some circumstances, similarly, the verification of an agreement, once it has been accepted, becomes a relatively trivial task. At other times, it becomes impossible, as each side is inexorably driven to fear the worst from its adversary.)

As we try to offer some generalization about trends, about where all this is headed, what can we predict about the likelihood of such mutual difficulties in determining an adversary's capabilities and determination, of the kinds of tiring contests in which each side assumes that the other is bound to capitulate and come to terms?

This kind of confusion may not be so much a function of the effectiveness of secret police forces or of iron curtains; it may be related more naturally to economic growth, and especially to unevennesses in such growth, as a new power compares its resources and strength with those of some other state that used to be preeminent. Who in 1910 could really tell whether Germany could outbuild Britain, given the entire century after Trafalgar when Britain had been able to outprocure everyone else in naval weapons? Who can tell now whether the Soviet economy can persist in its devotion of resources to tanks and missiles and to a new navy, as compared with the mature capitalist economy of the United States, beset with elections and the demands of its consumers?

Guerrilla revolutions have been very much of this form, where wars are concerned, as the radical revolutionaries bet on the future and on themselves, betting on an untested element, with their reactionary opponents not being sure whether to give in and escape to an exile on the Riviera, or instead to stick it out, on the guess that the guerrillas will run out of steam. To the extent that any conflict in the world is between a rising new force and an old established one, such inabilities to agree on terms will be more of a problem. When the conflict is instead merely between adversaries who have known and tested each other over decades, this kind of endurance contest, or game of "chicken," is a little less likely to emerge.

The Question of "Linkages"

The endurance contest phenomenon is very much tied to arguments about "linkages." Few concepts are indeed as prone to be as confused or as abused as this notion of linkages between arms control and the rest of politics. The term is often applied to diametrically opposed courses of policy, causing confusion for the press and the general public, and even for the people making decisions in a government. The worst of confusions, polemical or otherwise, occur when analysts and political figures begin defending or attacking the notion of "linkages" in the abstract. Given that diametrically opposed policy options can be associated with this term, this is hardly the most clarifying way to phrase a debate.

A very simple way to get around such a confusion about linkage could be outlined at the outset, in a proposal that everyone "get serious" about arms issues and avoid the gamesmanship of linking them to anything else. Arms agreements are either desirable or undesirable in their own terms, by this perspective, and should be decided entirely in these terms.[10]

If the agreement is undesirable, it should be avoided. If the agreement is desirable, it should be adopted, regardless of what is happening on human rights in Poland, and so forth. Arms issues are of paramount importance, by this perspective, affecting the likelihood of wars and the ways wars would be fought. They should thus neither be played with to extract concessions, nor played with to be offered as a concession directed to other issue areas.

Yet this rejection of all consideration of linkages might strike the professional negotiators of either side as far too unrealistic and high-minded. Either side may feel that it can get away with demanding some sweetener, or may feel that it has to offer one, as part of finalizing an arms control agreement. And either side may also see some larger organic connections to the rest of politics, by which the desirability of an arms restraint agreement has to be evaluated in broader terms.

One very typical argument for assigning importance to linkages is that the United States should demand some accommodating *political* behavior from its adversary before signing any disarmament or arms restraint agreement. In effect, this is a view by which arms restraints are not necessarily very valuable in their own right, or as least not so valuable that the United States should not consider holding out for something more. An arms control agreement that represents indeed a slight improvement for U.S. interests may mean more than a slight improvement for the other side. Perhaps the United States should withhold its approval of such agreements until the deal is made still better for its position.

Unless the Soviets stay out of Poland, or get out of Afghanistan, or unless the Soviet brigade is removed from Cuba, some would thus argue, the United States should not accept what might on the surface have been a sensible arms restraint agreement.

Reversing this argument, some other analysts (or the same analysts at another time) might conclude that it was the Soviets who needed some kind of a concession on the United States' part, a sweetener to make *them* ready to accept an arms control agreement. If the United States really cares about SALT II, let it offer the concession of not inviting Solzhenitsyn to the White House during the Ford administration, lest doing so be seen as too much of an insult by the Soviet leaders, leading them to reject the agreement in a burst of retaliation.

When arms control is important to both sides, the issue is thus still (as was noted in the earlier example of Anglo-German naval negotiations) one of "more important to whom?" If one side cares a lot, it may be exploitable for a sweetener concession. If the other side cares visibly much, perhaps it is the first side that should be demanding the concessions from them.

Just as the ending of a war (a war that is benefiting no one) is sometimes postponed as each side demands concessions from the other, so a moderation of the arms race may be postponed in a jockeying for similar concessions. Persons more passionately devoted to peace or to disarmament may despair of the behavior in this process, criticizing it as silly, selfish, and short-sighted.[11]

The defender of an emphasis on linkages might come back, however, to claim that the desirability of an arms control agreement can depend organically on the political and general military situation. Perhaps this is not a bargaining question anymore of asking for substantively unrelated concessions, or of treating arms restraints as a quid pro quo to be offered in exchange for substantively unrelated concessions from the other side. Rather, it would simply amount to a reminder to all sides that something like a limit on ASAT (antisatellite), or on MIRV (multiple independently targeted reentry vehicle), or on missile totals, can quite naturally change in desirability, depending on what else is happening in the world. The United States may have to steer its own policies on other questions with this idea in view, and it can reasonably remind the Soviets that they must take account of similar constraints.[12]

This version of linkages would thus claim to be in no real disagreement with the argument at the outset for simply treating arms issues on their own terms; it says that good arms restraint agreements should be ratified and bad ones should not, simply adding some additional parameters to what makes an agreement intrinsically good or bad in the first place.

Yet this is a slippery slope, then, as considerations of negotiation and bargaining come into play again. When trying to extract a concession from an adversary, it is always more effective to assert that the deal would simply make no sense without the concession. It makes for a tougher bargaining task, as was noted earlier, to let it be known that the agreement was desirable even without the concession, for it means that one is merely holding back in an endurance contest of "chicken."

Anyone trying to squeeze the adversary for an unnecessary concession will thus do well to make it look like a necessary concession. Anyone "playing games" with arms issues will do better at the game if he pretends that he is responding to the organic dictates of the issues and thus not at all failing to take arms control seriously on its own terms.

U.S. negotiators would thus claim that it makes no sense for the United States to ratify a SALT agreement if there is a Soviet combat brigade in Cuba (or—hypothetically—if Poland is being militarily invaded), rather than stating that the United States would cease negotiating a mutually beneficial SALT agreement simply out of anger and retaliation for such Soviet moves. And the Soviets would claim that they are similarly always following the dictates of the objective situation, asserting that it makes no sense for them to come to the INF (intermediate-range nuclear forces) or START (Strategic Arms Reduction Talks) bargaining table when Pershing II has been deployed, rather than admitting that they are spitefully retaliating by holding back on what might have been a mutually beneficial process.

We thus far have noted situations in which either side might find an arms agreement important, but may also guess that the other side would find it important too, and so will hope to hold out for some additional concessions from the other side in a nonmilitary category. But what if either or both of the sides were to conclude that the political categories were more important than the military? This category of issues may be hard to understand for the reader who assumes that the avoidance of wars and of arms races is the most pressing task for humanity. Yet people and statesmen have not always seen the priorities that way. Once again we must consider linkages of simple bargaining and gamesmanship and then some more "organic" linkages, with negotiators on each side at times pretending that the former are actually the latter.

If the East Germans were to dismantle some of their minefields along the border with West Germany, the action might be seen as an arms policy concession, dictated by the larger considerations involving West German economic credits being extended to the Communist regime. If the United States holds back on its sales of conventional weapons to Taiwan, it is not in exchange for any arms policy moves by the People's Republic of China, but rather because of more general political goals that the United States is pursuing vis-à-vis Beijing.

Relatively few such examples come to mind of an explicit swap of military concessions for substantively unrelated larger political counterconcessions. Any deemphasis of the military side of things will more normally shift the focus to organic linkages, much like those noted earlier, but measured in exactly the opposite direction. Rather than the political situation having to be "right" if military matters are to be set-tled, organic arguments would be involved by which the military situa-tion had to be more "right" to set up an atmosphere in which political matters could be settled.

A very different priority of importance for relationships of arms issues and other issues thus get advanced by those who would tout the political spinoffs from any and all arms restraint agreements. By this analysis, an arms control agreement that was not particularly desirable on its own, perhaps even a slightly one-sided sacrifice from the U.S. standpoint, should nonetheless be accepted, because doing so will sweeten the deal for all concerned in a way that will bring about a political improvement. Rather than extracting non–arms control con-cessions by dragging its heels on arms control, the United States would be making a concession in the field of arms control, as a way of getting things moving in a positive direction on some non–arms control front.[13]

As the reverse of this approach, U.S. negotiators might sometimes anticipate that the Soviets will be ready to make some material conces-sions on issues of arms policy because of political effects that they might desire. In such a case, the tougher problem for U.S. analysts is to determine whether the net package is still so desirable from the per-spective of U.S. national interests; or should what was an attractive concession on arms issues now be rejected, because the political objec-tives Moscow is seeking are too objectionable from the U.S. point of view?

To sort out these cases, one might use a diagram like that of table 16–1. One question is whether the issues of arms are more important than the non–arms control issues. And the other question is whether the possibilities of an agreement are altogether "more important" for the United States or for the Soviets.

All of these concerns about comparative concessions and about the relative need on each side for an arms control agreement, or for an overall agreement, still relate relatively little to the issue of verification introduced at the outset, but they relate very much to that other funda-mental problem of arms negotiations: determining who should give in first, and how much to give in.

Rather than condemning any alleged folly of those who "play games" with arms control and with linkages, one should note that such anxieties and contests are almost inevitable and that the games are very difficult to sort out. To concede too much is not only to betray

Table 16–1
"Linkages"

	Arms Issues over Political Issues	Both Kinds of Issues Important	Political Issues over Arms Issues
United States wants agreement more	United States makes substantively unlinked concessions on politics	United States makes concessions on all fronts	United States makes substantively unlinked concessions on arms issues
Both sides want agreement	"Organic linkage" I	"No nonsense"	"Organic linkage" II
Soviets want agreement more	USSR makes substantively unlinked concessions on politics	USSR makes concessions on all fronts	USSR makes substantively unlinked concessions on arms issues

one's own national interest; by conveying a signal of irresolution to the adversary, one may find agreements more difficult to achieve in the future.

Experience and Wisdom?

Have we learned anything or improved anything about the process of negotiating restraints on arms? How bad are things now, as compared with ten years ago? Are they just as bad as thirty or forty years ago? While such questions may sound blurry and excessively linked to intuitions and perceptions that cannot be scientifically tested, they are the questions that concern us very much. This negotiating process has ups and downs of its own, not identical to the likelihoods of peace and war, but much of what we need and want in the world may depend on the wisdom, experience, and competence of the negotiating leaderships of the important powers.[14]

Things may well have improved, at least as compared with the decade immediately following the end of World War II, for the U.S.–Soviet arms dialogue of the 1940s must certainly be rated as less productive than what was the norm for international arms negotiations in earlier decades. Part of the reason for this can be traced to the unique secrecy of Stalin's Soviet Union and another part to the Soviets' newness to this kind of international negotiation in general (as well as to the newness of the active U.S. participation in world politics?). Also playing a role was the suddenness of the constitution of a duopoly of power, as the Axis powers faded from the scene, and Britain and France showed great weakness.

When a younger person hears samples of the U.S.–Soviet dialogue in the middle of the 1980s, he might wonder whether there has been much of a mutual learning process by which each side becomes more used to the other and more tolerant. But examining the historical record of the years of the Berlin Blockade and the Korean War will offer a small degree of reassurance.

Mutual understanding and communication, especially when they are only partial, are not always a blessing, however. Perhaps the United States and the Soviet Union have mainly learned how to fight limited wars, how to use conventional weapons without also using nuclear weapons, how to use surrogate troops without using their own. If so, it is reassuring at one level and discouraging at another, and those who feared total war can relax a little, while those who hoped for total peace are doomed to disappointment.

Such partial communication could also be disastrous, moreover, if either side were mistakenly to assume that the other would back off in a crisis. The Cuban missile crisis did not emerge from any U.S. dialogue with the Soviets that was more vitriolic than (or even as vitriolic as) the rhetoric of the Reagan administration. Rather, it may have occurred because Khrushchev misread as a sign of weakness Kennedy's professions of an interest in peace. In short, the crisis may have illustrated more the "game of chicken" syndrome than a "prisoners' dilemma" syndrome; when steering among these syndromes, the tasks of "communication," "learning," and "diplomacy" become very difficult.

As part of the same process of mutual accommodation and mutual learning how to get along with the opposing superpower, the United States is still not at the end of a much longer evolution of and debate about core military strategy. Is a resignation to mutual assured destruction (MAD) appropriate or isn't it? Apart from whether it is appropriate or not, has such a resignation to mutual deterrence been accepted by the Soviets? And has it really been accepted by those in power in the United States, or have the planners in Washington and Omaha perhaps now copied the Soviets in a continued commitment to war-fighting instead of deterrence?

The idea that war would be as bad for the winner as for the loser is surely a new one, drawing its life only from the development of the atomic bomb after 1945, or perhaps only from the hydrogen bomb's development after 1952. Since new ideas take some time to replace the old, it would not be surprising to find one of the major powers taking the lead here, with the other one following. If Americans digested and internalized an understanding of the new nature of weaponry (of nuclear weaponry in particular) sometime in the 1950s and 1960s, does it follow that the Soviets would accept the same lessons a decade or so later?

Someone wishing to argue that the Soviets have indeed followed along could perhaps point to the ABM (antiballistic missile) treaty and to a few relatively frank Soviet statements of position; he could also point to the obvious facts of what thermonuclear weapons have done to the physical nature of any future war. Yet other analysts, including many who have seemed to be influential in the Reagan administration, would argue that this is an "ethnocentric" conclusion, belied by the bulk of published Soviet statements about nuclear strategy; these analysts would claim that the Soviets still care very much about victory in any nuclear war and are purchasing weapons and designing strategy with this goal in mind.[15]

Rather than the United States leading the Soviets into a new perception of the new nature of strategy, it seemed possible in the 1980s that the leadership was the other way round, as U.S. statements seemed to be copying those of the Soviets (either out of sincere academic emulation, or because of a feeling that Soviet toughness required a Western toughness in response). If the Soviets, as some have alleged, care so much about victory that they might not be deterred by the prospect of the assured destruction they would suffer, then the United States must care about victory too, seeing to it that any such "victory" would go its way in a future war, or else the Soviets would not be deterred from starting such a war.

Nations: Good, Bad, or Ordinary?

Analysts find it perhaps the most difficult to be objective and scientific about the next question on the list, the nature of the societies being dealt with.

Are all powers equally culpable in the conflicts of the world (a basic power-politics assumption)?[16]

Or is the United States, as the most capitalist country in the world, the most at fault for the wars that occur and for the arms races that occur? This became a very popular assumption on the campuses of North America and of the world during the Vietnam War; whether one is a Marxist or not, many intellectuals around the third world and around the free world, along with the official spokesmen of the Communist "second world," would endorse this view.[17]

Or is the world arms competition mainly the fault of states lacking free elections and politically democratic forms of government, since the Soviet Union is in truth an "evil empire," and since liberal democracies can note with pride that they do not fight wars against each other, having even managed to negotiate their way out of arms races with each other? The last analysis portrays the United States as relatively blameless for the Cold War and for any return of the Cold War in the breakdowns of negotiations such as SALT. It also tends to portray the Soviet Union as bad in the same way that Hitler's Germany was bad.[18]

Each of these three perspectives, the power-politics, the radical, and the traditional American self-view, have large numbers of adherents. But to assay the trends of prospects on arms restraint, we may wish to tune a little more finely than any one of the three.

One does not have to allocate blame equally between Washington and Moscow to conclude that Moscow may be much less of an evil force in the world than was Hitler's Germany. The leaders in Moscow (or in Washington) have the wherewithal to inflict much more devastation on the world than the Luftwaffe ever could have, but one must conclude that Moscow's relationship to other peoples of the world is very different from the outright hostility and hate (almost a zero-sum hate relationship at points) that Hitler and the Nazis felt for many non-German peoples.

Whether one likes it or not, one must face the possibility that the real conflict between Moscow and Washington is one of largely benign rather than hostile or malignant intentions. Moscow has one view of what would make Poland, Afghanistan, Nicaragua, or El Salvador happier places to live, and Washington has a very different one. If either side were a little less altruistic, there might be no possibility of a war breaking out over the future of these countries or of arms races being conducted in preparation for such wars. Peace would not be served if either Moscow or Washington became selfish to the degree of Hitler's Germany, but it would be served if they both merely became as self-centered as contemporary Switzerland. But people are not easily changed. Jefferson's United States and Lenin's Soviet Union will remain what they are, countries ideologically and intuitively committed to helping any other country exploit the liberal or Marxist model.

And what does this do for the prospects of successful arms control? In a few ways, it makes arms constraints more difficult to attain. In most ways, it should make them a little easier.

First the difficulties. Each side, in perhaps being genuinely altruistic itself, will be afraid of the logical tensions of admitting that the other side might be so as well. Hence there is a tendency toward projections of evil intention. Hence there is a communications difficulty that at the very least takes some time to overcome.

A "tough-minded" practitioner or advocate of selfish power-politics is usually much more willing to impute very similar motives to his adversaries, seeing no moral differences among nations, but simply an inherent competitiveness toward the game, by which there have to be losers as well as winners. By comparison, an ideological or moral approach to the conflicts of international politics is all too likely to dictate that immoral or ideologically incorrect motives be imputed to the adversary, since an image of symmetry would be in discord with the ideologies on each side.

Liberals will be fond of pointing out that freely elected governments have rarely, if ever, fought wars against each other. Hence the problem of war must be caused by the existence of unrepresentative governments.

Marxists used to contend (at least before the China–Vietnam fighting) that Communist states would never fight each other, with the wars of the world thus being the fault of capitalism.

While either ideological perspective may have some claim to its tenets of faith, what then receives too little consideration in such perspectives is the possibility that arms races and wars may be "nobody's fault," that such systemic difficulties as "prisoners' dilemma" or "mutual misunderstanding," and "tug of war" (exactly the inputs outlined earlier) may account for many of the difficulties, regardless of the domestic nature of states.

The advantages of such Soviet and U.S. motivations, as compared with those of some more predatory powers in history, or compared with Nazi Germany and World War II Japan, are also obvious. The Soviet Union or the United States might someday wind up destroying much of the world with nuclear weapons, but neither side genuinely would want to do so. The USSR might wish to bring the benefits of Communism to Paris or Rome, but would never look forward to the nuclear destruction of these cities. The United States would love to see freely contested elections held in Warsaw or Kiev, but similarly would never relish their nuclear destruction.

The world is thus considerably less burdened with the outright hatred that Hitler felt for the Jews or for the Russians. The importance of the SS-20 is misstated if it is simply graphed in terms of how much devastation it could inflict on West European cities. The real fear is whether it somehow would facilitate a Soviet "liberation" of those cities.

To repeat, one could design a plausible set of values for the major powers of this world that would make the arms management problem much less severe. If everyone agreed on a single perspective of the good society, the problems would be eased. The same would happen if everyone became indifferent to any good society models for the globe. Yet we would be in much worse dilemmas if everyone were aggressively interested in plundering the world, in taking resources away from some other ethnic group, or even in wiping out that ethnic group. Some such more general conflict has survived in the world, in the Middle East and perhaps in South Asia. Yet one blessing of the horrible example set by the Nazis was that much of any such sentiments lost their legitimacy by the end of World War II. Hitler might have enjoyed directing a nuclear-armed missile at New York or Tel Aviv as part of continuing genocidal policies. No current possessor of nuclear weapons can plausibly be accused of wanting to accomplish such mass murders for his own sake.

So, less worrisome than the current motives of the major nuclear powers is rather what might be done one day in retaliation, or in preemption, or by accident, or as part of some contest of demonstrating resolve.

The Comparison of Forces

Some observers of U.S.–Soviet arms confrontations are inclined to ground their entire analysis on the basic comparison of the two sides' nuclear forces. For them the significant shifts are not the ins and outs of verifiability, or of comparisons of willingness to endure the mutual burden of an arms race, and not any phases of the Cold War or détente, but rather the progression from the original U.S. monopoly of nuclear forces after Nagasaki, to subsequent stages of U.S. superiority, and then perhaps to "parity" (however defined), and then to a Soviet superiority (and then the next step?). The analysts who concentrate on such a focus are not always right-wingers lamenting the fading of U.S. superiority. Not a few more left-leaning analysts of "the origins of the Cold War" would point to the U.S. nuclear monopoly and to the alleged U.S. arrogance and Soviet fears that stemmed from this monopoly as being to blame for the end of the U.S.–Soviet cooperation that existed during World War II.

There is surely something to an approach that takes such basic force comparisons into account. Some of the very worst of Soviet and U.S. arms negotiation behavior may indeed have occurred not because the Soviets and Americans were so new to the process of negotiation and exchange, but because the United States held all the trumps (at least all the *nuclear* trumps; one cannot forget the Soviet strength in conventional forces in the late 1940s or the geopolitical advantage offered Moscow in its direct access to Europe).

Yet, before basing too much on the steps here, or leaping to some wrong conclusions as to the next step, we must ask ourselves *when* any real chance then occurred. As was noted earlier, the only really important change had probably already occurred in 1949 when the USSR acquired nuclear weapons and thus acquired an unignorable ability to destroy London, Paris, New York, and Washington. Compared to this difference between U.S. monopoly and U.S. "superiority" (nonmonopoly), all the other degrees of parity or of "superiority" for another side may be very minor.[19]

Above all, it would be a mistake to project some sort of symmetrical series here by which we moved along as follows:

U.S. monopoly
"U.S. superiority"
"parity"
"Soviet superiority" . . .
. . . Soviet monopoly   (?)

The worst of the scenarios for a "window of vulnerability" comes nowhere close to the equivalent of a Soviet monopoly, nowhere close to reducing the retaliation the USSR would suffer to what the United States would have suffered in 1948.

For the more general political future of the world, for the likelihood of peace and war, of Communist conquest or nonconquest, we moved from a logical extreme (nuclear monopoly) to the marshy and debatable center; we have not moved to the other extreme (Soviet monopoly), and one really cannot see any way to get us to that extreme. This remains good news for the West and good news for arms control, and it carries with it yet another suggestion that we are unlikely to return to the worst of where we have been.

To return once more to the subject of President Reagan's Strategic Defense Initiative (SDI), this proposal can be viewed as a nostalgic attempt to return the world to the 1948 situation of U.S. nuclear monopoly (it is often assailed this way by Soviet spokesmen, and it is sometimes defended this way by U.S. officials trying to explain to NATO allies how they would benefit from "Star Wars"). The Reagan administration's technologists can be criticized for simultaneously painting too threatening a picture of Soviet monopoly and too promising a picture of U.S. monopoly. Most outside observers are inclined to conclude that neither kind of nuclear monopoly is any longer possible; that is, that New York and Washington and Leningrad and Moscow will be continuously vulnerable to nuclear attack for decade after decade into the future. The important analytical point is that this reality should be treated more as a blessing than as a curse.

The Proliferation of Powers

The nonproliferation issue is a blessing for the arms control dialogue and not only in showing the Soviets that they might have a need for verification institutions. It also has more generally amounted to a great common interest for the Soviet Union and the United States, since each sees that it will be better off if countries like the Koreas, the Germanies, Pakistan, Libya, Argentina, and Brazil do not acquire nuclear weapons, and (laying selfish superpower interests aside) that the world will be better off as well.

Having a common enemy can convert enemies into partners and can convert adversaries into allies. The years of Hitler's menace to the world saw almost no U.S.–Soviet arms control problem, for each was too busy fighting off the Nazi menace to allocate much energy to distrusting the other. When Hitler departed this world, the Cold War was free to break out, amid the same kinds of layers of mutual suspicion that underline the general difficulty with arms restraints.

West and East Germany are not equivalent to Nazi Germany, and it would be a mistake to paint the U.S.–Soviet opposition to nuclear proliferation as equivalent to the outright enmity or hostility directed at the Axis in World War II. Cynics about the possibility of U.S.–Soviet cooperation, especially after the wearing down of détente since the middle 1970s, would indeed scoff at any picture of U.S.–Soviet closeness on any arms control issue.

Yet is it difficult to find any subject area in the world on which Moscow and Washington have been as close as on the risk of nuclear proliferation. The Law of the Sea negotiations and the North–South confrontations of UNCTAD may have rivaled this situation at times, but they did not match the close coordination and secret "smoke-filled room" conspiracy that went on between U.S. and Soviet representatives, discussing matters relevant to the nuclear Nonproliferation Treaty.

This U.S.–Soviet cooperation remains basically in place on nuclear proliferation, despite the conflicts that have grown on so many other issues. Whether the USSR and the United States can continue to work together on what clearly continues to be in their common interest may be a very nice test case for any and all theories of linkage.

With other countries seeing themselves, after 1968, as being in something of an adversary relationship with the U.S.–Soviet axis, the proliferation issue was oriented nicely at right angles to most of the normal arms disputes between the two superpowers. Within the domestic debate on arms issues inside the United States, a debate all too typically pitting "hawk against dove," the same refreshing reorientation of alignments was to be gained from the nuclear proliferation issue.

The menace of nuclear proliferation will not go away. This per se is bad news. Yet the good news, related to it, is that this leaves little reason to expect that U.S.–Soviet relations will really settle back to the low points of the 1940s and 1950s, when virtually every statement from one side could be interpreted as a propaganda attack on or a trap for the other.

Some Conclusions

The conclusions we might offer here are a mixture of optimism and pessimism. We might spot some slight improvements in the way arms

negotiations are handled and some slight regressions, and still not have a good handle on the bulk of what makes arms races or wars happen. The exogenous factors listed, including the tendencies toward prisoners' dilemma or "chicken" contests furthered by the nature of military weaponry, and perhaps the total number of powers in the system, may yet be the more important variables in this area.

Also important is a matter on which we indeed have very little leverage: the basic domestic nature of societies, whether they be liberal, Marxist, fascist, or traditional. The news on this last count is good as compared with 1939, and bad as compared with 1928.

What makes peace persist or makes wars break out is thus only partly a result of the way negotiations and formal agreements move along. Perhaps even more weighty for the settling of this most important of all questions will be whether the military technology itself supports stability—that is, discourages the taking of offensives in the event of a political crisis. One hopes that the arms negotiation process can be used to steer this technology in the good direction and away from the bad, but what scientists discover is in many ways still out of anyone's control.

If some group of scientists develop a perfect form of antisubmarine warfare, whereby all the submarines of the oceans can be discovered and destroyed in some quick attack, then peace will be very much in danger. If the same scientists, working just as diligently in the same laboratories, instead discover ways of making submarines much quieter and more invisible, then peace will be reinforced. Since submarine-based nuclear weapons look as if they will be secure against anyone's preemptive counterforce attack until well into the next century, peace may still be more secure than it was in 1953 or 1961.

We can indeed detect some improvements in the process of arms negotiations. A few of these will reflect the basic fact again that each side indeed has assured second-strike forces. As was noted before, another element in the improvement of the 1960s and 1970s was the result of a lessening of the comparative secrecy gap and the reemergence of some other states capable of deploying military strength and causing military problems, with a spread of nuclear weapons easily being the most menacing of such problems.

Should we now pessimistically expect that the Reagan administration and the Soviet leadership will let the arms negotiation process simply slip back to being as bad as it was in 1949? For all the reasons noted, it may indeed be impossible for this to occur; happily enough, there are some steps that cannot be retraced.

Notes

1. An example of what might fairly be described as such a realpolitik analysis is to be found in Hans J. Morgenthau, *Politics among Nations,* 3d ed., (New York: Alfred A. Knopf, 1963), 407–10.

2. For some other examples of attempts at an overview of the evolution of the process of arms negotiations, see Herbert York, *Race to Oblivion* (New York: Simon and Schuster, 1970), and Bruce M. Russett and Bruce G. Blair, eds., *Progress in Arms Control?* (San Francisco: Freeman, 1979).

3. On the failures and successes of earlier naval arms negotiations, see Jonathan Steinberg, *Yesterday's Deterrent* (London: McDonald, 1965), and Harold and Margaret Sprout, *Toward a New Order of Sea Power* (Princeton: Princeton University Press, 1963).

4. See Arthur H. Dean, *Test Ban and Disarmament: The Path of Negotiation* (New York: Harper and Row, 1966), for a good overall view of the style and substance of U.S.–Soviet arms negotiations in the 1950s and early 1960s. Also see John W. Spanier and Joseph E. Nogee, *The Politics of Disarmament; A Study in Soviet–American Gamesmanship* (New York: Praeger, 1962).

5. William C. Potter, *Nuclear Power and Nonproliferation* (Cambridge, Mass.: Oelgeschlager, Gunn, and Hain, 1982).

6. On the atmosphere of secrecy that had developed by the time of Watergate and Vietnam, see Morton Halperin and David Hoffman, *National Security and the Right to Know* (Washington: New Republic, 1977).

7. For an example of an analysis stressing the surprise and concealment of Soviet arms procurements even at the time of détente, see Albert Wohlstetter, "Is There a Strategic Arms Race?" *Foreign Policy* no. 15 (Summer 1974): 3–20.

8. Such a retrospective interpretation of the Vietnam War is in effect explored in Wallace J. Thies, *When Governments Collide* (Berkeley: University of California Press, 1980).

9. See Steinberg, *Yesterday's Deterrent.*

10. For an example of this kind of argument, see William H. Baugh, *The Politics of Nuclear Balance* (New York: Longman, 1984), 218–19.

11. For a more general analysis of the "linkage" phenomenon at the termination of wars as well as of arms races, see Gorden A. Craig and Alexander L. George, *Force and Statecraft* (New York: Oxford University Press, 1983), especially pp. 227–35.

12. Such an organic notion of linkage is in effect the approach defended in Richard Burt, "Reassessing the Strategic Balance," *International Security* 5, no. 1 (Summer 1980):37–52.

13. This interpretation of an organic link *from* arms control *to* politics is exemplified in Charles Osgood, *An Alternative to War or Surrender (Urbana: University of Illinois Press, 1962).*

14. On the U.S.–Soviet mutual learning process, see Alexander George, *Managing U.S.–Soviet Rivalry: Problems of Crisis Prevention* (Boulder, Colo.: Westview, 1983). For a discussion of the possibility that China and the United States have actually been learning how to get along with each other so that experience produces wisdom about the management of issues, see Jan Kalicki, *The Pattern of Sino–American Crises* (New York: Cambridge University Press, 1975).

15. For a typical argument that the Soviets have their own view of military strategy, see Richard Pipes, "Soviet Strategic Doctrine: Another View," *Strategic Review* 10, no. 4 (Fall 1982):52–58.

16. For a representative example of the power-politics view, see Kenneth W. Thompson, *Understanding World Politics* (South Bend, Ind.: University of Notre Dame Press, 1975).

17. For an example, see Gabriel and Joyce Kolko, *The Limits of Power* (New York: Harper and Row, 1972).

18. A good illustration of this view that blames foreign dictatorships rather than any defect of the American system can be found in W.W. Rostow, *The United States in the World Arena* (New York: Harper, 1960).

19. For a clear concession that the end of the U.S. nuclear monopoly had in effect eliminated much of the relevance of any comparison of the two sides' nuclear forces, see Henry A. Kissinger, *Nuclear Weapons and Foreign Policy* (New York: Harper and Row, 1957), chap. 6.

Index

ABM. *See* Antiballistic missile
Absolute Weapon, The (Brodie), 69,
  122–123
Abu Dhabi, 277
Academia's perspectives on war, 53–56
Accuracy of missiles: counterforce tendency
  and, 149; ethnic targeting and, 173,
  179–180; morality and, 111, 113; of
  MX, 17; negative consequences of, 111;
  Reagan administration and, 244;
  renewed interest in strategic nuclear war
  and, 217–218; strategic stability and,
  76–77
Ackerman, T.P., 143*n*.1
Afghanistan, 276, 277, 279–280, 281
Air warfare, 61–65; morality of, 67;
  mutual assured destruction and, 61–62;
  predictions on the nature of, 125–126;
  strategic considerations in, 149. *See also*
  War(s)
Aircraft carriers, 233
Airplanes, 232–233. *See also* specific planes
Albert, B.S., 175, 182*n*.3, 226*n*.2
Albertini, L., 57*n*.5
Alliances, changed nature of, 86–87
Allies. *See* Extendability of deterrence;
  NATO; Western Europe
Alperovitz, G., 72*n*.9
Amendment, Mansfield, 272
"American liberal" perspective: "entangling
  alliances" notion and, 266–267; on
  foreign policy, 252, 255–256
American self-image, 258–262, 270–271
Andriole, S.J., 199*n*.5
Andropov, U., 167
Antiaircraft guns, 155
Antiballistic missile (ABM): criticisms of, 9;
  effectiveness of, 76; population defense
  through, 117, 236–237; Soviet, 158;
  treaty, 312
Antibomber defense, 117
Antisubmarine warfare (ASW), 76, 155

Antitank guided missiles (ATGM), 191,
  234, 247
Arab–Israeli conflicts: mobilization systems
  and, 232; Six Day War (1948), 188,
  233; Yom Kippur War (1973), 188; as
  "zero-sum" conflicts, 42
Arms control, 1–25, 293–321; choices of
  international security and, 1–4; critics
  of, 4–5; disarmament and, 5, 6–10;
  endurance contests and, 303–305; formal
  negotiations vs., 10–14;
  ideological conflicts and, 312–315;
  improvement in U.S.–Soviet dialogue
  on, 310–312; "linkages" notion and,
  305–310; military strategy and, 19–24;
  nature of societies and, 312–315; North
  American dissatisfaction with, 54–55;
  nuclear proliferation and, 116,
  317–318; "prisoners' dilemma" and,
  294–296; U.S.–Soviet forces and,
  315–317; verification and, 296–302
Arms race stability: defined, 23; weapons'
  impact on, 52
Arms races, wars vs., 51–52
Asia: Southeast, 261; Soviet power in, 276,
  280–283, 287–288
Assured second-strike retaliation. *See*
  Mutual assured destruction; Second-
  strike capability
ASW (antisubmarine warfare), 76, 155
ATGM (antitank guided missiles), 191,
  234, 247
Atomic bomb, 79, 122–123
Attack, surprise, 187, 248
Australia, U.S. commitment to, 257

B-47 bombers, 14
B-52 bombers, 220
Bailey, T.A., 274*n*.8
"Balance of terror," 80
Ball, D., 166, 228*n*.20
Barton, J.H., 119*n*.4

About the Author

George H. Quester is chairman of the Department of Government and Politics at the University of Maryland, where he teaches courses on defense policy and arms control and on U.S. foreign policy. He previously was chairman of Cornell University's Department of Government, and in 1981–82 he was a professor in the Department of Military Strategy at the National War College. Dr. Quester is the author of a number of books and journal articles on international politics and international security, and he is a member of the International Institute for Strategic Studies and the Council on Foreign Relations.